D1288315

EARTH IN DANGER

TOWARD A NEW PLANET

Edited by Eung-kyuk Park

50 Great Stories to Save the Planet

The collection of articles examines ideas and ways to protect
the environment and look out for the well-being of mankind.

The Korea Institute of
Public Administration

ISBN: 978-89-5704-431-5 93530

Published by The Korea Institute of Public Administration (KIPA)
459 Eonjuro Gangnam-gu, Seoul 135-706, Korea
Tel: 82-2-564-2001
Fax: 82-2-564-2013
An audio version of this book in MP3 can be freely downloaded at KIPA homepage.
Website: www.kipa.re.kr

copyright © 2012 by The Korea Institute of Public Administration (KIPA).
All rights reserved.

A word of gratitude

This book is made from articles

published as a 50-part series in a collaborative project

between the Korea Institute of Public Administration

and The Korea Times between February and July of 2012.

The Korea Institute of Public Administration

and The Korea Times express their deep gratitude

for the valuable contribution from each and every writer.

Prologue

There is no denying that the Earth, as we know it, is in danger. The entire planet is suffering from environmental devastation, including climate change, every conceivable type of pollution, ecological destruction and the depletion of natural resources.

The results are mind-numbing. There is widespread flooding and droughts, typhoons and tsunamis, heat waves and a wide range of other natural disasters.

As if the environmental predicament was not enough, the world is facing every conceivable type of threat and instability, from the breakdown of the global financial system to economic recession in all corners, and the subsequent damage to the most basic quality of life.

Increasingly, there is recognition that the Earth and its inhabitants no longer have the luxury of waiting and hoping for the best. It is high time that the realities are accepted at face value and the world must make concerted efforts to determine in more exact terms what the current situation implies for mankind and bring this information to people everywhere.

This is no longer a set of problems that can be effectively addressed by a handful of powerful countries; it requires the undivided attention of every single element here on Earth.

Korea, for its part, must play an active role as a prominent member of Northeast Asia and help identify environmental problems as they exist and build a case for turning things around.

As part of facing up to this enormous challenge, the Korea Institute of Public Administration, in collaboration with The Korea Times, has jointly launched an intensive series of contributions from experts from around the world, to review the nature of the problem and through their experience, research and wisdom identify viable solutions at local and global levels.

This book is the collection of 50 contributions from the joint project.

No work is accomplished alone. A debt is owed to many. First of all, appreciation must be expressed to many distinguished individual experts in respective fields at home and abroad who have contributed in-depth articles pertaining to the environment.

I wholeheartedly thank The Korea Times for allowing vast space to publish the articles on environmental issues in time for the publication of this book. I would like to extend deep-hearted thanks to President Moo-jong Park of The Korea Times, Chief Contents Editor Jake J. Nho, and Managing Editor Young-jin Oh for their efforts in selecting contributors and serializing articles. Special thanks go to chief editorial writer Nho who has been creative, dynamic and speedy in dealing with serial articles in step with the publication of this English version.

When all is said and done, the warmth of understanding of this publication, shown by the National Research Council for Economics, Humanities, and Social Sciences (NRCS) and its Chariman Dr. Chin-keun Park, is recorded with a renewed sense of gratitude.

I wish to thank to Deputy Minister Yunsik Hong of the Office of National Agenda, and Director General for Planning and Coordination Kyun Oh of the Office of National Agenda at the Prime Minister's Office for their constant support to the Korea Institute of Public Administration and this project.

I also would like to express my deep appreciation to Bernard Rowan, professor of political science and chairperson of the Department of History, Philosophy and Political Science at Chicago State University for his final editing of this volume.

Finally, I would like to express my deep appreciation to Dr. Yongseok Seo, a research fellow at the Korea Institute of Public Administration, for his devoted contribution in shaping the volume into its present form by taking overall charge of planning, editing and compiling the articles.

Eung-kyuk Park
President
Korea Institute of Public Administration

Foreword

Together, we will overcome.

We are all concerned about the environment. There are constant reports and research about climate change and global warming and how it is affecting the lives of mankind and the generations to come.

There are serious problems and their implications. The most obvious are heavy carbon footprints, depletion of energy resources and thus the need for efforts to generate clean energy.

Fortunately, the world as a whole is in clear recognition of the dangers that we face and constant and numerous steps are being taken to reverse or at least prevent further progress.

In Korea, the frequency and concentration of rainfall has been changing at speeds that are difficult to keep and hard to forecast with sufficient amount of accuracy.

The increase in droughts and flooding is indicative of the violent contrasts in our environment, one which is singular and one which we must do whatever is necessary to protect, and enrich, for our children and their children for generations to come.

It is in this sense that we need to disseminate information to anyone and everyone because here and around the world because knowledge comes the determination to make a contribution to change. Now, more than ever, change is in dire need.

Change and modifications for protecting our environment comes in many forms.

It can be in leaving your car at home a couple of days a week to reducing the amount of detergent that we use to do our laundry and to leaving a clean a plate at the end of a meal.

The world is in constant search of cleaner sources of energy--energy we cannot live without-- and we are finding some through nuclear, wind, and solar power.

But the reality is that we need more, much more if we are to ensure that the air that we breathe and the water we drink are safe and healthy, for us and our future generations.

I emphasize the commitment we must make for future generations because they are not here yet. And we have the responsibility make certain that we do not leave them a world that is polluted and helpless.

Together, we must have the courage, wisdom, commitment and determination to overcome the challenges that are facing us and our Earth.

From these perspectives, it was a valuable and meaningful project for the Korea Institute of Public Administration to work with The Korea Times to generate a greater focus on the imminent need to protect our environment and look out for the well-being of mankind.

Chin-keun Park
Chairperson
National Research Council for Economics, Humanities and Social Sciences

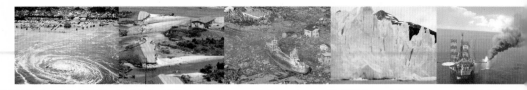

Contents

Prologue
Foreword

Chapter 1. Global Leader

Making a future we want together	13
Green growth essential to saving 'Earth in Danger'	17
Growth can go with environmental protection	23
20 years lost in the environment	27
Leading the way to a green energy era	34

Chapter 2. Scholar

Asia-Pacific fighting climate change	39
Disaster management and federalism	45
Are we prepared?	51
Mitigating revelations of climate change	57
Adaptation critical in changing climate	63
Future of tourism within the environment	69

Chapter 3. International Organization

A new paradigm of economic growth	77
Little Ice Age	83
Decisions have to be made	89
Accelerating investment in green growth	95
Women's role vital in disaster prevention	101
Essentials of consumerism	105
Consequences of climate change on oceans	115
World needs better alternatives to oil	121
Taking advantage of urbanization	127

Chapter 4. Government (Executive and Legislature)

Green growth is a revolutionary paradigm shift	135
A new way to meet the environment	141
People, nature converge at 4 major rivers	147
Why I work in shorts and sandals	151
Are environmental conflicts all bad?	155
In pursuit of low-carbon growth	161
Achieving shared growth through green ODA	167
Environmental governance in NE Asia	173
Geopolitics of energy and Korea's choice	177
Can policies prevent environmental accidents?	185
Yeosu Declaration to bring life to ocean	191

Chapter 5. World Governments

Pricing, partnerships key to green growth	199
Addressing challenges with integrated policy	203
The failure of disaster diplomacy	209
Green energy growing in Arab World	215

Chapter 6. National Think Tank

Making perpetrators pay the price	223
Climate change, resource depletion trigger dramatic global change	229
Mt. Baekdu eruption's impact on NE Asia	239
Risk governance in age of uncertainty	245
Environmental for Future Generations	251

Chapter 7. Journalist

Does Earth really need our protection?	259
Ocean pollution and int'l cooperation	265

Chapter 8. Entrepreneur

Smart grid for smart energy   273
The marvels of green construction   277
Learning to promote sustainability   281
Little things that count   285

Chapter 9. Civil Society

Environment through the lens   293
Nuclear technology: to have or not to have   299

Epilogue
Contributors
Index
Appendix

Chapter 1

Global Leader

Making a future we want together
Green growth essential to saving 'Earth in Danger'
Growth can go with environmental protection
20 years lost in the environment
Leading the way to a green energy era

Making a future we want together

Myung-bak Lee

President Myung-bak Lee addresses the Rio+20 United Nations Conference on Sustainable Development in Rio de Janeiro, Brazil, early Thursday morning (KST). *Yonhap*

The following is an edited version of remarks by President Myung-bak Lee of the Republic of Korea at the Rio+20 United Nations Conference on Sustainable Development in Rio de Janeiro, Brazil, June 2012.

Since the 1992 U.N. Conference on Environment and Development was held 20 years ago, we are now witnessing the successful opening of the summit here in Rio de Janeiro. So I would like to offer my congratulations.

In the 20 years since, the world has experienced many changes.

The accelerated pace of the global economy has greatly increased the size of the global economy. On the other hand, as we can see from recurring crisis and polarization, we are experiencing not just opportunities for growth but also vulnerabilities.

However, a greater change is taking place. And that is global warming. The rapid pace of climate change is shaking the very nexus of life, from water to energy to food resources. Desertification is spreading rapidly, while biodiversity is rapidly decreasing. Surely, this is not the future we dreamed of at Rio+ some 20 years ago. Surely, this is not the legacy we intend to bequeath to our future generations.

We need a new way of thinking and acting and a new concentration to our efforts. It is for this reason that the Republic of Korea chose a new path. In 2008, the first year that I took office as President, I declared low carbon, green growth as the new development paradigm for Korea.

Thinking outside the box

Green growth is thinking outside the box to respond to climate change and to solve energy and environmental issues in a way that the solution itself becomes a new growth engine and a new way of life. To this end, the Presidential Commission on Green Growth was established and a green growth five-year plan was formulated that comprises all administrative agencies, invests two percent of our GDP (gross domestic product) annually.

We launched a policy council encompassing industry, finance, science and technology and NGOs (non-government organizations) to expand public-private partnerships. As a result, although we still have some way to go, many changes as well as innovation are taking root in Korea.

Transcending party lines

The Basic Act on Green Growth and the act on greenhouse gas emissions trading were both passed through inter-party cooperation in the National Assembly. Green industries and technologies, including new and renewable energy, are experiencing rapid development.

Korea's project to improve the water infrastructure will help us overcome floods and droughts successfully and prepare us against extreme weather whose probability of occurrence is once in two centuries.

Also a new 1,800-kilometer-long riverside bicycle track has been laid so that cyclists can ride across the nation, a new turning point for green life.

The shift from highways to high-speed railways is taking place, and the era of electric automobiles has begun. The popularity of green buildings is spreading throughout local communities, and some local governments are taking the process one step further to build a clean development mechanism for their cities in cooperation with UNEP (the United Nations Environment Programme).

Even in the midst of the global economic crisis, this "green new deal" policy has led to 750,000 jobs over the past three years. Many of the newly created jobs helped the lower income class.

From these perspectives, green growth is an inclusive action strategy that implements the three goals of sustainable development: economic development, social cohesion and environmental conservation.

The challenges that confront us are global in nature and require our response to be global in scale. It is against this backdrop that we share the common destiny through a global green growth institute launched two years ago. With the support of the international society and thanks to the passionate participation of many, the GGGI (Global Green Growth Institute) was launched to mobilize international cooperation for green growth and to support developing countries. It has evolved into what it is today, and we will have an official signing ceremony tonight (Wednesday local time) here in Rio de Janeiro to convert it into an international body. On that note, I would like to take this opportunity to extend my deepest appreciation to all those people for their warm support.

Energy efficient power generation

I pledge to you that GGGI, as a strategic cooperative body for prompting collective actions, will make the utmost effort to become an enduring asset of international society. GGGI, through the green growth knowledge platform launched together with the World Bank, UNEP and OECD, will strive strenuously to systematically disseminate green growth.

Beginning next year, the Korean government will begin to expand the total size of green ODA (official development assistance) to $5 billion by 2020 and use this as a basis to deploy global green growth partnerships following the East Asia Climate Partnership, scheduled to end this year.

Through this initiative, we will provide focused and targeted support for areas such as energy efficient power generation, power grid development, renewable energy and energy storage systems, green transport and buildings, and water and agricultural infrastructure development.

In addition, the Green Technology Center that was established this spring in Seoul will be fostered as a bridge for technology cooperation, while a platform for training and education will be strengthened to nurture global talent.

Green climate fund

To achieve sustainable development through green growth and transition to a green economy, we need a strategy, technology and, most of all, supportive resources.

In this regard, I highly evaluate the agreement reached at the Conference of the Parties to the UNFCCC (United Nations Framework Convention on Climate Change) in Durban, South Africa, at the end of last year on the establishment of a green climate fund. What remains to be done now is to successfully launch the green climate fund so that a green triangle links strategy, technology and resources and works organically.

The Republic of Korea, for its part, will stay fully dedicated to ensuring that this triangle reaches advanced and developing countries alike to become a world architecture. We will gather the energy and wisdom of the international community together so that new jobs and opportunities for growth spread evenly and continuously across the world.

There is a saying that the best way to predict the future is to make the future the way we want it to be. That is correct. The future we want is in our hands. Let us not forget. It is we ourselves who are to blame, so we must move ourselves to the future we want.

Green growth essential to saving 'Earth in Danger'

Myung-bak Lee

President Myung-bak Lee, at center, waves to passers-by while participating in a cyling festival in Changwon, South Gyeongsang Province. *Korea Times file*

First and foremost, I am grateful to the staff of The Korea Times for their hard work in publishing the feature series "Earth in danger" over the past six months. My thanks should also go to UN Secretary General Ki-moon Ban and all other contributors from various sectors.

As many have noted with great concern, Earth is now in danger. Global warming caused by greenhouse gases emitted during industrialization now poses a threat even to the very nexus of life, from water to energy to food resources. Accelerated climate change adds to the sharp increase of disasters and the ensuing damage, rapid expansion of desertification and the reduction in biodiversity on a daily basis.

A new path we have to take

The conclusion I arrived at after much hard thought was that we should not pass on an earth in danger to our posterity. Novel ways of thinking and behavior were needed. We should choose a new path that would ensure sustainable prosperity and safety for future generations.

In the first year of my presidency in 2008, I announced "Low Carbon, Green Growth" as a new paradigm to guide the nation's development.

Low carbon, green growth is a new policy of thinking outside the box, which is aimed at making efforts to deal with climate change and to resolve environmental and energy issues and turn them into new growth engines and lifestyles.

As part of efforts to realize these goals, the Presidential Committee on Green Growth was launched to facilitate collaboration in deliberating and coordinating various green growth policies across ministries and agencies at the government level.

Green growth committees were also set up under local governments. Both the central government and local governments worked out five-year green growth plans and have invested 2 percent of GDP in the sector annually.

On top of this, the government was the first in the world to lay the groundwork for the continued pursuit of green growth by enacting the Framework Act on Low Carbon, Green Growth. It also paved the way for reducing the greenhouse gas emission in a groundbreaking manner through a market system by legislating the Greenhouse Gas Emissions Trading Act, supported across various political parties.

As such, the government prepared the legal and institutional groundwork as well as the framework for putting green growth, the new paradigm for national progress, into practice.

Transition to green growth

Though we still have a long way to go, numerous changes have resulted from such endeavor in Korea after about four years.

First of all, green growth is changing the economic landscape.

Green industries are emerging as a new growth engine. Investments by private businesses in green industries, including new and renewable energy, have skyrocketed every year. As a consequence, the green industry is growing rapidly, and the export of green products is rising sharply.

An increasing number of businesses are putting green management into practice. The number of businesses that practice low carbon and environment-friendly management principles is on the rise. In businesses, advocating green management is now establishing itself as a marketing trend that is the most effective in appealing to consumers.

Thanks to the government efforts to expand R&D in green technology, a growing number of companies have come to have top-notch green technologies that are grabbing attention in the international arena.

Second, green growth is bringing about changes to the environment.

Environment-friendly spaces have increased. Green areas, including urban forests, eco-friendly streams and ecotourism destinations, are sprouting up in the neighborhood.

Air and water quality in urban areas is also improving. In addition, some local governments have recently begun to implement the urban clean development mechanism. These all combine to bear testimony to the expansion of eco-friendly spaces where people coexist with the environment.

Green buildings and green transportation systems are also on the increase. The construction boom of energy-saving green buildings in both public and private sectors is spreading all over the nation. An eco-friendly transition in the transportation system from expressways to high-speed railroads is taking place. The era of electric automobiles is also dawning.

On top of this, bike paths that can be easily used in our day-to-day life have increased, and it has become possible to ride a bike across country on the 1,800km-long bike path stretching along the four major rivers.

The abilities necessary to respond to climate change have strengthened. The Government has come up with strategies to adapt to climate change as a hedge against global warming. The Four Major Rivers Restoration Project made it possible to secure and manage water resources in a stable manner, which is needed to prepare against floods and drought that had in the past only occurred once in two centuries. Furthermore, the stability of the food supply has been enhanced by efforts to prevent disasters resulting from climate change and develop new varieties of crops.

An increase in the accuracy of weather forecasts and reliable computation of climate change scenarios helped to bolster the abilities to cope with disasters caused by climate change.

Third, green growth is changing lifestyles

Most people are aware of the seriousness of climate change. More than 90 percent of the people believe that green growth policies have to be continuously pursued under all administrations. As such, the national consciousness on green growth has been awakened.

On the basis of these changes in consciousness, green living is spreading: green consumption is rising among the general public and domestic waste is being reduced. On top of this, environment-friendly leisure activities, including bicycling, ecotourism and urban farming, are on the rise, which attests to the fact that green practices are becoming natural parts of the lives of ordinary people.

International proliferation of green growth

As such, there is a dramatic green growth-based transformation in many aspects of human life. But it will take a long time for green growth to reach full fruition. In fact, change has just started in earnest and is moving forward in the desirable direction. For this reason, I am very sure that it will succeed.

No matter how successful our transition to a green way of life is, however, green growth by Korea alone does not mean much. That is because all life is bound by a collective destiny. The peoples of the world owe it to themselves to build a planet-responsible civilization to cope with climate change and the energy crisis. This is why I have tried to work with the international community for global green growth even before my August 2008 declaration of the national vision of low-carbon green growth.

At the expanded G8 Summit in Toyako in July 2008, I volunteered to act as an "early mover" in responding to climate change. I also proposed the East Asian Climate Partnership (EACP), promising Korea would gladly play the role of a bridge linking the developing and developed nations.

From next year through 2020, the Republic of Korea will increase the amount of its green Official Development Assistance (ODA) to more than $5 billion. As our EACP commitment ends this year, Korea's green ODA will shift to the Global Green Growth Partnership.

In order to more systematically support green growth in developing countries, Korea will work through the Global Green Growth Institute (GGGI), which was founded in June 2010.

The Institute will expedite cooperation between developing and developed nations, while encouraging partnerships between the private and public sectors. In this way, developing countries will more efficiently receive the necessary policy support as well as skills and know-how.

Last March, the Green Technology Center Korea (GTCK) was launched and will be nurtured as a hub for technical cooperation needed to support green growth in the developing world. The Center will also be responsible for training and educating international experts in relevant fields.

In September 2013, the Korean government is planning to establish still another higher educational institution in Hongneung in Seoul. The Green Growth Graduate School will be entrusted with nurturing professionals who will maintain a sustainable green growth system, such as green growth engineers, green managers and green policymakers. Hongneung, the cradle of Korea's rapid economic development, is poised to emerge as a center of global green growth in charge of advancing green growth technology and expertise as well as fostering high-caliber global experts.

Recently, with the Presidential Committee on Green Growth playing a pivotal role, the Korea Meteorological Administration, Korea Forest Service and the Rural Development Administration built a collaboration system for climate change adaptation and green growth. The results of the cooperative work will in turn be relayed to GGGI so that it can actually be used in administering meteorological, agricultural and forest affairs in developing countries, contributing to international proliferation of green growth.

Action strategy for 'Earth in danger'

It is significant that the international community is accommodating green growth as the action strategy to deal with the earth in danger.

OECD adopted green growth as a core strategy for achieving sustainable economic growth in its 50th Anniversary Vision Statement and has implemented green growth projects by sector. The Rio+20 and G20 Summits have also decided on green growth as a main objective to be carried out. Along with GGGI, World Bank, UNEP and OECD are propagating green growth systematically through the Green Growth Knowledge Platform.

I would like to thank the international community for enthusiastically endorsing Korea's initiative to officially convert GGGI into an international organization this coming fall. I take great pride in the fact that GGGI is becoming a viable common asset for all nations.

As an international organization, GGGI will be the centerpiece of global green growth strategy. The GTCK will be the technology arm of green growth in developing countries. The Green Climate Fund, which was created as the result of the United Nations Climate Change Conference in Durban, South Africa last year, will provide financial resources for green growth strategies and technologies.

Now that a green triangle has been perfected with the three sides representing strategy, technology and finance, our hopes have been elevated that we will not necessarily leave the earth in danger for our descendants.

Korea will continue to strive to make the green triangle an impeccable green growth architecture for all, going beyond the developing and developed countries.

I hope coming generations will remember the passions and agonies that we suffered for their sake. I hope they remember us for how hard we worked and how much we sacrificed not to leave them an Earth in danger.

To the extent that the next generation appreciates what we did for them, they will do the same for the generation coming after them, continuing a virtuous cycle.

I certainly trust that our contemporaries will be long remembered as a generation that the earth in danger and transformed it into a planet characterized by harmonious coexistence between nature and humanity.

Growth can go with environmental protection

Ki-moon Ban

Hundreds of people put on a performance, forming a human "SOS" symbol, asking for plans to preserve the Cheonsu Bay at the Sambong Beach in Taean, South Chungchong Province, as part of campaigns to save the environment from further pollution. *Korea Times file*

Twenty years ago, when world leaders met in Rio de Janeiro for the Earth Summit, 5.5 billion people inhabited our planet. Nearly half were living in extreme poverty.

Today, even with the global population exceeding 7 billion, the proportion is down to just over one quarter. Over the same period, food production has kept pace, so much so that were it distributed adequately, there would be enough to feed every person on Earth.

That is some of the good news. The bad news is that hunger and poverty are a daily burden for billions, and the environmental services on which human safety and well-being depend are under increasing pressure.

According to the latest "Global Environment Outlook" report, issued by the UN Environment Programme in June to coincide with the Rio+20 conference on sustainable development, there has been significant progress on only four of ninety of the most important internationally agreed environmental goals.

The world continues on a dangerous path in which economic growth has been achieved at the expense of natural resources and ecosystems.

We can no longer continue to burn and consume our way to prosperity while avoiding responsibility for the effect of our actions on the planet and the future well-being of generations to come.

Climate change is an existential threat. Biodiversity loss is accelerating, desertification and land degradation are imperiling lives and incomes in all regions, and the marine environment is under assault from pollution to over-fishing. Deforestation and forest degradation will likely cost the global economy more than the losses in the 2008 financial crisis. Increasing urbanization is generating ever more waste, including e-waste and other hazardous byproducts of industrialization.

Combating climate change

To extend the benefits of progress to all - and to ensure that the gains we have made can be sustained - we need to change our development model, giving equal weight to the economic, social and environmental dimensions of sustainable development.

Most urgently, we must combat climate change by meeting current pledges to keep increases in the global average temperature to less than 2 degrees Celsius above pre-industrial levels. To do that, we must move decisively towards a low-carbon economy.

It is often claimed that moving in this direction will be too costly and disruptive. But the international community has already proven, through the landmark Montreal Protocol on Substances that Deplete the Ozone Layer, that it can collaborate successfully to tackle such a challenge, with the benefits far exceeding the costs.

Phasing out polluting technologies

Scientists identified an urgent problem. Governments agreed on a legally binding approach to address it. The private sector came on board. Funding was made available for developing countries to phase out polluting technologies. The result is a drastic reduction in both the production and use of ozone-depleting substances. A catastrophe has been averted.

The example of the Montreal Protocol shows that where there is commitment and initiative, common solutions can be found to common problems. More reasons for optimism can be seen in the outcome of Rio+20.

Rio was the first step towards creating a new model for a 21st-century economy that rejects the myth that there must be a zero-sum trade-off between growth and the environment. Rio recognized that with smart public policies, governments can grow their economies, alleviate poverty, create decent jobs and accelerate social progress in a way that respects the earth's finite natural resources.

The results in Rio can lead us to a more sustainable future. World leaders renewed and strengthened political commitment to sustainable development. Governments agreed to launch a process to establish universal Sustainable Development Goals, building on our advances under the Millennium Development Goals.

Sustainable consumption

Sustainable consumption and production was endorsed, as was the potential of the green economy for poverty reduction, economic growth and environmental care. Doors were opened to help us to identify new financing for sustainable development.

Partnerships were strengthened among countries, businesses and civil society to promote initiatives on energy, food and nutrition, transport and oceans. More than 1,000 corporate leaders from all continents delivered a common message: business as usual no longer works.

Perhaps the most tangible legacy of Rio is that it galvanized action. More than 700 commitments were registered, and many of them will take us far towards the transformative change we are looking for. Among them is a commitment by eight multilateral banks, led by the Asian Development Bank, to shift $175 billion over the next decade to sustainable transport. More than $50 billion was committed by the private sector to my Sustainable Energy for All initiative - with tens of billions more from governments and other players pledged to the initiative and other energy programs. These commitments will benefit more than a billion people over the next two decades.

Golden thread

Energy is the golden thread that connects development, social inclusion and environmental protection. It literally brings light into people's lives, and generates hope and opportunity.

Our aim is to ensure universal access to modern energy services for the one in five people worldwide who lack them; to reduce energy waste by doubling energy efficiency; and to double the share of renewables in the global energy mix. The deadline is 2030. If we succeed we can raise people's well-being while helping to bring down the global thermostat.

When I was a child I knew energy poverty first-hand. I also knew hunger. In Rio, I launched the Zero Hunger Challenge. In a world of plenty, no-one should go hungry. This is my vision. All people should have access to nutrition year-round - those cannot buy or grow food should be able to receive it through a social safety net. No child should grow up stunted. Food systems should be sustainable, small farmers, especially women, should be empowered, and - from farm to market - food should never be wasted.

By 2030, we will need 50 percent more food, 45 percent more energy and 30 percent more freshwater - just to continue to live as we do today. These are major challenges. Rio helped to emphasize their scale and the urgency of addressing them.

But it also highlighted that we have the tools we need - from treaties to technology, from programs to partnerships. We have wasted too much time, too many opportunities. We must get to work. Let us use all the tools at our disposal to eradicate poverty, promote prosperity and preserve a healthy planet that can support the well-being of future generations.

20 years lost in the environment

Jeffrey Sachs

Major national projects like the development of Saemangeum in North Jeolla Province cause severe environmental conflicts among residents and interest parties but also provide related parties an opportunity to reach viable solutions. *Korea Times file*

I have one basic message, which is not exactly a surprise and that is that we are in very deep trouble. Things are not working and the international system is not solving problems that humanity has never had to solve together.

At Rio+20, we could not go celebrating and we had to go with our heads held down taking in the reality that the Rio Summit 20 years ago which produced three tremendous treaties: to avert human-induced climate change, to avert the destruction of biodiversities and to avert the desertification of the earth's drylands have all failed to do what they set out to do.

Twenty years on, not one of these treaties is working yet. As a result, we have more urgent tasks at hand because we have squandered 20 years.

I think one of the main problems is that we don't realize the scale of the challenge that we face. This is not an issue to feel good about because of a demonstration project here or a nice example there, as the world is overwhelming us in the reality of environmental wreckage and risk far more than we are accomplishing by our combined efforts over these 20 years.

And I want to take climate change as the core case to put forward, but one could also talk about the loss of biodiversity and indeed many other ills that are at front and center as well.

The climate change is of course an issue of the emission of greenhouse gases, mostly from sources of the fossil economy and that global fossil fuel economy continues to grow rapidly and that is at the heart of all successful middle and high level economies in the world.

Nature of the challenge

Fossil fuel made the modern economy possible and it has carried economic growth for two centuries. And the infrastructure system, the energy and transport systems and the industrial processes that we live on are largely driven by a fossil fuel economy.

The point is therefore sometimes hard to appreciate the real nature of the challenge that we have in front of us.

Currently, the world is emitting about 32 billion tons of carbon dioxide per year and with that rate of emission the atmospheric concentration of carbon dioxide is rising two to three parts per million each year.

From the pre-industrial level of 280 parts per million, we are not at about 395 parts per million.

Many climate scientists say that the safe level to avoid dangerous enthroprogenic interference is in the rear-view mirror, probably at a level of around 350 parts per million.

And yet we continue to see a relentless rise in greenhouse gas concentrations and CO_2 concentrations because of the rapid growth of the world's economy.

The role of fossil fuels, which are the main sources of CO_2 emissions, are so deeply entrenched that our economic structures are shockingly similar despite what seems to be wasteful when you come down to it.

In the world as a whole, we use about 0.2 kilograms of oil equivalent for each dollar of national production measured in purchasing power parity

And for that kilogram of oil equivalent, we emit about 2.4 kilograms of carbon dioxide when it is burned because the mix of coal, oil and natural gas that goes into producing that kilogram of oil equivalent energy.

When you combine 0.2 kilograms of oil equivalent per dollar of GDP and 2.4 kilograms of carbon dioxide per kilogram of oil of oil equivalent and you multiply them together, you get approximately 0.46 kilograms of carbon dioxide for each dollar produced in the world.

And since the world economy is currently running at $68 trillion and you multiply by that, you get the 32 billion tons of carbon dioxide.

Now, when you look around the world, there is not much difference in how our energy systems work. At a world's average, it is 0.19 kilograms of oil equivalent per dollar of GDP; in China it is 0.2; it is 0.2 in Korea; and 0.19 in the United States.

Hard-wiring of energy

The hard-wiring of energy is not so different across the vastly different sets of economies because we have industry, transport and buildings that have similar technologies that exist in all of these economies.

If you look at the energy mix, there is a little bit of difference because the world as a whole produces 2.4 kilograms of CO_2 per kilogram of oil equivalent of energy. In Korea, it is 2.2; 2.4 in the U.S.: and 3.1 in China because of the higher concentration of coal in the energy basket. But not so much difference across the economies.

This means that to change direction is to change deeply the hard-wiring of our economic systems. This is what we need to do.

Consider the following: The world economy is growing at about 4 percent per year. That is a doubling every 18 years. By 2050, we will have approximately a four-fold increase of GDP and of world production if development continues as we hope it does.

That would mean a world economy of $270 trillion at today's purchasing power prices.

Now what the climate models and scientists tell us is that simply continuing with the carbon and energy concentrations that we have would be a path of suicide and recklessness. We would not have a viable food supply for the world in such a trajectory. We would have profound instability. We will not have only 200 million Africans suffering from extreme drought in the south horns of Africa but we would have all regions around the world incapable of assuring their food security.

Efficient energy use

And yet, what do we have to do? If you look at the most efficient economy right now in energy use, instead of 0.2 kilograms of oil equivalent per dollar, its 0.1: That's where Japan is, and that's where Denmark is, at half of the world's average.

Suppose we get to a $270 trillion world output and we cut to 0.1 rather than 0.2 of energy efficiency, the world becomes as efficient as the most efficient economies today.

Even if we are to have a chance for safety, we will have to have half our emissions at most in the world by mid-century.

If you do the arithmetic, what would be required is a reduction of about 80 percent of the carbon concentration of that energy.

Essentially, we would have to become as efficient as the most efficient economies in the world and decarbonize at the same time to accommodate both growth and the deep reduction of emissions that we need. That's what a green economy and green growth really implies. It is really deep, deep decarbonization of energy systems.

There is no place on this earth that is remotely on this path right now, no matter if countries are doing clean energy systems, solar power systems, nuclear or wind power, none of them, with the possible exception of Denmark - I would say because of its great wind resources and great governance - are on the trajectory that we need.

We don't even set goals that way nationally. We set goals to 2020 which is a very easy game to play because it does not force us to think about the depth of change that is needed.

In the United States, the trick is to close down some coal plants and use more natural gas but that is a dirty joke. From an environmental point of view, that doesn't even begin to address the real challenge of decarbonization that we face globally.

So my point is that this is an issue that is so unprecedented, so deep in its structure, we are so close to the edge that we, humanity, have not really taken on this base reality in our discussions, negotiations and political processes; our white papers are not even close.

Of course, I come from a country which has denied this reality for the last 20 years where one political party insists that it doesn't even exist and the other party dares not speak the name of climate, so that the world's largest economy is out of this story in any real way.

And in the rest of the world of talking nobody is actually doing anything at the depth that is required. This is a fundamentally unsolved problem and almost no government in the world and no country in the world have even identified pathways that are realistic in how to decarbonize.

Of course, technologically, we can think about how that can be done. In fact, it is surprising at how low cost this can be. Not for free: it would cost real resources.

I don't believe for a moment that this green economy is free in the sense of today's market prices but it is less costly than denial.

But in my view, it is reckless that we don't pay the price that is required. And we can see how this can be done: nuclear power, and renewable energy, carbon capture and sequestration, mass electrification of transport systems and green buildings. The range of technologies exists.

They are expensive, we don't have good storages and many of these carbon capture sequestrations are on paper or a few demonstration models, nothing of scale. No one is building in scale and no one of planning in scale. Many countries are closing down their nuclear programs, but we are not going to run the global economy on intermittent energy sources because you need base energy to run an economy and so we have unsolved problems at the fundamental level.

We can see where we need to go but we are not on that trajectory right now.

The UN framework process has failed for 20 years. There have been fine treaties but have not been successful in turning the needle in terms of global emissions.

What we need is a mass mobilization of society rather than international laws and diplomatic negotiations.

I believe that we have left climate change in the hands of lawyers for the last 20 years and the lawyers are good at prolonged negotiating and they have spent the last 20 years on negotiating what is binding, how you measure it and what is verifiable and almost nothing has been accomplished. Certainly nothing compared to the scale of the challenge.

What we should think about is waking up the eyes of world society, especially young people and universities, experts and businesses to the scale of the reality.

We should not be thinking about new new legally binding agreements but sustainable development goals that our morals and global goals need for our shared survival. Because, at least that way, we will be able to state the way that the world wants to save itself, that these goals are not to be negotiated or whether they are binding or not. That is what the world stands for.

And based on those goals, we create a new generation of problem-solving tools, bring together expertise, activism and social mobilization to understand the depth of the challenge, the magnitudes and the technological options and to induce our society to take steps without asking who moves first.

Leading the way to a green energy era

Jeremy Rifkin

The development of the Pusan Science Industrial Park, near the southern port city of Pusan, is an exemplary development with deep consideration for the environment. *Korea Times file*

We are approaching the sunset of the oil era in the first half of the 21st century. The price of oil on global markets continues to climb, and peak global oil is within sight over the coming decades.

At the same time, the dramatic rise in carbon dioxide emissions from the burning of fossil fuels is raising the earth's temperature and threatening an unprecedented change in the chemistry of the planet and global climate, with ominous consequences for the future of human civilization and Earth ecosystems.

While oil, coal and natural gas will continue to provide a substantial portion of the world's and the European Union's energy well into the 21st century, there is a growing consensus that we are entering a twilight period where the full costs of our fossil fuel addiction are beginning to act as a drag on the world economy.

During this twilight era, the 27 EU member states are making every effort to ensure that the remaining stock of fossil fuels is used more efficiently and are experimenting with clean energy technologies to limit carbon dioxide emissions in the burning of conventional fuels.

These efforts fall in line with the EU mandate that member states increase energy efficiency 20 percent by 2020 and reduce their global warming emissions 20 percent (based on 1990 levels), again by 2020.

Convergence of new energy

But greater efficiencies and mandated global warming gas reductions, by themselves, are not enough to adequately address the unprecedented crisis of global warming and global peak oil and gas production. Looking to the future, every government will need to explore new energy paths and establish new economic models with the goal of achieving as close to zero carbon emissions as possible.

The great pivotal economic changes in world history have occurred when new energy regimes converge with new communication regimes. When that convergence happens, society is restructured in wholly new ways.

In the early modern era, the coming together of coal-powered steam technology and the printing press gave birth to the first industrial revolution.

It would have been impossible to organize the dramatic increase in the pace, speed, flow, density and connectivity of economic activity made possible by the coal-fired steam engine using the older codex and oral forms of communication.

In the late nineteenth century and throughout the first two-thirds of the twentieth century, first generation electrical forms of communication - the telegraph, telephone, radio, television, electric typewriters, calculators, etc. - converged with the introduction of oil and the internal combustion engine, becoming the communications command and control mechanism for organizing and marketing the second industrial revolution.

A great communications revolution occurred in the 1990s. Second generation electrical forms of communication - personal computers, the internet, the World Wide Web, and wireless communication technologies - connected the central nervous system of more than a billion people on Earth at the speed of light.

And although the new software and communication revolutions have begun to increase productivity in every industry, their true potential is yet to be fully realized. That potential lies in their convergence with renewable energy, partially stored in the form of hydrogen, to create the first "distributed" energy regimes.

The same design principles and smart technologies that made possible the Internet and vast distributed global communication networks will be used to reconfigure the world's power grids so that people can produce renewable energy and share it peer-to-peer, just like they now produce and share information, creating a new, decentralized form of energy use.

We need to envision a future in which millions of individual players can collect, produce and store locally generated renewable energy in their homes, offices, factories, and vehicles and share their power generation with each other across a Europe-wide intelligent intergrid. (Hydrogen is a universal storage medium for intermittent renewable energies; just as digital is a universal storage mechanism for text, audio, video, data and other forms of media)

Renewable energy

The question is often asked as to whether renewable energy, in the long run, can provide enough power to run a national or global economy?

Just as second-generation information system grid technologies allow businesses to connect thousands of desktop computers, creating far more distributed computing power than even the most powerful centralized computers that exist, millions of local producers of renewable energy, using hydrogen storage and intelligent utility networks, can potentially produce far more distributed power than the older centralized forms of energy - oil, coal, natural gas and nuclear - we currently rely on.

The creation of a renewable energy regime, partially stored in the form of hydrogen and distributed via smart intergrids, opens the door to a third industrial revolution and should have as powerful an economic multiplier effect in the 21st century as the convergence of mass print technology with coal and steam power technology in the 19th century or the coming together of electrical forms of communication with oil and the internal combustion engine in the 20th century.

European industry has the scientific, technological, and financial know-how to spearhead the shift to renewable energies, a hydrogen economy, and an intelligent power grid and, in so doing, to lead the world into a new economic era.

Europe's world class automotive industry, chemical industry, engineering industry, construction industry, software, computer and communication, and banking and insurance industries, give it a leg up in the race to the third industrial revolution.

By fostering renewable energies, a hydrogen infrastructure, and a continent-wide intelligent intergrid, the European Union can help create a sustainable economic development plan for its 500 million citizens in the first half of the 21st century.

The third industrial revolution will require a wholesale reconfiguration of the transport, construction, and electricity sectors, creating new goods and services, spawning new businesses, and providing millions of new jobs.

Being first to market will position the European Union as a leader in the third industrial revolution, giving it the commercial edge in the export of green technological know-how and equipment around the world.

Producing a new generation of renewable energy technologies, manufacturing portable and stationary fuel cells, reinventing the automobile, transforming Europe's millions of buildings into power plants to produce renewable energy for internal consumption or distribution back to the grid, reconfiguring the electrical power grid as an intelligent utility network, as well as producing all of the accompanying technologies, goods and services that make up a high-tech third industrial revolution economy, will have an economic multiplier effect that stretches well toward the mid-decades of the 21st century.

Distributed communication

The coming together of distributed communication technologies and distributed renewable energies via an open access, intelligent power grid represents "power to the people." For a younger generation that's growing up in a less hierarchical and more networked world, the ability to produce and share their own energy, like they produce and share their own information, in an open access intergrid, will seem both natural and commonplace.

The key challenge that every nation needs to address is where they want their country to be ten years from now: in the sunset energies and industries of the second industrial revolution or the sunrise energies and industries of the third industrial revolution. The third industrial revolution is the endgame that will take the world out of old carbon and uranium-based energies into a non-polluting, sustainable future for the human race.

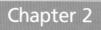

Chapter 2

Scholar

Asia-Pacific fighting climate change
Disaster management and federalism
Are we prepared?
Mitigating revelations of climate change
Adaptation critical in changing climate
Future of tourism within the environment

Asia-Pacific fighting climate change

Komal Raj Aryal

NASA's Terra satellite captured this natural-color image of Typhoon Muifa on Aug. 4, 2011. The eye of the storm is east of Taiwan, and clouds overlap Okinawa. Storms in the Asia-Pacific region have been getting more violent in recent years. *AFP- Yonhap*

There is mounting evidence that Asia and the Pacific are experiencing weather patterns more extreme than previously experienced, attributable to the effects of global climate change. Reduction of the impact of climate change is gaining importance in the international agenda.

Increasing intensity and frequency of climatic hazards impact negatively upon environmental and socio-economic systems. Disasters of flooding, mudslides, forest fires, cold waves and heat waves, storm surges, and decreases in ground water are issues in the arena of governance of sustainable development in the region.

Many countries from the region are struggling to cope with frequent disasters believed to originate from climate change. In the last three years, we have seen major floods and mudslides induced by high intensity rain in Korea, Vietnam, China, Sri Lanka, Nepal, India, Thailand, Myanmar, Vanuatu, Pakistan and Bangladesh. Disaster risks associated with climate change have the potential to affect us all; the indications are that the risks, both in Asia and the Pacific region and globally, are likely to increase in the future.

Finding ways to avoid the impacts of climate change is a major challenge to us all. The geography of Asia and the Pacific is complex, encompassing as it does, everything from the rural mountainous area of Nepal to the urban and sophisticated area of Songdo Future City of Incheon. In rural Asia, the economy relies upon agriculture, whereas in urban Asia the economy is dependent upon industries and infrastructures.

In the past 50 years, Asia has been extensively engaged in industrial production for local, regional and global consumption. At the same time, various urban centers of Asia have emerged as major hubs for the global economy. The by-products of high-tech manufacturing are increasing, and as a result, climates are changing, leading to frequent localized disasters that affect the global economy.

The experience of flooding for Thailand's economy, according to BBC news on Feb. 20, 2012, is as follows: "Thailand's economy has declined sharply. Major local and multinational companies including Honda and Sony have been affected by flooding. These industries have had to cut their profit margins as production disruptions became commonplace."

People in Asia and the Pacific have been living with risk for a long time. The history of climate change-related disasters in the region is notorious and well-documented. Recent events include the following: Cyclone Nargis, which killed a reported 138,000 people in Myanmar in 2008; the 2010 floods in Pakistan, which directly affected an estimated 20 million people; 2011 flooding in Australia, Thailand and the Philippines; 2011 urban landslides and heavy rain in Korea; and extensive wildfires in Russia during 2010, attributed to a combination of drought and extreme temperatures.

The impact associated with such events is widespread and increasingly complex, as society, infrastructure and our relationship with the environment become more intertwined and interdependent.

My experience with historical disaster events in Nepal shows that repeated climatic disasters push already affected communities to vicious poverty cycles. On the one hand, frequent small-scale disasters have a greater impact in terms of casualties than large-scale ones. On the other hand, repeated disasters encourage industries to relocate to areas where the frequencies of disasters are low, thereby reducing economic opportunities for the people living in and around the disaster-prone areas. This leaves local communities at risk of hunger.

It is time to work together to reduce risk at the local level so as to control our future changes in the way we operate within our world. First, we need to bring together people from different disciplines of endeavor, ranging from the natural, social, physical and engineering sciences, to work for disaster risk management. Second, we need to reach consensus about how to integrate risk management as a foundation within science. The United Nations World Conference on Disaster Risk Reduction adopted the Hyogo Framework for Action HFA (2005-2015) in 2005.

Since then, United Nations organizations have been accelerating disaster risk reduction activities as a way to improve the capacity of all nations to reduce the impact of natural hazards. Significant funding has been allocated to facilitate the implementation of existing plans.

However, the midterm evaluation report recommends more education and training activities before implementing HFA local level plans. Sustainability and effectiveness of initiatives depend on leadership that initiates resilience building in the region.

In the context of disaster risk reduction in Asia and the Pacific, we need a thorough local socio-political risk analysis to support current objectives. At present, local level interventions are primarily of the "project" and not of the "process" type; they fit notions of risk management initiatives at a local level rather than local based risk management as such.

Ownership and sustainability of processes and results are therefore in question and, consequently, so is the role that local risk reduction can play in sustainable development governance. Disaster effects are wide-reaching. Disasters are increasing.

Unless everyone is involved in relevant risk avoidance activities, somebody (and it might be you) will suffer the consequences. But the worst thing is the likelihood that the population impacted will be universal. Disaster effects at a local level seem avoidable, but repeated disaster events of increasing magnitude will soon be unavoidable.

Resources in the disaster impact areas will become increasingly difficult to access or generate, and this will have a national impact through food supply and industrial manufacturing, which will then generate an international impact.

This is not an isolated phenomenon; disasters are proliferating, and climate change is involved in the process. Halt climate change and you will at least slow the process of deterioration.

On using local analyses of vulnerability, risk would promote a more comprehensive, localized view of risk and its causal factors. But participatory local climatic risk analysis is still organized from the perspective of disaster risk and very often not as part of an overall diagnosis of local development activities needed and the factors that promote disaster resilience locally. More often than not it is climate change and therefore climatic disaster risk that is at the center of concern and not development in a more general sense. It is of global and local importance that Asia and the Pacific get a handle on this situation while we still have the opportunity.

Hyogo Framework for Action 2005-2015

1. Ensure that disaster risk reduction is a national and local priority with a strong institutional basis for implementation
2. Identify, assess and monitor disaster risks and enhance early warning
3. Use knowledge, innovation and education to build a culture of safety and resilience at all levels
4. Reduce the underlying risk
5. Strengthen disaster preparedness for effective response at all levels

In recent years every government in Asia and the Pacific has had to cope with the effects of a substantial number of weather-related incidents exposing the vulnerability of their populations. Climate change can affect sustainable development governance in two ways; a slow onset impact (drought, prolonged wet periods) and sudden rapid impact (typhoons, floods, heavy snow, long dry or wet spells, glacial lake overflow, landslides).

Often, the sudden rapid impact of climate change will come without warning, leaving the population little or no time to react. Experience of previous incidents has shown that such events are rarely straightforward and often leave victims in a vulnerable state. Government departments at all levels are then faced with complex situations.

People have survived the slow onset impact of climate change for many years and have developed adaptation strategies. Recent increases in the sudden rapid impact of climate change mean that governments in Asia and the Pacific region should expect these types of incidents every year.

To manage the complex and multiple impacts of sudden and rapid climate change events, government departments have a responsibility to integrate risk reduction and adaptation strategies jointly and apply a crosscutting approach for sustainable development governance. Following the publication of HFA reports from NGOs, development banks and other agencies have repeatedly highlighted the role and duties of government in overseeing disaster risk reduction (DRR) and climate change adaptation (CCA) integration.

However, it is seldom the case that strategies for strengthening institutional capacities are identified. The focus is often on improving community awareness, so that all too often cultivating awareness within and across governmental communities is overlooked.

While it is reasonable to expect that all heads of government departments have an understanding of the vulnerability, risks, hazards and principles of DRR and CCA, it is likely that specialized training will be required for individuals charged with developing and implementing policy, depending on the scale and complexity of the local situation. The extent to which DRR-CCA policy integration for sustainable development governance is carried out is a matter for individual department heads, and it is likely that decisions will be based on comprehensive pre- and post-disaster risk assessments.

A proactive stance allows sustainable development governance through government integration of DRR and CCA. For this reason, pre-disaster risk

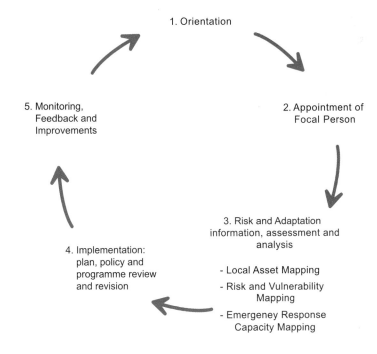

1. Orientation

5. Monitoring, Feedback and Improvements

2. Appointment of Focal Person

3. Risk and Adaptation information, assessment and analysis

- Local Asset Mapping
- Risk and Vulnerability Mapping
- Emergeney Response Capacity Mapping

4. Implementation: plan, policy and programme review and revision

assessment is a key component of the approach. For this purpose, I recommend a procedural approach for integrating DRR and CCA into development planning across all sectors of national government using the following five-steps:

Many governments in Asia and the Pacific region have separate central departments for dealing with disaster risk and for dealing with climate change adaptation. Both departments are designed to tackle risk locally. These departments should either be combined, forming a new DRR and CCA department, or be encouraged to form a joint coordination body at the central (national) level to oversee integrated risk and adaptation policy formulation.

Both departments consist of team members who have valuable knowledge on DRR and CCA in regional and international contexts. A merging of this information would facilitate a more streamlined and efficient perspective for evolving DRR and CAA strategies for sustainable development governance plans.

All national government departments should liaise with the centralized DRR and CCA department or joint coordination body to ensure that they obtain an operational knowledge base for integrating risk reduction and adaptation into departmental policies and programs. This will also ensure continuing interoperability with HFA 2005-2015 and the National Adaptation Program and procedures as government officials develop their own capacities and understanding.

The purpose of the five steps (in the diagram) is to provide awareness about integrated DRR and CCA policy, departmental coordination and operational procedures relevant to minimize the impact on sustainable development governance in Asia and the Pacific region. It must be emphasized, however, that this is only guidance. Each disaster is different and each government will need to exercise professional judgment to reduce the local impact according to the circumstances present.

For sustainable development governance to be successful, local risk assessment needs to be implemented at all levels of government, and across all sectors. Cross-sector working will be essential to avoid the emergence of duplicated or conflicting policies.

Best practices and policies should be disseminated between local, national, regional and international levels to maximize knowledge-sharing and strategy effectiveness. As well as information dissemination in the form of seminars, providing those in other sectors with the opportunity to observe practical examples of local risk assessment policies being implemented on the ground should strengthen the understanding of what sustainable development governance can achieve.

Disaster management and federalism

Bernard Rowan

A man clears snow from his window near the city of Kukes some 160 km (100 miles) north of capital Tirana in Albania. Heavy snow and other erratic weathers have reached disaster levels across the globe, mostly as a result of climate change. *Korea Times file*

The United States is one of the world's most powerful countries if one considers GDP or military might, but in other respects it is not so powerful. If we look at national debt, balance of trade, or economic diversity with respect to industrialization, the standing of the U.S. would be considerably less remarkable.

The same would be true regarding America's infant mortality, literacy, and divorce rates, money spent on police, fire, and other safety agencies vis-à-vis education, and the list could go on. Being powerful does not preclude being less powerful at the same time, or underdeveloped, depending upon the subject at hand.

The same must be said for the United States' preparation and ability to deal with natural disasters as a federal system. Due to its political genesis, America is one of relatively few countries that prosecute politics through a system that defines and distinguishes authority for national, state, and local governments through written constitutions. Americans believe fervently in keeping power local when it can be kept local and delegating power to the federal or national government only when the object is one that meets constitutional limits. Every so often, a new leader comes along who wishes to invigorate the federalist components of our political system. Such is one of the dialectics of American political life and history.

Disaster Reduction

As we approach the 10th anniversary of the World Conference on Disaster Reduction, it is instructive to remind ourselves of its five stated priorities for disaster management:

1. Ensure that disaster risk reduction is a national and a local priority with a strong institutional basis for implementation.
2. Identify, assess and monitor disaster risks and enhance early warning.
3. Use knowledge, innovation and education to build a culture of safety and resilience at all levels.
4. Reduce the underlying risk factors.
5. Strengthen disaster preparedness for effective response at all levels.

I would argue that the disaster preparedness, response capacity, early warning systems, and reduction of risk factors in the United States all leave much to be desired. In a political system much more concerned with anti-terrorism, immigration policy, health policy, and economic recovery, there is too little discussion of this subject. In a presidential election cycle now entering full swing, disaster management should be discussed as a matter of national security and national development for this century. And all of these needs are only accentuated by the nature of our federal system of government.

As other essays in this series have elaborated, the consequences of human use and abuse of natural ecosystems, the under provision of resources and planning, and the need to integrate risk reduction and response structures into economic development priorities and policies are going to become more prominent parts of global public discourse.

There should be no overreaction or notion that the end-time is near, but there should be every effort to protect and preserve our peoples, lands, and infrastructure through the application of public and private resources to disaster risk reduction and management.

The American federal system is ill-equipped to manage and to reduce the risks attending natural disasters in its current configuration. It has failed to do so in the case of Hurricane Katrina and other recent cataclysms. It is time to nationalize further the security of our national borders so as to permit federal government authority to supervise the states in dealing with natural disasters - both response and recovery efforts and even more for risk reduction.

Nature's movements

According to a recent report, there are 12,479 miles of coastal borders in the states of the United States of America. There are thousands of additional miles of Great Lakes and connecting waterways or coastlines. This constitutes a vast stretch of territory that must be considered if we want to take seriously the need to anticipate nature's movements and limit the effects of natural disasters.

If we wish to draw a parallel to national security, the country already has nationalized much of the air safety management apparatus. This makes sense given that on any particular day there are 80,000 or more commercial air movements alone, not including international flights or those of civil aircraft. While few would question the need for the United States government - the national or federal government - to protect our skies and airspace and to secure it from enemies at home or from abroad, the same logic doesn't prevail with respect to disaster prevention along coasts that have the same quality, i.e. international borders.

Florida and Texas are among the most vulnerable states in terms of disaster management. Many of the other areas more likely to experience natural disasters are in the Southeast and south central sections of the country. They also include the states with the highest percentages of land lying in floodplains. This context creates a disproportionate burden for these states, and it is likely that current investments do not come close to meeting the needs in terms of forecasting, limiting impacts, and response, relief, and recovery.

It is time to nationalize our coastal waterways and coastal borders so that the power of the nation and our people, both in terms of the federal government and in terms of the centralization of decision-making and funding that can reap economies of scale and bring uniform and systemic solutions to common problems, may be brought to bear.

Thomas Birkland and Sarah Waterman have written about the over-emphasis on homeland security and the relative de-prioritization of non-terrorist threats such as natural disasters. Hurricane Katrina was much more of a disaster than it needed to be because the federal government's disaster management structure and processes were left to relative neglect. State and local counterparts were wholly inadequate.

Birkland and Waterman describe the current era in American federalism, relying on Tim Conlan, as one of "opportunistic federalism," which extends a mindset that seeks short-term benefit from federal dollars and attention to the exclusion of longer-term needs and coordination. Too many in this country continue thinking of disaster planning and management as something to be done when or after the unthinkable happens - too much more at that time along with too much less in the years that precede disasters. This is an expensive and dangerous mindset.

Fiscal dilemmas

Many of the states, perhaps most, are in dire fiscal condition at this point; the effects of the first great recession of this century in the United States have reached and continue to mire the states in fiscal dilemmas. We cannot afford the illusion that standing on opportunistic federalism will suffice for fulfilling the responsibilities of America's governments to the people.

The National Response Framework, which remains the basic law for organizing federal relationships around disaster management, should be scrapped, or at minimum revisited and revised. State and local governments lack the capacity to do the heavy lifting as to natural disaster planning and response in this day and age, and the costs and requirements will only increase this century.

As Birkland and Watermann also have noted, when Hurricane Katrina occurred, and in its aftermath, the chief scapegoat and party to blame was the federal government.

This points to an underlying perception that the mitigation of and preparation for natural disasters is a national governmental issue, not one to be left to the vagaries of state and local provision. But as yet, America's policymakers and the public have not demanded associated actions and change.

Federalism should be invigorated with a stronger national component, but it should not be eliminated. The Army Corps of Engineers is generally welcomed to facilitate the development of infrastructure projects throughout the country. Think of the benefits in terms of jobs that disaster management industries could provide, working in tandem with the Corps and other agencies of the federal, state, and local governments. Following Richard Weitz of the Hudson Institute, there will always be a role for non-governmental organizations, public-and private partnerships, and the development of a national culture around disaster management.

Disaster management apparatus

But whereas Weitz is content to modify the disaster management apparatus with regional structures and law enforcement information sharing established via the Department of Homeland Security, I think this approach does not go far enough. Regional institutions such as those for the Federal Reserve, national defense, and courts are fine, but the principal center for policy development and implementation needs to be re-vectored to a single agency or policy platform under the U.S. Congress. Disaster management is more appropriately considered a part of national security.

Paying homage to federalism should not amount in the final analysis to leaving the planning, preparation, and execution of prevention, relief, and recovery efforts to the vicissitudes of state and local funding and development.

Too many times each year we see the President doing flyovers and then declaring areas ravaged by flooding, hurricanes, or some other disaster as "national disaster areas." Then, with the consent of state and local authorities, the National Guard and national agencies begin to respond. What this country did to its airports following 9/11 has been to create and ensconce an entire federal apparatus to support state-level efforts to prevent acts of terrorism.

On any given day, year, or decade, there is an even greater need to do the same for disaster management. As the articles of this series detail, the costs of clinging to old ways continue to rise, and the associated loss of life and all forms of capital stands as a call to action for long-term development that enhances human possibility.

Federalism and disaster management constitutes a field for 21st century technologies and change. A new cooperative federalism, guided by a much more robust federal government role and presence, from planning to funding, should be implemented to involve state and local cooperation and working teams that will implement associated national policies, plans, and initiatives. We are way behind, but the way forward is right before us.

Are we prepared?

Sang-ok Choi

Hurricane Hatteras Island, N.C., 2011

Recent natural and human-made disasters have forced our societies to re-consider existing emergency management systems and plans. Last year was a memorable one for many Americans impacted by disasters. Massive blizzards and floods affected dozens of states across the country. Texas and other states fought dangerous wildfires for months. Last spring, the United States was devastated by the deadliest tornadoes since the 1950s over just a few weeks. In August, a magnitude 5.8 earthquake struck Virginia that was felt as far away as New York City. This was just one of 5,017 earthquakes experienced in 2011, according to the U.S. Geological Survey. As a result, emergency management systems are being tasked to reflect global changes in the environments of ecosystems, politics, economy, society, technology, and international situations. So as we reflect on the past year, many wonder what lessons we learned.

Weather-related disasters

In 2011, more than 1,100 American people died in weather-related incidents and more than 8,000 were injured. The year also included a record of at least 14 individual events that caused economic damage of over $1 billion and carried a collective price tag of more than $55 billion. Events such as the southern drought contrasted with flooding across the northern United States to represent the extreme temperature and precipitation swings that climate scientists project will become more common in the future amid a warming climate. Trends such as urban sprawl and conversion of rural land to suburban landscapes increase the likelihood that a tornado will impact densely populated areas. The wild weather of 2011 reminds us all of our increasing vulnerability and prompts an initiative to build a weather-ready nation.

Weather warnings are critical to protecting people and property. Nationally, the average lead-time for tornadoes is 12 to 14 minutes, but during various outbreaks of severe weather in 2011, tornado warnings were issued with an average lead-time of approximately 25 minutes, while some exceeded half an hour. Not long ago, the average lead-time was half as long. Warnings for flash floods, another leading cause of weather-related fatalities, have also improved greatly with a nationwide average lead-time of one hour or more. An effective warning requires that the threat be detected, notice communicated, and that people in impacted areas take action to protect themselves. By helping atmospheric scientists and the emergency management community better to understand how weather information is received and what triggers people to take action, we can communicate the threat more effectively and save more lives.

Pollution-related disasters

Various types of major pollution incidents continue to occur, which have an important impact on the ecological environment, people's health and social development. The U.S. Environmental Protection Agency (EPA) established the Environmental Response Laboratory Network (ERLN) to assist in addressing chemical, biological, and radiological threats during nationally significant incidents. The ERLN is managed by the EPA's Office of Emergency Management and serves as a national network of laboratories that can be accessed as needed to support large-scale environmental responses and to provide consistent analytical capabilities, capacities, and quality data in a systematic, coordinated response. The ERLN integrates capabilities of existing public sector laboratories with accredited private sector labs to support environmental responses.

The ERLN provides an environmental laboratory testing capability and capacity to meet EPA's responsibilities for surveillance, response, decontamination and recovery from incidents involving release of chemical, biological, or radiological contaminants; facilitates coordination of laboratories capable of responding efficiently and effectively to incidents; and establishes relationships and priorities with other federal laboratory networks through the Integrated Consortium of Laboratory Networks (ICLN) in preparation for a major environmental event. Implementing the concept of scientific development and constructing a harmonious society is necessary to solve environmental risks properly. Based on an analysis of the main problems to the regional emergency management of sudden environmental incidents, a major suggestion is to develop an environmental emergency management system (E2MS) for regional emergency pollution accidents. E2MS is concerned with constructing a regional emergency management information system, improving the environmental protection and risk management infrastructure, building a regional environmental emergencies sudden decision support system, perfecting an emergency management mechanism and increasing the level of risk management.

Reform of EM systems

Structurally, emergency management systems should be established in terms of three basic principles: integration, organic operation, and collaboration. Emergency management agencies and functions should be centralized. These centralized emergency management systems are characterized as operating designated leading emergency management agencies responsible for coordinating and managing emergency management resources and information to deal with specific types of disasters. The United States created the Department of Homeland Security (DHS) to coordinate national security services including emergency management and risk management after 9/11. Likewise, in 2008 Korea introduced roles of coordinating emergency management services. The change from decentralized to centralized emergency management systems enables designated emergency management agencies to monitor and control entire emergency management activities, to increase the efficiency of managing and using limited resources, and to consistently operate emergency management activities with clear roles and responsibilities for each agency across disaster types and situations. In particular, there needs to be a serious awareness of new hazards such as global warming and terrorist attacks. It is imperative that we better understand such threats and find ways to limit and more effectively deal with such possibilities.

Shared governance

The Korean government has made efforts to emphasize its role for emergency management, without equally supporting the activity of other players such as voluntary organizations, business corporations and the local community. That is partially why the Korean government has not substantially succeeded in managing all kinds of disasters. Residents and their communities have to deal with emergencies more directly than anyone else. Since the establishment of the National Emergency Management Agency, many residents have increased their awareness of disasters and emergency management, although there is still room for improvement. When an emergency receives national attention via mass media or the Internet, awareness among residents and their communities dramatically increases. However, a majority have not attempted to set up their own written emergency operation plan, though some have done so verbally.

Another challenge to be overcome is the ongoing belief that planning is all that is required to prepare for disasters. Instead of writing emergency operations plans, we need to find ways to reduce vulnerability and enhance capabilities. Ways must be found to improve communication among all pertinent actors during disasters and work harmoniously to promote recovery in the aftermath of such events. Voluntarism has not historically been a popular activity in Korea, although its activity has recently increased. However, the virtue of cooperation has been very popular as seen in the giving and taking of diverse forms of emergency assistance. To elaborate, cooperation entails the reciprocal exchange of service.

Building an effective defense network: US case

In 1950, two important laws shaped emergency management in the United States. The Federal Disaster Relief Act authorized the federal government to provide disaster assistance.

The Civil Defense Act created the Federal Civil Defense Administration to deal with possible attacks from foreign enemies on U.S. soil. Over the next several years, the government would witness poor coordination of disaster assistance programs because they were broadly dispersed across many federal departments.

In 1979, President Jimmy Carter created the Federal Emergency Management Agency by executive order. FEMA mandated that state and local governments plan and prepare for disasters. Emergency management was slowly recognized as a profession. The Robert T. Stafford Disaster Relief and Emergency Assistance Act (Stafford Act) in 1988 specified how federal assistance could be given following on a presidential disaster declaration.

However, all these changes did not prevent the failure of the federal government during Hurricane Katrina. President George Bush and Congress were reminded of the impact of major natural disasters and the need to be prepared for all types of hazards. In 2005, Congress passed the Pet Evacuation and Transportation Standards Act to avert the kind of evacuation challenges witnessed during Hurricane Katrina. It also instituted the Post-Katrina Emergency Management Reform Act in 2006. The latter reinstated ties between the FEMA Administrator and the President, as well as directed additional monetary and personnel support to the Federal Emergency Management Agency.

It appears as if the federal government was trying to undo many of the mistakes made after the introduction of the Department of Homeland Security, although the priority given to terrorism remains.

The creation of the Department of Homeland Security (DHS) was perhaps the most visible policy response to the events of Sept. 11. A common problem is the creation of emergency operations plans without the development of capacity to implement them in any meaningful way. For instance, poor policy formulation and lack of training also limit the ability of public officials to prevent disasters or react to them effectively.

Culture may be another cause of disasters in the United States. People tend to disapprove of government regulations that could keep them safe. Individuals and families often downplay risk or make decisions that render them vulnerable to disasters.

Meanwhile, the federal government mandated the National Incident Management Strategy as a way to promote interagency communication and coordination.

The President also repealed the Federal Response Plan and put in its place the National Response Plan, which downplays FEMA's role in disasters and seems to be overly consumed with terrorism alone. Many of the laws passed during this time focus on the prevention of terrorism through intelligence gathering, counter-terrorism operations and law enforcement functions.

Mitigating revelations of climate change

Geoff O'Brien

Industry leaders meet in Korea to discuss the relevance of nuclear energy and security implications prior to the Nuclear Security Summit Monday and Tuesday. Korean Prime Minister Hwang-sik Kim delivers an address to participants Friday. *Korea Times photo*

Accelerated climate change and increasing variability is one of the greatest threats to the international objectives of sustainable development and the Millennium Development Goals (MDGs).

Addressing climate change requires reducing greenhouse gas emissions. These gases retain heat that is radiated from the planet; the greenhouse effect. Without the greenhouse effect, the average temperature of the planet would fall to about minus 14 degrees Celsius.

Life will not be forever sustainable if this trend continues. We are increasing the concentration of greenhouse gases in the atmosphere and warming the planet. A sharp rise in the average global temperature could lead to catastrophic consequences.

The international community is trying to find ways of reducing or mitigating the emission of greenhouse gases through the United Nations Framework Convention on Climate Change (UNFCCC). Progress has been slow!

The problem is that energy is so fundamental to our lives (the production of electricity, fuels for transport, cooking, heating, industry and commerce, etc.), and most of the energy we use, some 87 percent, is produced from fossil fuels.

Fossil fuel use produces carbon dioxide, a greenhouse gas. We are emitting huge amounts of that gas (and other greenhouse gases) into the atmosphere. The concentration of carbon dioxide has risen from 280 parts per million (ppm) to about 390 ppm since the Industrial Revolution and is increasing at about 1-2 ppm per year.

The use of fossil fuels is predicted to continue rising. If we are to effectively address the issue of climate change mitigation, then we will have to find ways of reducing their use and deploying low or no carbon technologies. This is an immense challenge.

There are four ways of addressing climate change mitigation: nuclear power, renewable technologies, geo-engineering and efficiency. Each has its associated problems. In short there is no easy answer to the challenge of mitigation. Each of these areas is discussed below.

Nuclear power

Nuclear power production from fission is an established technology. It is not without problems as both Chernobyl and Fukushima have taught us. Recently Germany and Japan have decided to phase out nuclear power, citing safety concerns.

There are other problems such as nuclear waste. Nuclear waste is very toxic and has to be safely stored, possibly for thousands of years, until it has decayed to a safe level. Deep underground storage seems to be the preferred option, but we have little experience, and this raises concerns.

The uranium needed to make fuel for nuclear reactors could be in short supply. Sir David King, the former U.K. chief scientist, predicts that uranium supplies will begin to run out in 2023 if the current global plans for nuclear power stations are implemented. For the U.K., and perhaps other nations, this may mean that plutonium stocks will have to be reprocessed to make nuclear fuel. Considerable investment would be needed. Though nuclear stations do not produce greenhouse gases at the point of production, fission technology does not offer a safe or sustainable future. Its value is as a stopgap measure.

However there is considerable hope for nuclear fusion. This technology is based on fusing two isotopes of hydrogen to make helium. The advantages of this technology are that the fuel is almost limitless and the fusion reaction does not produce any toxic waste. In Europe the International Thermonuclear Experimental Reactor (ITER) is being developed to further research fusion at a cost of some 16 billion euros.

Though there are some indications that fusion reaction is achievable, to date it has only been sustained for a small fraction of time. At present, the amount of energy needed to start the reaction has exceeded the output from the fusion reactor. There is uncertainty about our ability to make this work. Even if fusion power is possible, then it is unlikely that commercial plants will be available before 2050.

Renewable technologies

Renewable energy is all but unlimited. There are three sources of renewable energy: the sun, gravity, and geothermal heat from the earth's core. Renewable technologies such as solar water heaters and photovoltaic cells capture energy from the sun to produce electricity and heat. Wind energy can be used to generate electricity.

Hydroelectric power, a mature renewable technology, relies on rainfall from river systems stored behind dams. Tides, driven by the gravitational interaction of the moon and earth, can be harnessed to produce electricity.

Geothermal energy from hot rocks in the interior of the earth can be used to produce steam to generate electricity. There are limitations associated with these technologies. Wind and geothermal energy, tides, and dams are location specific. Solar hot water and solar and wind generated electricity are variable; without the sun or wind they do not produce energy.

Alternative fuels such as hydrogen and biomass have considerable potential. Hydrogen is the most abundant element in the universe and ,when combined with oxygen, produces heat or electricity and water as a waste product.

The problem is the production of hydrogen. Conventionally, stripping methane or natural gas has produced hydrogen. The byproduct of this process is carbon dioxide. Hydrogen can be produced by the electrolysis of water. If the electricity used were produced from renewable sources such as wind, then hydrogen production would not contribute to global warming.

Hydrogen can be used directly, for example, in the internal combustion engine, or used in a fuel cell to produce electricity. Hydrogen is a low energy density fuel when compared to, for example, gasoline. When used for transport systems, hydrogen has to be stored either at very high pressures or as a liquid at cryogenic temperatures.

Many vehicle manufacturers are developing electric vehicles that rely on batteries to store electricity. At present, it is unclear if the battery or hydrogen will emerge as the dominant technology for transport. Electric vehicles have limited battery life, and re-charging is time consuming. If charging points use electricity produced from fossil fuels, then this would contribute to global warming.

Biomass resources, such as wood and crop residues, are essentially carbon neutral; they release carbon dioxide when used and absorb it when grown. Biomass has been used as a fuel for millennia. Biomass is used to produce electricity in dedicated power stations. The technology is not complex and can work well, provided biomass supplies are readily available.

Despite the potential for renewable resources, new technologies such as wind and photovoltaics only produce a small fraction of global energy. Biomass is used throughout the developing world and only produces a small amount of energy in the developed world. Investment in the development and implementation of these technologies is needed if meaningful reductions in emissions are to be made.

Energy use could be reduced by some 20 percent through efficiency measures to both supply and use. The Laws of Thermodynamics limit the efficiency of conventional power stations, typically about 40 percent for a coal-fired station. The wasted energy can be used either for heating or industrial processes. This is known as Combined Heat and Power (CHP).

Energy efficiency

For gas-fired power stations, the Combined Cycle Gas Turbine produces electricity in two ways. Gas is used to drive a turbine to produce electricity, and the waste heat generates steam for electricity production.

But carbon dioxide is still produced, and for a low carbon pathway this must be addressed. Carbon Capture and Storage (CCS) and carbon sequestration are two methods that can be used. CCS captures carbon dioxide either pre or post combustion methods and then stores it underground in depleted oil or gas wells. This technology is currently being tested. CCS will add to the cost of electricity by some 10-15 percent according to current estimates. Carbon sequestration involves enhancing natural carbon sinks such as forests and peat bogs and improving agricultural practices.

More efficient end-use means less energy is needed. Buildings use some 40 percent of energy for heating, cooling, lighting, equipment and appliances. Improved thermal efficiency of buildings would reduce the amount of energy used.

The Passive House, developed in Germany, has high thermal efficiency and can maintain a comfortable environment with little additional energy, even if the external temperatures fall to minus 20 degrees Celsius. More efficient lighting and appliances can reduce domestic demand.

Embedded renewable capacity such as solar hot water, photovoltaics and heat pumps can make a building almost self-sufficient in energy terms. These ideas can be applied to all buildings. Cities could be both energy producers and users.

Geo-engineering works by removing greenhouse gases from the atmosphere or by limiting the amount of sunlight reaching the planet's surface. Artificial trees that absorb carbon dioxide using plastic polymers have been proposed.

There are issues of commercial viability and storage of collected carbon dioxide to be addressed. Other proposals aim to increase the amount of carbon dioxide absorbed by the oceans through adding large quantities of lime to the water.

Spraying sulphate aerosols into the stratosphere can reflect sunlight back into space. Unmanned ships could increase above-ocean cloud cover by spraying seawater into the air. Placing thousands of tiny mirrors in space between Earth and the sun could reflect sunlight back into space. These ideas have received much criticism, since they mask the carbon dioxide problem and can lead to serious side effects, for example, the oceans becoming more acidic.

Any energy technology has positives and negatives. The challenge for policymakers is to balance both supply and use. Low carbon supply options need to be deployed, and we must use energy more efficiently. This is not a technological issue, and there are three main problems to face.

First, politics and economics. Within UNFCCC, getting all 194 nations to agree on a low carbon strategy is fiendishly difficult. Without an international deal that sets targets for all, no one nation can be certain that others will pull their weight. At present, the rich nations are transfixed by the economic crisis, and there appears to be little appetite to really tackle the climate crisis. Governments are fearful of being first and will not act until something actually goes wrong. By then it may be too late.

Second, distorted markets. Renewable energy is plentiful. But their transformation into usable energy supplies appears too costly, much more so than fossil fuel polluting alternatives. This hides the fact that the fossil fuel industry received $409 billion in handouts in 2010, compared with $66 billion for renewable technologies. More investment in renewables is needed. In addition, the external costs of fossil fuel use are not reflected in price mechanisms. The market is distorted.

Third, technological lock-in. We are still trapped in thinking about energy systems where high-density fuels are transformed into energy services, often at a gigantic scale. We are unable to think differently. This is worrying as renewable sources imply that we need a new approach to energy system architecture, an architecture that is based on typically low-density variable sources such as wind and solar power.

Low carbon energy

The shift to a low carbon energy economy needs a concerted effort to address both supply and demand. To date, the main concern has been on supply of energy. More recently, concerns have been raised that fossil fuels will run out in the near future.

Unconventional fossil fuels such as shale gas, tar sands and heavy petroleum are plentiful. Some estimates suggest that there could be sufficient fossil fuels to last into the next century. But their exploitation will have severe environmental consequences.

It is not a question of shortage of fossil fuels but more a question of whether we should continue to use them. This is not a technological question but a question of values. If we want a sustainable future for future generations, then we really need to do things differently.

Parts of the material for this article were sourced from: O'Keefe, P. O'Brien, G. Pearsall, N. (2010) The Future of Energy Use. Earthscan, U.K. ISBN 9781844075041

Adaptation critical in changing climate

Geoff O'Brien

A general view of the leading edge of Perito Moreno glacier in the southern Patagonia region near El Calafate. While most of the world's glaciers are melting away because of warmer temperatures, scientists say the Perito Moreno ice field, known as "The White Giant" is gaining as much as 3 meters (10 feet) a day in some parts, pushed forward by heavy snowfalls in the Patagonia region. This picture was taken Jan. 3, 2009. *Reuters-Yonhap*

From a climate change perspective, adaptation is a series of precautionary or anticipatory adjustments to shifts already happening or likely to happen in the near future.

Accelerated climate change and increasing variability are among the greatest challenges we face. The Intergovernmental Panel on Climate Change

Table 1: Examples of possible impacts of climate change

Phenomena and direction of trend	Agriculture, forestry and ecosystems	Water resources	Human health	Industry, settlement and society
Over most land areas, warmer and fewer cold days and nights, warmer and more frequent hot days and nights	Increased yields in colder environments; decreased yields in warmer environments; increased insect outbreaks	Effects on water resources relying on snow melt; effects on some water supplies	Reduced human mortality from decreased cold exposure	Reduced energy demand for heating; increased demand for cooling; declining air quality in cities; reduced disruption to transport due to snow, ice; effects on winter tourism
Warm spells/heat waves. Frequency increases over most land areas	Reduced yields in warmer regions due to heat stress; increased danger of wildfire	Increased water demand; water quality problems e.g., algal blooms	Increased risk of heat-related mortality, especially for the elderly, chronically sick, very young and socially-isolated	Reduction in quality of life for people in warm area without appropriate housing; impacts on the elderly, very young and poor
Heavy precipitation events. Level excludes frequency increases over most areas	Damage to crops; soil erosion, inability to cultivate land due to waterlogging of soils	Adverse effects on quality of surface and groundwater; contamination of water supply; water scarcity may be relieved	Increased risk of deaths, injuries and infectious, respiratory and skin diseases	Disruption of settlements, commerce, transport and societies due to flooding; pressures on urban and rural infrastructures; loss of property
Area affected by drought increases	Land degradation; lower yields/crop damage and failure; increased livestock deaths; increased risk of wildfire	More widespread water stress	Increased risk of food and water shortage; increased risk of malnutrition; increased risk of water- and food-borne diseases	Water shortages for settlements, industry and societies; reduced hydropower generation potentials; potential for population migration
Intense tropical cyclone activity increases	Damage to crops; windthrow (uprooting) of trees; damage to coral reefs	Power outages causing disruption of public water supply	Increased risk of deaths, injuries, water- and food-borne diseases; post-traumatic stress disorders	Disruption by flood and high winds; withdrawal of risk coverage in vulnerable areas by private insurers, potential for population migrations, loss of property
Increased incidence of extreme high sea level (excludes tsunamis)	Salinisation of irrigation water, estuaries and freshwater systems	Decreased freshwater availability due to saltwater intrusion	Increased risk of deaths and injuries by drowning in floods; migration related health effects	Costs of coastal protection versus costs of land- use relocation; potential for movement of populations and infrastructure; also see tropical cyclones above

Adapted from Table, Statistical Parametric Mapping 1 (IPCC, 2007)

(IPCC) has said there is clear evidence human actions are exacerbating the natural variability of the climate system; we are responsible for producing changes. Though there is general agreement about the urgent need to reduce greenhouse gas emissions, there is also recognition that we will have to adapt to the changes driven by the emissions already in the atmosphere.

There seems little likelihood of an international agreement to reduce emissions before 2020, meaning that climate change could further accelerate. There is the possibility that we will enter an era of dangerous climate change where extreme events could severely threaten communities and livelihoods throughout the world, even causing irreversible damage to ecosystems. Adaptation is an urgent need.

Climate change risks

Broadly speaking, accelerated climate change risks are meteorological in nature. For example, when temperatures rise, droughts and floods are likely to become more severe and less predictable. Table 1 highlights some of the possible risks we will face.

The lack of an international agreement to limit emissions means that many of the impacts listed in Table 1 are likely to be exacerbated.

This will make adaptation even more challenging. It is highly probable that we will have to adapt to significant changes. We may have already reached tipping points for irreversible change.

A tipping point occurs when for example, warming of the tundra releases methane into the atmosphere. Methane is a powerful greenhouse gas that further accelerates warming. It is clear that adaptation is needed urgently in this context.

Adaptation is a process of adjustment to disruptive events. It is not a new concept. Societies have adjusted continually throughout history. From a climate change perspective, however, adaptation is precautionary or anticipatory adjustment(s) to shifts already happening or likely to happen in the near future. It is defined by IPCC in its Third Assessment Report as follows:

Adjustment in natural or human systems is in response to actual or expected climatic stimuli or their effects, which moderates harm or exploits beneficial opportunities. Various types of adaptation can be distinguished, including anticipatory and reactive adaptation, private and public adaptation, and autonomous and planned adaptation (IPCC, 2001).

Adaptation is not only adjustment to an average climate condition but also a response to reduce vulnerability to extremes, variability, and rates of change at all scales.

Though the aim of adaptation is to reduce or mitigate vulnerability, its focus is on adaptive capacity, which is the ability of societies to adjust to climate disruptions. Vulnerability is the degree to which societies are unable to cope with the adverse effects of climate change, including climate variability and extremes.

Adaptive capacity refers to the potential or ability of communities to adapt to the effects or impacts of climate change, to adjust to actual or expected climate stresses, and to cope with the consequences. The determinants of adaptive capacity comprise factors such as wealth, technology, education, information, skills, infrastructure, access to resources, government and stability and management capabilities.

Wealthier nations have greater adaptive capacity than do poorer nations, other things equal. A term increasingly used in adaptation is resilience, meaning the ability of communities to respond and cope with disruptive events. Resilience entails building up the capacity of communities to be more self-reliant.

Resilience also is a function of learning from experience and using the determinants of adaptive capacity to better prepare for future. In this sense, resilience is an on-going process.

This is an important aspect of adaptation to climate change as we will have constantly to assess climate hazards and make judgments about the risks that they will produce.

Adaptation strategies

Adaptation strategies will differ from place to place. There is no single solution. Adaptation strategies should reduce risks to communities, promote food and water security, protect critical infrastructure and ensure that people are prepared.

The types of measures that can be used may be characterized in two ways. The first are structural measures comprising any physical construction to reduce or avoid possible impacts of hazards, or the application of engineering techniques to achieve hazard-resistance and resilience in structures or systems such as flood levies, ocean wave barriers and evacuation shelters.

The second type is non-structural measures that comprise measures not involving physical construction but using knowledge, practice or agreement to reduce risks and impacts, in particular through policies and laws, public awareness raising, training and education. Common non-structural measures include building codes, land-use planning laws and their enforcement, research and assessment, information resources, and public awareness programs.

Local knowledge, climate science

Short measures can range from the building of flood defenses to the introduction of drought resistant crops. It is important that adaptation measures build on local knowledge as well as good climate science.

There needs to be an interchange of information concerning what works best and why. Adaptation measures build resilience through this kind of learning.

But there are likely to be some very difficult decisions. Many of our cities and critical infrastructures are in coastal areas highly vulnerable to rising sea levels and storms. New Orleans is a graphic example of what may happen. Even today there is discussion of whether some low-lying areas of the city should be re-developed. In the future we will have to consider whether or not to abandon some areas, since the costs of defending them are likely prohibitive.

In Asia there are many cities that will be threatened by rising sea levels and extreme storms. Countries such as Bangladesh will lose land and many will be displaced. This raises the prospect of climate refugees. How will we deal with such problems?

Costs of Adaptation

This is a contentious area. A 2006 study by Stern on the economics of climate change concluded that it would more cost effective to act now as opposed to dealing with the consequences. Stern suggests that spending roughly three to five percent of GDP would avoid the loss of some 15-20 percent of GDP if we do nothing (Stern, 2006). 2007 Oxfam and UNDP studies (UN Development Programme) estimated costs of between $50 and $109 billion per annum (Oxfam, 2007; UNDP, 2007).

The UN Framework Convention on Climate Change (UNFCCC) estimated that the global funding needed for adaptation by 2030 could amount to between $49 and $171 billion per annum, of which between $27 and $66 billion would accrue in developing countries (UNFCCC, 2007). More recent analysis suggests that these figures underestimate the costs.

Adaptation is complex, and studies need to include all relevant sectors, including agriculture, water, ecosystems, coastal systems, human health and infrastructure. An analysis by Parry et al (2009) of the UNFCCC study suggests that in some sectors, estimates may need to be two or three times higher. A 2010 study by the World Bank of infrastructure costs alone suggests an annual amount of between $75 and $100 billion (World Bank 2010).

One of the problems is deciding on what areas and sectors to protect. This implies that a concerted effort is likely to be much higher that current published estimates. Given that the recent World Bank study only focuses on infrastructure, it is not unreasonable to assume that a comprehensive approach is likely to cost over $100 billion per annum.

Cost and lives

According to The Global Humanitarian Forum (2010), the costs of climate related losses amount to $125 billion per annum and some 300,000 lives every year; the quality of countless other lives is downgraded because of climate change. It is impossible to put a value on such losses and suffering.

Through UNFCCC, the global community has established a Green Climate Fund. The Fund has identified that developed countries should commit to providing $30 billion in fast-start finance for developing countries in 2010-12 and mobilize $100 billion a year in public and private finance by 2020 for adaptation and low carbon initiatives. Don't hold your breath as the global economic slowdown may mean this commitment will not be fully met.

Climate adaptation is urgent. However, there seems to be a lack of action. This is odd since adaptation is about protecting people and the assets we need. Many of the measures will require innovation, in particular the move to a greener economy.

A greener economy would require new products. This should result in long-term benefits, particularly if we decide to adapt the global energy system to new and alternative energy resources. What is clear is that many of the options are realizable.

The question remains: do we have the political will? Many of our leaders are transfixed by Giddens Paradox (2009); they will not act until something goes wrong.

Future of tourism within the environment

Jim Dator

Snow is seen on Mt. Mauna Kea in Hilo, Hawaii, a popular tour site that attracts people from around the world. Tourism has been suffering from not only the economic downturn on a global scale but because people in general are looking for more economical ways of travelling. *Korea Times file*

If I were to convene a group of decision-makers now, in 2012, to talk about the futures of tourism in Hawaii (or anywhere), most people would want to talk about the fact that tourism is one of the biggest and most important industries in the world today.

They would want to discuss all the ways tourism will continue to grow, and that every community that intends to prosper in the futures must focus on developing its "hospitality" resources.

I, on the other hand, would want to talk about "the unholy trinity, plus one" that suggests that we are nearing the end not only of tourism in Hawaii, but everywhere - as well as the end of the global neoliberal political-economy of which tourism is a major part.

But before we consider the futures, we must first understand the past. How did something as "frivolous" as tourism become one of the most important global industries?

Imagine we are attending a meeting taking place in Hawaii a scant 236 years ago - in 1776. Whoever we are and whatever we are doing, we aren't worrying about the future of tourism! Neither are we discussing the possibility that our way of life, secure after 2000 years of spectacular growth and development - is about to come to an end. But it did.

Next imagine our meeting taking place 110 years ago. Now we might be talking about tourism. The Moana Hotel in Waikiki had been built a few years earlier. Tourists, few in number - 2,000 a year, and almost all very wealthy with lots of spare time - arrive by steamship which in itself was a relatively new invention, replacing the earlier sailing ships. A few more hotels are being built or planned, and even though airplanes are just beginning to fly, we certainly are not planning for them at all, viewing them as mere dangerous toys.

Increase in tourism

Imagine our meeting taking place 80 years ago, in 1933. All tourists still arrive by steamship, but in a few years, the first Pan American Clipper will be flying between San Francisco and Hawaii. An airplane ticket costs $360 one-way. In 2012 dollars, that is roughly $6,000. Moreover, the gruesome flight takes almost 22 hours. Nonetheless, the number of tourists increased over the next decade to about 40,000 per year.

By 1956, the tourist count reached well over 100,000 per year. But are we planning for the impact of statehood in three years? How about the arrival of the first passengers by jet plane also in only three years? By the early 1960s tourists numbered almost 300,000 annually, and hotels were beginning to spring up like mushrooms after the rain.

And so on, with many ups and downs - but mostly mainly ups - to the present count of 8 million tourists per year and rising. It is Hawaii's only industry, by far. All livelihoods depend on it.

I focused mainly on one thing in the past that created the present of tourism - the transforming power of new transportation technologies: from voyaging canoes, to sailing ships, to steamships, to propeller airplanes, to jet airplanes, beyond which (it is very important to remember) there have been no major advances since the 1970s. Aircraft have gotten bigger recently and there are more and bigger airports. But no breakthroughs in transportation technology.

There are many more crucial causes of tourist growth than just changes in transportation. One is the invention of the credit card so that anyone with enough cards with some credit left on them can fly now and pay later.

Electronic ticketing

That was not possible 40 years ago. For most folks then, "you no pay, you no go." Tourist growth itself might have stopped long ago without consumer credit available worldwide by merely flashing a piece of plastic. A true miracle.

Another revolution was in electronic ticketing and reservation systems, like Sabre, which would not have been possible without Arthur C. Clarke envisioning telecommunication satellites in space, making instant global communication possible.

People had to know about Hawaii and want to come here for tourism to grow. It is not a place that most people just happen to stumble across. Locations like Hawaii are the most remote - and last discovered - spots on the planet.

But more fundamentally, for all of these things to happen, the world had to transform from being a labor-intensive agricultural society dependent on horse power, wind power, water power and human power into an industrial society dependent on oil, electricity, and machines, and then into an information society dependent on people who sit around all day reading and sending electronic messages to each other while producing absolutely nothing at all but more messages.

To have mass tourism you need masses (including retired masses) that are rich, numerous, idle and healthy enough to want to travel for fun. If people still had to work for a living on a farm or in a factory, as most people did until about 50 years ago, there would be no gigantic tourist industry.

A lot of absolutely unbelievable things had to happen to create jobs in tourism - things that were so totally unbelievable that you would have laughed at anyone who told you about them before they existed.

One final important point before we leap into the future: The owners and managers of hotels and other tourist attractions went from being essentially small mom and pop innkeepers to local business magnates to global corporations and now to global corporations who only care about making money, and don't care whether it is via tourism or not.

They will drop tourism like a hot potato the minute before it stops making them lots of money. They will gladly change hotels into condos or homeless centers or homes for fish if that is the most economical thing to do.

That is the nature of the world we live in now. While this logic makes total sense to economists and the managers of industry, it means that tourism, the flagship - as well as most of the flotilla - of the economy, is fundamentally very fragile and dependent indeed.

And so here we are at the present. Recently, after the hiccups of 9/11 and 2008, tourism has had one fantastic year after another. Tourists and money are pouring in.

What's next?

No one can say for sure. Most people answer the question "what's next" by responding, "more of whatever is happening now." Maybe. But here is my answer, presented not as a prediction of what will happen, but rather as a forecast of what might happen, and for which we should be prepared. I call it the unholy trinity, plus one. It is a trinity because it is composed of three things that people consider to be separate, but which in fact are deeply joined as one.

The first person of the unholy trinity is:

1. The end of cheap and abundant oil before any equivalent replacement takes over.

Hawaii is almost totally dependent on imported oil for everything. In spite of abundant sunshine, wave, wind, geothermal, and ocean thermal energy conversion potentials, about 90 percent of our energy comes from imported oil - more than anywhere else in the U.S. And yet, the brief 100-year era of cheap and abundant oil is over.

While the daily price will certainly go up and down with the economy, oil is becoming more and more scarce, difficult to get, and hence progressively more expensive from now on until it essentially "runs out."

Of course, many energy solutions exist in principle, but none are nearly ready to take over from oil. A gap of uncertain duration awaits us before other energy forms take over - if they will be able to take over at all within our lifetime.

This will be a disaster for mass tourism of course. It simply will be too expensive for most people to travel. More seriously, almost all of the food we in locations like Hawaii currently consume is flown or shipped in. It will take a lot of money and time to solve our energy problems. Where will that money come from? Do we even have time?

2. The focus of life globally and locally will switch from the production and consumption of goods, to addressing long-neglected - and exacerbated - environmental issues: Climate change, sea level rise, water shortages, new and renewed diseases, environmental refugees. All of these will very seriously impact us in Hawaii. Where will the money, energy and time come from to adapt effectively to them?

3. Collapse of the global neoliberal political-economy: Our global and local economy is built very largely on debt and financial tricks, not on markets, productivity or hard work.

Over the past 75 years, we have faced a series of economic crises that we "solved" each time by inventing new and ever-confounding debt instruments, thus kicking the day of inevitable reckoning into the future for our children and grandchildren to deal with - not by our inventing a sustainable economy.

When will the economic system finally collapse? Tomorrow? Next year? Ten years later?

So that is the unholy trinity: the end of cheap and abundant energy, environmental change and economic collapse. They are all part of the same thing.

We can't solve one by making the others worse. We certainly can't solve the end of oil by using ever-more polluting energy sources, as we are currently doing. We can't solve environmental change by throwing money at it. We don't have enough time, money or credit to throw anything at it but hard work and prayer.

What is the "plus one?"

Many concerned economists say, "The government, by Keynesian measures, should fund new energy, infrastructure, and environmental research and jobs, thus preventing total economic collapse." That won't work because of the other two persons of the unholy trinity.

But even if this were not so, government can't help because of 30 years of bad-mouthing - the mantra that all government is bad and that we should each take care of ourselves entirely. This has resulted in under-resourcing, downsizing, privatizing, outsourcing and debt, each of which has been intended to drive nails into the coffin of effective government.

And while massive national debt is the final nail, please understand that, as the Republican candidates for the American presidency have recently made completely clear, this is the purpose of our debt - to cripple and kill all government functions. The huge debt is not an unfortunate consequence of certain policies. It is their fundamental intent.

We have driven the government and ourselves deeper and deeper into debt not to solve current problems but rather to make it harder and harder for people to act collectively through the government in the future, leaving everything up to private forces.

As a consequence, the United States has become a strong nation with weak states - that is, while many Americans remain wildly entranced by certain American icons, they have allowed the government to become too weak to aid ordinary Americans when communal help is needed. This seems to be the road to rejection and ultimately revolution.

It is far too late to prevent the consequences of the unholy trinity, plus one. We can only adapt to them.

Chapter 3

International Organization

A new paradigm of economic growth

Little Ice Age

Decisions have to be made

Accelerating investment in green growth

Women's role vital in disaster prevention

Essentials of consumerism

Consequences of climate change on oceans

World needs better alternatives to oil

Taking advantage of urbanization

A new paradigm of economic growth

Richard Samans

Natural resources are the heart of the economy

Green growth is a relatively new concept characterized by the Organization for Economic Cooperation and Development (OECD) as "fostering economic growth and development, while ensuring that natural assets continue to provide the resources and environmental services on which our well-being relies." It is closely related to the concept of a green economy, which the United Nations Environment Program (UNEP) defines as one in which "growth in income and employment should be driven by public and private investments that reduce carbon emissions and pollution, enhance energy and resource efficiency, and prevent the loss of biodiversity and ecosystem services."

In any discussion of economic growth, an important caveat is in order: growth is not an end in itself. The fundamental objective of economic policy is not growth but rather broad-based progress in living standards. After all, growth in GDP per capita is a measure of mean, not median, progress. Moreover, it is only a partial measure insofar as it captures the production of most but not all goods and services, omitting or undervaluing some of those that improve a society's health, security and the environment.

But while GDP growth is an imperfect proxy for the pace and breadth of progress in living standards and may not be sufficient for economic success, it certainly is necessary. In all but very wealthy societies, major socioeconomic progress is simply not possible without rising employment, incomes and wealth. The ultimate objective of economic policy must be to generate what might be called "BIG" growth: strong GDP growth that is also "Balanced" in the sense of being resilient and stable rather than prone to disruptive booms and busts; "Inclusive" in the sense of generating broad-based social gains rather than exacerbating inequality and social exclusion; and "Green" in the sense described by the OECD and the UNEP.

Green growth is therefore best understood as one part of a three-part quest to enlarge the very conception of economic growth — to create a new economic model that produces faster but also wider, more resilient and more environmentally sustainable economic progress. Construction of this new paradigm begins with the recognition that the quantitative and qualitative aspects of growth require equal and integrated attention from policymakers.

Allocative efficiency

This may sound obvious and uncontroversial in the aftermath of a systemic international financial crisis and during a period of rising income inequality and widespread ecological degradation. However, the challenge such parallelism poses to economists and policymakers should not be underestimated, as it represents a departure from the way economics has been taught and economic policy practiced for over a generation.

While important, measures that promote the allocative efficiency of markets and quantitative side of growth (e.g., deregulation, privatization, trade liberalization and fiscal balance) have been systematically overemphasized relative to the three more qualitative parameters of BIG growth, sometimes to catastrophic effect, as illustrated by the recent sharp rise in unemployment, poverty and social upheaval in some countries and deterioration of fisheries and fresh water supplies in others.

Rhetorical recognition of the need for a new growth model may now be widespread, as evidenced by G20 leader communiques and similar pronouncements by heads of the major international economic institutions. But actual change in policy and pedagogy has only just begun. What is needed next is a more specific investigation of how and when the promotion of financial stability, social inclusion and environmental sustainability can complement and even accelerate allocative efficiency and top-line GDP growth. What specific policies and initiatives promote win-win, BIG growth outcomes, and how can governments and other stakeholders most effectively pursue them?

Such an investigation in respect of green growth is the very purpose of the Global Green Growth Institute, which was created by Korea a year and a half ago through an act of leadership by President Myung-bak Lee but now involves more than a dozen governments and numerous other state and non-state actors such as international organizations, research institutes, companies and civil society organizations.

Enabling green growth

Green growth's connection to GDP growth is comparatively straight forward, since it is fundamentally concerned with increasing the efficiency and sustainability by which economies utilize one of their most important factor inputs, like natural resources, through the application of new resource efficient technologies and practices. As a resource productivity agenda, green growth is intrinsically a total factor productivity agenda — i.e., a pure allocative efficiency play that also promotes social well-being by reducing environmental externalities that often accompany the exploitation of natural resources in the form of pollution and biodiversity loss.

There is a long and geographically diverse history of government policy and public-private cooperation along these lines. The general aim is to improve the enabling environment for private investment in industries deemed to have significant potential to generate large productivity gains for the economy as a whole. Far from picking winners and losers, these interventions seek to build the underlying infrastructure of new markets by removing obstacles that distort market signals or deter the entry of a wider range of competitors and investors. They create the playing field, the rules and sometimes the basic inputs necessary to support a major expansion of investment and competition in areas considered to have a broader potential economic and social payoff.

Judging from the history of industries as diverse as accounting, information technology, aviation, electricity and asset management — all of which have had a far-reaching impact on economic productivity — public-private cooperation has a vital role to play in enabling the acceleration and scaling of industries related to green growth.

Architecture for green growth

In recent years, international environmental governance in general and the U.N. climate change negotiations in particular have focused on building top-down political architecture, i.e., national environmental commitments and international environmental goals. GGGI is helping the international community to construct a complementary economic architecture that more directly supports country-led and industry-led (i.e., bottom-up) progress on green growth.

Organizations, including GGGI, are doing this by helping developing and emerging economy governments to design rigorous green growth plans that integrate environmental considerations into their core economic development strategies, conducting research to improve our understanding of the nature and transformational potential of green growth, and facilitating public-private partnerships that reduce risks, uncertainties and market imperfections which impede the engagement of additional private resources and actors into a wider competition for resource-related efficiency gains.

The green growth agenda has an inherent economic and environmental justification. But by moving more quickly and directly to mainstream sustainability in core economic policy and business strategy, it could also have the political co-benefit of improving the chemistry of international environmental negotiations by demonstrating that the United Nations' objective of "a green economy in the context of sustainable development" is indeed possible for countries rich and poor, and by improving the readiness of countries to implement climate, biodiversity, fisheries, water and other treaties whenever the international community ultimately gets around to reaching consensus on them.

International cooperation

The year 2012 is shaping up to be a crucial year for both international economic and environmental cooperation, with crises and corresponding opportunities looming on both fronts. We do not have the luxury of time to engineer a greener growth model. Investments in power, industrial and construction systems over the next 10 years will lock in environmental consequences for the next 40.

As governments prepare for the Group of 20 and United Nations Rio+20 summits in June of this year, they would do well to recognize the potential benefit of building this bottom-up, enabling economic architecture, viewing it as a natural complement to the traditional focus of international environmental governance on top-down legal frameworks and institutions. In the remaining months, they should work hard to cultivate a series of initiatives that increase support for developing countries seeking to design and implement green growth development plans as well as for public-private partnerships that have the potential to scale green investment and innovation in the power, transport, fisheries, construction, water and agricultural sectors.

Little Ice Age

John L. Casti

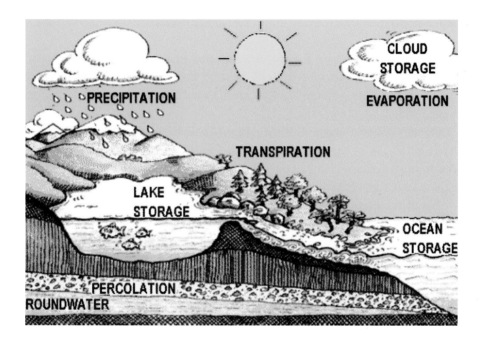

One of the charms of living in the center of Vienna is the opportunity to regularly visit the Kunsthistorisches Museum, a place that's on everyone's list of the world's great art museums. One of the museum's highlights is Pieter Brueghel the Elder's 1565 painting "Hunters in the Snow."

This haunting work shows three hunters returning from a hunting expedition accompanied by their dogs. By appearances, the expedition was not successful: the hunters seem to trudge wearily through the deep winter snow, and the dogs look pretty miserable themselves.

The weather depicted in the painting appears to be a calm, cold, overcast day; the trees are bare of leaves; wood smoke hangs in the air, and in the background we see ice skaters skimming over a frozen lake.

Little Ice Age

In fact, according to many climatologists, these two paintings fairly accurately bound a period now called the Little Ice Age (LIA), which seems to have begun around 1550 and lasted for about three centuries.

During this time, winters in Europe and North America were considerably colder than previously, with the River Thames in England and canals in Holland often freezing over. In Turkey, this climatic change showed itself when the southern section of the Bosphorus froze over in 1622.

Not to be outdone by Europe, it's reported that Lake Superior in North America had ice until June in 1607, and in the winter of 1780, New York harbor froze solid enough so that people could walk from Manhattan to Staten Island.

Perhaps the best account of the entire LIA is the book of the same name by Brian Fagan of the University of California. Fagan says that peasants of the time suffered not only bone-chilling weather but also famines, bread riots, and the appearance of brutal leaders.

Fagan writes that by the late 17th century, agricultural production had dropped so precipitously that "alpine villagers lived on bread made from ground nutshells mixed with barley and oat flour." He goes on to note that life was especially difficult for those in the French Alps. Advancing glaciers moved forward "over a musket shot each day, even in the month of August." And when the glaciers finally retreated, they left land so barren that no crops would grow.

Interestingly, the evidence of this global cooling period is somewhat less detailed for other parts of the world, especially the southern hemisphere. But this is not to say that the LIA was any less severe below the equator, only that documented evidence in the form of paintings, writings and the like is simply much scantier. However, ocean sediment cores from Antarctica to Africa seem to point to the same phenomenon.

Prolonged period of cooling

Leaving aside causes internal to the global climatic system itself such as oceanic currents, interactions between the atmosphere and the seas, surface reflection (albedo) and the like, climatologists have narrowed the search for the proximate cause of the LIA to two factors: sunspots and volcanic activity.

In the first, solar radiation takes a nosedive so that radiation striking the

Earth was severely reduced, while in the second case, volcanoes spew forth massive clouds of dust and volcanic ash leading to the same type of reduction in solar radiation striking the Earth's surface. Finally, there is the endogenous cause involving a shutdown of the famed "Great Ocean Conveyor," which moves warm water from the equatorial regions across the north Atlantic as the Gulf Stream current that warms northern Europe. If this dynamic is shut down by, say, an injection of large amounts of fresh water to the north Atlantic by means perhaps of a period of warming, then something akin to the LIA could be expected again. We'll return to this point a bit later, as it is a process that climatologists worry about today.

The example of the LIA shows that there are several possibilities for setting off an ice age. Volcanoes and sunspots are but two of a long list of possible culprits. So before proceeding, let's take a page or two to detail the "Top 10" possible causes of a new ice age.

10 ways to start an ice age

The 2004 film, "The Day After Tomorrow," is based on a disruption of the ocean conveyor that brings warm water to the Northern Hemisphere. The plot of the film revolves around melting polar ice that leads to a lot of fresh water from the northern polar region disrupting the flow of warmer water.

In the movie, three massive storms gather across the Earth and then combine into a planet-wide storm. The eye of this "perfect storm" is able to suck very cold air from the upper atmosphere to the ground, causing a flash freeze anywhere it touches.

The United States becomes a vast tundra reminiscent of Siberia at its worst, and even the southern half of the U.S. tries to relocate to Mexico. The Mexicans then briefly close the border, but it's re-opened when the U.S. President agrees to forgive all Latin American debt.

We should immediately note that there is not a shred of climatological science in the events portrayed in the film. All this having been said, the take-home message of this fanciful expression of some of the possible consequences of global warming is that the climate can do stranger things than are dreamed of in our philosophies.

So we should be alert to even highly unlikely scenarios for rapid climate change. In particular, ice ages can come quickly or slowly from many sources.

There are basically three different sources for an ice age: actions taking place in outer space, geophysical events on earth, and harmful human activity. Let's quickly review 10 different scenarios within these three broad categories:

The first three entries on our Top 10 list involve various changes in either the Earth's orbit around the Sun or in the Earth's planetary alignment, all of which would reduce the solar radiation falling on the planet's surface.

Widening of the earth's orbit around the sun: Presently, the earth moves about the sun in an orbit that is very nearly a circle. This means that the amount of solar radiation falling on the earth is pretty much constant throughout the year, although of course some regions get more radiation than others due to the tilt of the earth's axis of rotation. But the earth's orbit is widening very slowly, and in about 50,000 years it will be much more elliptical rather than circular. At that time there will be less solar radiation, on average, than there is today. Specialists believe that this is the primary cause of ice ages.

Change of the tilt of the earth's axis of rotation: The axis of the Earth's rotation is not straight up-and-down but is tilted a bit with respect to the plane of its movement around the Sun. As the Earth moves around the Sun, this tilt is what causes the change of seasons. But the axis slowly tips and then moves back more toward the vertical. When the axis is straight up-and-down, we have warmer winters and cooler summers. In these periods, there will be more snow at the poles, and in the summer less ice will melt. Presto! An ice age in the making. Fortunately, the axis of rotation won't be vertical again for another 20,000 years or so.

Wobble of the earth's axis of rotation: When a spinning top loses energy, its axis of rotation starts to wobble before it finally falls over. The Earth's axis of rotation also wobbles in just the same way as the top, one wobbly rotation taking about 23,000 years. Some researchers believe that this wobbling gives rise to temperature changes on the surface of the Earth that can also lead to an ice age.

Meteor dust: Out beyond Neptune there is a large region consisting of many small bodies left over from the formation of the solar system. These bodies consist mostly of frozen methane, ammonia and water, and they form what's called the Kuiper Belt. Some astrophysicists believe a big asteroid from this region could explode, giving rise to a cloud of dust that would surround the Sun. The resulting reduction of solar radiation could then trigger an ice age on Earth.

Space clouds: Out in deep space there are vast clouds of dust and gas. Occasionally, our solar system passes through one of these clouds in a passage that takes millions of years. This passage blocks out solar radiation causing "super" ice ages that occurred hundreds of millions of years ago. Or so theorists say.

Earth

Volcanoes: Volcanic eruptions of the "super" type that occurred in Yellowstone National Park more than 600,000 years ago can also cause an ice age.

Such an eruption blows so much soot, gas and dust into the atmosphere that sunlight is blocked out for years. The cooling Earth then experiences "eternal" winter and, hence, a very long ice age.

Collapse of the Gulf Stream: We've already outlined how the Gulf Stream current across the North Atlantic can sometimes shut down, an effect that most likely caused the Little Ice Age discussed earlier.

Thinning of the atmosphere: There are several processes, including a human induced reduction of greenhouse gases that can remove carbon dioxide and methane from the atmosphere.

Interestingly, without these gases, the Earth would cool dramatically from the loss of its "heat blanket," and almost surely touch off an ice age.

Tectonic shifts: The Earth's continents slowly move around into different configurations on a geological timescale. At times, they form one huge super continent. At other times, the landmasses break up into many smaller continents like we see today. A continent like Antarctica at a pole is especially dangerous, since if it breaks up, huge amounts of ice would be deposited into the seas, triggering off conditions for a new ice age.

Human activity

Nuclear war: the phenomenon of "nuclear winter" occurs when ground-burst nuclear weapons in a war send vast amounts of dust, soot and other contaminants into the atmosphere, much like the situation described above for a big volcanic eruption. The end result is the same: a large reduction in sunlight striking the surface of the Earth for many months, if not years, leading to cooling and some type of ice age.

This list is by no means exhaustive. But it provides much ammunition supporting the contention that the dawning of a new ice age is definitely not science fiction. It's happened before, and it will definitely happen again.

Adding it all up

It's important to again emphasize that transitions between radically different climatic regimes can take place over very short time periods, often just a decade or two.

These transitions are what system theorists would term an "extreme event," and there is an emerging theory of such events suggesting they occur in "bursts." Thus, extreme events involve a transition from one qualitatively different state to another in a time period very short relative to the overall time frame of the phenomenon, here global climatic change, followed by a very long period in the new state.

Hot or cold

On one side, we have the global warmers. The upward thrust of the Earth's temperature, along with consequent phenomena like melting of polar ice, is incontrovertible - whether or not it's caused and/or exacerbated by human activity.

Following the by-now-standard scenario, this temperature change will continue for many decades and ultimately shift populations and lifestyles to entirely new regimes. It's not necessary to detail these matters here, as the scientific and popular presses have decimated several forests already with their account of these dire straits.

On the other side of the ledger are what we might term the "global coolers," who argue for a trip to the deep freeze rather than the oven is at least as likely a scenario. Our story in this article has given the main reasons underlying this rather unfashionable, and certainly much less chronicled, view.

While the majority of climatologists pooh-pooh the likelihood of the freezer as opposed to the oven, it is a scenario that is not at all implausible or in any way unscientific.

It has happened before and will surely happen again. The only question is how and when. Our assessment is that it's more than a long shot, thus probably not the way to bet, at least if your timescale is a few decades.

Decisions have to be made

Leena Ilmela

This is one of the homes in Nam-dong in Incheon which is facilitated with sublight energy panels which are gaining popularity around the world, mostly because it is environment-friendly and produces no greenhouse gases causing pollution. *Korea Times file*

Not a single transaction between European banks is possible due to the once-in-a-century floods in Central Europe. One farm is contaminated; all food imported from Europe to Russia is cancelled. Climate change is a political challenge; 20 percent of exports are disappearing.

Three European examples of environment-related shocks that shake the economy. How do we make decisions in a world dominated by man-made (global financial system) and environmentally generated (climate change) uncertainties?

Climate change requires quick decisions. Climate change is studied widely, but still we have two groups of experts with totally opposite views. The Intergovernmental Panel on Climate Change (IPCC) anticipates that the critical level of global warming has already been reached, and the warming of the climate is faster than predicted. At the same time, there are other scientists who claim that a new small ice age is more of a potential threat. In between these groups is a third group of moderates who see the current warming trend as a normal cycle; they expect automatic balancing dynamics to take place.

Scientists criticize governments about slow and non-sufficient reactions to climate issues. But how can we as scientists expect that political decision makers define risk levels and adequate actions when even we cannot agree on the probabilities for the options presented above?

This is especially true since we know that climate change is only one topic on their agenda.

Politicians are fully occupied with the economic problems of the public sector, slow growth of the global economy, pensions, the feeble financial sector and the rapidly increasing cost of national health care. And their primary attention is focused on the next elections.

First, I will describe three different environment-driven extreme events (by extreme event we mean a low probability and high impact event), and then I will present one way to meet these decision-making challenges.

Surrender?

Decision makers can apply two different main strategies in this situation. The decision maker may invest in an anticipation system and try to detect early signs of the risks as soon as possible. Or decision makers can surrender to increasing uncertainties and invest in resilience. The former strategy is the right one for risks that we know well-enough to define their probability, the latter is the only way to prepare for extreme events that have a low probability but potentially high impact. The systemic nature of both the global environment and the global social system generates surprises that you cannot manage with traditional risk management methods. Let me present three examples, all from Europe: one concerns mitigation of climate warming, one a weather problem and the third a health safety challenge.

The European Union (EU) has set a very strict target to cut all environmental emissions as fast as possible. This choice has been justified by alarming data about climate change. Europe wants to be a forerunner and carry its share of responsibility.

The Baltic Sea is a very fragile ecosystem, and the recent development has generated serious discussions about preventive actions. The EU is planning to apply a new, tighter CO_2 emissions regulation that decreases emissions to as low as 0.1 percent by 2015. Sea transportation becomes more expensive. If the EU applies this regulation, it will end the pulp and paper industry in Finland (one third of the price of exported paper consists of transportation costs), and Finland will lose 20 percent of its exports. The unemployment rates will double and the countryside will be desolated.

Efficiency has been for a long time the leading goal of the economic system. Financial institutions of the 32 European Union countries have built an efficient payments transaction system called Inter European Payment System that started operations in 2011. Now Europeans can pay all their bills very easily to other European banks using debit cards. Efficiency emerges from the fact that all payments between banks are cleared in one center, Luxemburg, in the heart of the Europe.

What does this have to with environmental risks? A lot. We have recently seen an increasing number of severe storms and floods in the Northern hemisphere, and climate change scientists warn us that extreme weather is increasing. Let us presume that all of Central Europe will once again flood next spring, but that the flood beats the 100-year record and destroys a vast amount of infrastructure. Too high a level of flooding water in the wrong place can stop all payment transactions in the 32 countries.

The third example is very different. In Spring 2011, some people in southern Germany and tourists developed a very dangerous stomach disease, caused by e-Coli bacteria. Almost 40 victims died and the only information available was that the contamination had something to do with vegetables.

Germans blamed Spanish vegetables (Spain is a big exporter of farming products in Europe). Russia used the situation in order to deny all vegetable product imports from the EU region. It is easy to understand that as an outcome, 80 percent of Spanish vegetables were driven to the garbage dump, but the same happened also in France. And French farmers did not have anything to do with the problem! After three weeks of trouble, the origin of the problem proved to be in a small farm in Southern Germany. This plot was far too absurd for any risk management professional even to imagine.

All of these examples reveal how intertwined different systems of our world have become. All of the cases describe only the linkages between the environmental system and the socio-economic system, but still the dynamics vary a lot. The first example is an interplay between environment and regulation, the next describes technology's vulnerability to changing weather patterns, and the third was almost totally composed within a social system, media. None of these were covered by traditional risk management methods.

Resilience as a solution?

At the beginning of the article, I mentioned two different strategies for the management of such surprises. Anticipation is problematic for these three low probability events, but what about resilience?

In our studies, resilience consists of three elements: adaptability, agility and active learning. To be resilient means to adapt to changed environments. We are agile enough to use the opportunities the new kind of environment offers. We use the surprise - or shock - to actively improve our system.

The challenge is that even for the three examples I presented above, it is very hard to be prepared. Each one requires a totally different kind of resilience. The forest industry should have recognized early enough that the structure relying on transportation is not sustainable in the long run. But efficiency requirements have led to large units and long logistic distances.

The EU regulation is only going to speed up the development that was occurring. Efficiency is also the driver of the second example; Inter European payment contract leads to a centralized system that is fast, but a temporal failure disrupts the entire continent. The third example is more challenging. French farmers could not be prepared for this situation. Or could they?

Surprises are increasing

Surprises are increasing, and there is no way that we could invest in building dedicated buffers for all of the shocks the environmental system presents to our brittle centralized systems. The only solution is to try to find actions that increase resilience across all of these different events.

One method developed in collaboration with Aalto University (Finland) and International Institute of Applied Systems analysis (IIASA) is based on portfolio analysis. Method in a nutshell: the chosen uncertainties/shocks (such as climate change) are used for describing two extreme outcomes of the uncertainty in question (average temperatures rise at six degrees Centigrade, temperature drop representing a mini ice age). In the next phase, we describe success strategies for both of the extreme situations and then choose those actions useful in both of the environments. All this is determined for all of the uncertainties to be analyzed.

Let us do the test and analyze these three cases to find a couple of actions that are worth investing in. It is very evident that increasing logistical cost would be more bearable if the exported products were either more valuable or lighter.

Many backup centers for the SEPA system may be expensive but needed if weather is getting extreme. Extensive quality checks for all of the food will also allow French farmers to prove that their products are safe. But all of these examples do not help for the other two cases. And they are expensive to implement.

In our analysis, we identified one common feature in successful actions across all of these shocks. If you have a distributed production model, the paper production takes place in local mills that are able to use various raw materials, the SEPA system is organized as a distributed network of national computer centers (as the Internet is operating now) so that if one center fails, there are other centers that automatically take care of the duties of the failed unit, and distributed food production is arranged so that we use mainly local food, not only ecological but also safer.

The generic feature of all these solutions is a distributed structure. Perhaps the distributed structure is not as efficient as a centralized system, but it is much more resilient. We may not be able to control weather, but we are able to make decisions that build a resilient and weatherproof society.

Accelerating investment in green growth

Brindusa Fidenza

Volunteers from Korea, including school students, plant trees at a high school in a village near the Cambodian capital of Phnom Penh. Many countries and companies around the world have been investing to improve environmental conditions in countries like Cambodia. *Korea Times file*

As the world economy continues efforts to regain balance, emerging markets are forecasted to contribute most to global growth by 2015 and, according to the OECD, are likely to account for 60 percent of global gross domestic product (GDP) by 2030.

This global growth path could lift a further three billion people in developing countries out of poverty and into the mostly urban middle classes within the next two decades - an economic forecast celebrated in the midst of more challenging growth estimates for Europe, the United States and Japan.

However, the associated rise in demand for energy, water, urban development, transportation and agricultural infrastructure to help meet this anticipated growth is unprecedented. A cumulative investment in infrastructure of $18.1 trillion will be needed by 2030, according to a recent analysis undertaken for the World Economic Forum's Infrastructure Initiative.

Close to $1 trillion a year on average is a huge investment challenge to meet. In addition, a gathering body of analysis suggests that the business-as-usual approach to investment in traditional emissions-and resource-intensive infrastructure will not result in the sustainable growth that many developing countries seek, and might even decrease economic resilience in some cases.

For example, by 2030 there could be a 40 percent gap between global water demand and supply, with the situation worse for those developing countries in the Middle East and Asia that are already using freshwater supplies in an unsustainable manner.

In the agricultural sector, investment in traditional practices to meet an expected doubling of demand for production by 2030 could increase land under cultivation from 1.5 trillion hectares to 3.2 trillion hectares, leading to large-scale deforestation with negative land, water and climate change consequences.

Increase in energy demand

The energy sector also creates tremendous challenges. The International Energy Agency forecasts a 40 percent increase in energy demand by 2030, driven almost entirely by growth in developing and emerging countries. Without action to decarbonize energy infrastructure, investments in the energy sector will continue to accentuate the world's reliance on emissions-intensive fossil fuels for close to 60 percent of total power generation for this period.

In addition to increasing greenhouse gas emissions, following such an approach will expose developing countries to increased volatility in fossil fuel prices, as imports of oil and coal rise.

The consequences are potentially dramatic. Given these scenarios, scientists and other observers warn that the world is heading for a global average increase in land temperature of between four and six degrees Celsius by the end of the century, when in fact the average global temperature increase should be maintained within two degrees to avoid the negative impacts of climate change. The latest scientific analysis suggests the world has already experienced an average landmass warming of one degree since 1950; for every degree rise in average land temperature, scientists estimate an increase in the potential for more extreme weather events.

Rio+20 negotiations

Some commentators suggest that we are already seeing the early signs of bad things to come, with changing weather patterns (droughts and heavy rainfall) in many parts of the world such as the recent floods in Thailand, the Philippines, and Pakistan that claimed many lives, left millions of people affected and created billions of dollars in economic damage.

Fortunately, some good news exists. A multitude of initiatives and policy and business-driven commitments that are being announced in the wake of the Rio+20 negotiations stand as proof of the potential for public and private sectors to work together for sustainable growth. Supported by international agencies, an increasing number of governments in developing countries are changing their approach to infrastructure and industrial planning to make economic growth more sustainable and resilient.

This is not just an abstract concept. China has devoted key parts of its last three five-year plans to developing a green growth strategy for energy, agriculture and infrastructure, investing over $51 billion in new renewable energy projects in 2010 alone, according to Bloomberg New Energy Finance.

Recently, Mexico enacted a national law making a 30 percent reduction in greenhouse gas emissions a legal commitment by 2030. Other emerging economies such as Brazil, South Africa, South Korea, Kenya, Vietnam, and India are promoting green growth policies to enhance the resilience of their economic development.

Many other developing countries are following suit. According to the Global Status Report of the Renewable Energy Network (REN21), by the end of 2010, 96 countries had enacted renewable energy targets, 60 had bio-energy mandates and at least 30 were developing some form of low-carbon growth path. The goal of these national strategies, which include policies on renewable energy, energy efficiency, transport and agriculture, as well as market-based carbon tax and trade mechanisms, is to direct significant investment flows into resource-efficient, job-creating growth.

The role that organizations such as the Global Green Growth Institute (headquartered in Seoul) are playing in helping developing countries design comprehensive green growth strategies is already showing initial successes in countries such as Ethiopia and Indonesia.

The move among many developing countries to make their infrastructure investment and their growth strategies green in general has important economic implications. Bloomberg New Energy Finance again shows that in 2011, global investment in new renewable power plants - estimated at $187 billion - surpassed that of power plants fuelled by natural gas, oil and coal - at $157 billion - for the first time. 2011 was also the first year when expenditure on renewable energy in developing countries, driven by China, exceeded that of the industrialized world.

These conditions present a window of attractiveness for investment into growth markets. In the current economic circumstances, the fiscal outlook is more optimistic in developing countries, where debt to GDP ratios have been falling in recent years, as growth has been maintained and where, as a consequence, risk premiums have continued to decrease.

The economic performance of emerging markets, including several in sub-Saharan Africa, has improved greatly in recent years, as is the case with emerging market countries such as India that can attract more investment and are in a better position to absorb capital flows aimed at an expansion in investment.

Sustainable world economy

To support the dramatic increase in private investment needed to transform toward a sustainable world economy, this past July at the Mexican Business 20 (B20) Summit, the World Economic Forum launched a new public-private partnership initiative entitled the Green Growth Action Alliance, with Mexican President Felipe Calderon taking the role of Honorary Chair.

The alliance aims to deploy public money to unlock and utilize private sector investment for clean energy, transport, agriculture and other green growth areas. It will feed results into key international processes such as the G20 and climate change international negotiations.

The alliance has defined five areas of action: it will work to promote free trade in green goods and services, to achieve robust carbon pricing across the world market, to end inefficient subsidies and other forms of fossil fuel support, to accelerate low-carbon innovation and to increase efforts to direct public funding toward the most effective mechanisms and instruments that can help leverage private investment.

Nearly fifty of the world's largest energy companies, international financial institutions, and development finance institutions have already joined the alliance. The coalition also will work closely with governments and non-governmental organizations, including existing initiatives such as the United Nations' Sustainable Energy for All initiative, the Green Climate

Fund, the International Development Finance Club currently chaired by Germany's promotional bank KFW, and the San Giorgio Group -a policy research collaborative initiative of the Climate Policy Initiative, the World Bank and the OECD; its main objective will be to enable, support and scale up existing projects that can achieve real impact.

Among others, the World Economic Forum, in collaboration with the members of the alliance, will support the piloting of new mechanisms for green infrastructure and adaptation investments in specific countries, building new innovative financing models for green infrastructure that leverage private sector finance, identified through work in Mexico, India, Kenya, and Vietnam, among others.

Unlocking private finance

Concretely, as an example, it will assist Mexico in unlocking private finance for investments in businesses and technologies that will help achieve its legal requirement to reduce greenhouse gas emissions 30 percent by 2020. In partnership with governments, the alliance will identify key green growth initiatives, design strategies to overcome obstacles, and draw in private investment.

In Kenya, the forum has already been working with the national government, as well as with international and local businesses, to understand the various bottlenecks to deployment of private finance of clean energy at scale and to work collaboratively to design and develop potential solutions.

Mexican President Felipe Calderon said, "The G20 Mexican Presidency welcomes this initiative and supports its efforts to define the practical steps business can take, in partnership with government, to deliver the green growth agenda. The Alliance will also play an important role in tracking our progress in leveraging private finance for green growth."

Accelerating investment in green growth

Women's role vital in disaster prevention

Margaret Arnold

Yoshie Murakami cries as she holds a hand of her dead mother in the rubble near the spot where her home used to be on March 16, 2011 in Rikuzentakata, Iwate Prefecture in Japan following the devastation of a tsunami in which many women and children were victimized. *Yonhap*

Natural disasters are not neutral in the way that they impact people. They compound social exclusion and existing vulnerabilities, disproportionately impacting the poor, women, children, the elderly, the disabled, minority groups and those marginalized in other ways.

Certain groups are particularly vulnerable to disasters, for example, female-headed households, children, the disabled, indigenous groups, landless tenants, migrant workers and other socially marginalized groups.

The root causes of their vulnerability lie in a combination of their geographical context; their financial, socio-economic, cultural, and gender status; and their access to services, decision making and justice.

More than 90 percent of the estimated 140,000 fatalities following the 1991 cyclone in Bangladesh were women. In India, up to three times as many women as men died in the 2004 tsunami, while in Indonesia, this figure rose to up to four times the number of male casualties. The limited mobility and social status of women increased their vulnerability to these events.

Importantly, reconstruction and recovery interventions are also not neutral. They can increase, reinforce or reduce existing inequalities. In a post-disaster context, the poor and marginalized face obstacles to accessing government relief or recovery assistance. They are less likely to understand how to work through the bureaucratic system or may not have access or entitlement to key documentation, such as national identity cards. Certain groups are therefore not only more vulnerable to the impacts of natural disasters but they may also be more vulnerable to ending up in a worse situation as a result of the recovery process.

Disaster risk management

Within the disaster risk management community, we often speak about the window of opportunity that opens after a natural catastrophe to do things differently going forward. The idea is that while devastating, the disaster brings a momentary period of raised awareness of risk, monetary resources and both a real and metaphorical blank slate upon which people can build more resilient communities or initiate other social changes on issues that may not advance during "normal" times.

Hence, the resounding calls after Hurricane Mitch devastated Central America for "transformation, not reconstruction." We heard about "building back better" after the Indian Ocean tsunami, and the "peace dividend" that the tsunami brought to Aceh after decades of fighting between the Government of Indonesia and the Free Aceh Movement (GAM).

Experience has taught us that this window of opportunity is not a given and must be managed carefully. The pressures to get people out of tents and back into houses, or to spend donor money quickly, often trump the need to ensure quality in construction or the adequate engagement of communities to ensure sustainability. Most would agree that Central America has yet to be transformed, and that the tsunami failed to deliver a peace dividend in Sri Lanka.

However, a key area where much progress has been made after disasters is gender equity, which can often be addressed easily and speedily in the recovery process. Support to disaster recovery can be designed to empower women at a grassroots level, build more resilient communities and initiate long-term social change and development.

Women have often been active leaders in rebuilding their communities after disasters. They take the initiative in calling grassroots community meetings and organizing disaster response and recovery coalitions. In Maharashtra, India, after the earthquake there, a local NGO negotiated with the government to secure the appointment of women as communication intermediaries, placing them at the center of the reconstruction process. The women's groups underwent training to build technical capacity and monitor reconstruction.

Over time, they became community development intermediaries. After the 1999 earthquake in Turkey, local NGO KEDV began creating public spaces for women and children to rebuild disrupted community networks and promote women's participation in the public sphere. These women and children's centers started out in tents and then moved to temporary housing settlements.

Women's empowerment

Disaster aid agencies can support women's empowerment after disasters by deeding newly constructed houses in both the woman's and man's names, including women in housing design as well as construction, promoting land rights for women, building nontraditional skills through income-generation projects, distributing relief through women, and funding women's groups to monitor disaster recovery projects. These are a few of the practical steps that can be taken to empower women and at the very least avoid the reinforcement of existing gender inequities.

Promoting women's empowerment in disaster recovery not only contributes to more effective and efficient recovery but also establishes opportunities for women and communities to shape a more sustainable development. Moreover, the experiences of grassroots women leading disaster recovery efforts have grown to include their engagement with local, national and regional authorities to inform the development of policies and programs that support pro-poor, community-driven resilience building.

As the head of the ProVention Consortium, I had the opportunity to support the networking and knowledge sharing of grassroots women leaders, led for years by GROOTS International (http://www.groots.org/) and the

Huairou Commission (http:// www. huairou.org/). These include groups such as the Comité de Emergencia Garifuna of Honduras, which began with organizing emergency relief after Hurricane Mitch and went on to reduce the impact of future hazard events and climate change by restoring indigenous food crops and reforesting coastal areas.

On a recent trip to Peru, I met with women representing a network of grassroots organizations working on resilience building in the slums of Lima who are partnering with the National Institute for Civil Protection (INDECI) to inform their efforts and formalize the role of grassroots community leaders in the national dialogue.

Grassroots organizations

At the global level, grassroots women are organizing under the Community Practitioners' Platform for Resilience. Endorsed by the United Nations International Strategy for Disaster Reduction (UNISDR) in 2010, the CPPR aims to demonstrate, teach and build alliances with governments and development institutions and take strategic policy and program actions to promote pro-poor, resilient development.

All of these efforts grew out of the experiences of women in poor communities devastated by disasters who organized to take charge of their recovery and development paths. The window of opportunity opened. While it was seized upon for basic survival, it also has resulted in long-term, positive social transformation.

Climate change, perhaps the mother of all disasters, provides the mother of all windows of opportunity for positive social transformation. There are countless examples demonstrating that empowering women to exercise leadership within their communities contributes to climate resilience, ranging from disaster preparedness efforts in Bangladesh, Indonesia and Nicaragua, to better forest governance in India and Nepal, and to coping with drought near the Horn of Africa.

There is also strong and mounting evidence at the country level that improving gender equality contributes to policy choices that lead to better environmental governance, whether through increased representation of women within their communities, in society at large and at a political level or through increased labor force participation.

Climate change hits the least protected people and regions

Climate change has major social implications. Many of the world's poorest and most vulnerable people already feel the effects of climate change, and adverse impacts are unavoidable for millions more. The negative impacts of climate change push those living on the margin closer to the edge and can hamper the development pathways of entire regions by impeding the fight against poverty, disease, and hunger.

In addition, policies and interventions to both mitigate and adapt to climate change entail significant distributional, poverty and social impacts. Mitigation policies and measures can have significant distributional impacts, including opportunities and risks for the poor and other vulnerable groups. For example, a greener urban transportation system that reduces CO_2 emissions could mean higher travel costs, making it less affordable to the poor. Similarly, programs like Reducing Emissions from Deforestation and Forest Degradation (REDD) need to promote low-carbon livelihood options that deliver development co-benefits for the poor, particularly in the areas of agriculture, forestry and sustainable land management.

Poor people in developing countries bear the brunt of climate change impacts while contributing very little to its causes. However, the human and social dimensions of climate change have been woefully neglected in the global debate. The World Bank focuses on climate change as an integral part of its mission to fight global poverty and enhance growth with care for the environment by helping to realize climate-smart policies and operations in client countries that advance the interests of those who are most vulnerable to the effects of climate change.

The starting point to understanding vulnerability to climate change is a clear understanding of existing levels of socioeconomic vulnerability and adaptive capacity. However, climate change impacts entail a number of characteristics that require a more dynamic view of vulnerability and new ways of working: they are diverse, long-term and unpredictable. Adapting to these traits is challenging since they require making decisions under high levels of uncertainty.

The 2010 World Development Report: Development and Climate Change, echoes this by stating, "Climate change adds an additional source of unknowns for decision makers to manage", and "Accepting uncertainty (is) inherent to the climate change problem."

There is a need to revise existing concepts of vulnerability and integrate approaches into development efforts to help the poorest and most vulnerable access financial, technical and institutional resources necessary to adapt to climate change impacts and climate action. Proper attention to the social dimensions of climate change can greatly enhance the effectiveness and sustainability of development. Climate change presents the world with perhaps the biggest challenge of our time. It also presents an opportunity to do things differently. - M.A.

Environment info Air pollution

Air is the ocean we breathe. Air supplies us with oxygen that is essential for our bodies to live. Air is 99.9 percent nitrogen, oxygen, water vapor and inert gases. Human activities can release substances into the air, some of which can cause problems for humans, plants, and animals.

There are several main types of pollution and well-known effects of pollution that are commonly discussed. These include smog, acid rain, the greenhouse effect, and "holes" in the ozone layer. Each of these problems has serious implications for our health and well being as well as for the environment.

One type of air pollution is the release of particles into the air from burning fuel for energy. Diesel smoke is a good example of this particulate matter. The particles are very small pieces of matter measuring about 2.5 microns or about .0001 inches. This type of pollution is sometimes referred to as "black carbon" pollution. The exhaust from burning fuels in automobiles, homes, and industries is a major source of pollution in the air. Some authorities believe that even the burning of wood and charcoal in fireplaces and barbeques can release significant quantities of soot into the air.

Another type of pollution is the release of noxious gases, such as sulfur dioxide, carbon monoxide, nitrogen oxides, and chemical vapors. These can take part in further chemical reactions once they are in the atmosphere, forming smog and acid rain.

Pollution also needs to be considered inside our homes, offices, and schools. Some of these pollutants can be created by indoor activities such as smoking and cooking. In the United States, we spend about 80-90 percent of our time inside buildings, and so our exposure to harmful indoor pollutants can be serious. It is therefore important to consider both indoor and outdoor air pollution.

Essentials of consumerism

Randell Krantz

Consumers, who are the most important part of protecting the environment, take part in an event to promote a campaign for reducing the emission of CO_2 to the 350ppm (parts per million) level at the Hanok Village in central Seoul. *Korea Times file*

Global consumption of resources continues to grow rapidly. Over the past four years, an estimated 450 million people have been lifted out of poverty and the number of households in the emerging and developed world living on an income of more than $3,000 per annum has increased by 28 percent. Looking ahead, more than 150 million new consumers will join the middle class each year until 2030. Despite what many see as a double-dip recession, 36 countries grew at a rate of over seven percent last year.

As incomes rise in emerging markets, new members of the middle class demand more meat and dairy products, which require more resources to produce. This generation of mostly young, urban consumers from emerging markets presents huge opportunities for social progress and market development. These same consumers also will create new demand for products and services and place additional strains on the planet's finite resources. Current approaches to manage our resources are already struggling to address this additional demand.

Let's look at the price volatility of several agricultural crops, those where the past 10 years of growth has unwound over 100 years of declining prices. Between 2000 and 2010, prices of widely used commodities such as cotton, palm oil and cocoa increased by 75 percent, 230 percent and 246 percent respectively. In July of last year, cotton prices were the highest they had been in 300 years.

What is sustainable consumption?

While various ideas around sustainability have been floating around for the past 40 years or so, the link between sustainability and consumption of products and services we use every day is a much more recent phenomenon. The conjunction of these two words risks being confusing, or even worse, a paradox.

But what does it actually mean to consume sustainably? Coming up with a technical definition for sustainable consumption can be quite a challenge. After all, what is sustainability? From whose perspective? Over what time period?

For the sake of argument, we define sustainable consumption as consumption that meets the needs of the present without compromising the ability of future generations to meet their needs. The intrinsic values of this definition are simple to understand, while the details tend to be much debated.

Sustainable consumption is a complex issue because it encompasses the interconnected impacts from a range of environmental and social issues, including water, food, energy and climate change. A few examples illustrate the scale of the challenge:

- Water consumption already outstrips demand in many parts of the world, and analysis suggests that by 2030 the world will face a 40 percent global shortfall between forecasted demand and estimates of available water supply. This is not just in arid countries or poor countries, but already evident in Australia, the U.S. and Spain. The amount of water needed in households for personal use is trivial, while the water embedded in the food and products of everyday use is substantial.

- While enough food is grown today to comfortably feed seven billion people, roughly 50 percent of all produce grown is wasted in the EU, the U.S., and Sub-Saharan Africa, according to the FAO. In addition, experts project that annual meat production will need to rise by 75 percent - to 470 million tons - by 2050, incurring significant environmental impacts. Livestock production alone accounts for 70 percent of agricultural water use, 30 percent of global land use and 18 percent of global greenhouse gas emissions.

- As these same economies develop, and as population increases, energy demand is expected to increase 40 percent by 2050. With the majority of this estimated increase expected to come from non-OECD countries, and with 1.5 billion people worldwide still lacking energy access, a huge challenge presents itself as these countries cannot be denied their development rights. With advanced technologies, the consumer will play an increasing role in lowering energy consumption. McKinsey estimates that customer demand response, known as "demand side management," could reduce peak energy demand in the U.S. by 20 percent between 2009 and 2019.

- The scientific consensus that we need to limit the global temperature by two degrees means that our current trajectory is not sustainable. Greenhouse gas emissions are generally calculated by their origin; however nearly 20 percent of China's emissions are produced on behalf of other countries, and emissions in the U.S. would be eight percent higher if counted by consumption.

So what can we do? Traditional responses to these complex challenges tend to have two flaws: 1) they focus on a single issue that cannot be solved in isolation, and 2) they focus on the sustainable supply of resources rather than the demand that drives consumption.

If each of these issues is so complex in its own right, how can we possibly look at everything together? By taking a systems view, it can actually be simpler to look at the way each of these issues interacts and to manage the whole rather than the disparate parts. Let's look at a simple system to understand how these pieces fit together.

Systems thinking

Imagine a simple system with a city surrounded by agricultural land that generates its power from locally mined coal. Water from a lake is used for household use for citizens, cooling the power plant and irrigating agricultural fields.

A well-intentioned policy to lower carbon emissions might easily end in a vicious cycle that upsets our simple system. Let's say that citizens vote to lower emissions by co-firing biomass to replace 25 percent of the coal at the coal-fired power plant and a policy to promote the use of biomass in the coal plant and corn ethanol for cars. This in turn would promote cultivation of fast growing biomass stocks such as alfalfa for biomass pellets and additional planting of corn.

Between land use displacement and direct use of existing corn supplies, food prices might suffer drastic swings, while increased irrigation would create challenges to the water supply, which would cause both the citizens and the power plant to suffer from water scarcity. Lowered agricultural yields could then exacerbate the issue, as would the potential for deforestation and longer-term climate change.

This need not be the case, as a better set of policies could help drive a much more virtuous cycle. Recently, there has been a rush to look at the way some issues interact in groups, such as the "water-food-energy-climate nexus" promoted in a recent book by the World Economic Forum.

Imagine the same simple system in which the drive to remove emissions is addressed via the demand for electricity, rather than the supply. Educating citizens and placing price premiums on overuse of energy could easily yield a 20 percent reduction in household and industrial electricity use. This not only would saves emission, but also money, as less fuel would be required to meet the energy needs of the city. Additional energy supply could come from wind turbines that take only limited land from agricultural production. No-till farming could reduce the emissions from agriculture, while reductions in food waste would reduce in the value chain and in the home demand on the agricultural system.

A win-win-win for water, food and energy is indeed possible. It does however require more thorough thinking about the impacts of each action and reaction, as well as tracking of indicators across more than one part of the system.

Demand management

In this example, we can see that the systems solution needs to look beyond just the supply of energy, food and water. In fact, the demand for these resources and the associated waste along the way present a huge opportunity for net benefits at reduced costs.

Survey data repeatedly show that moral or ethical arguments will only drive 10-15 percent of consumers to make more sustainable choices, even while more that 50 percent state that they are doing "everything they can" to protect the environment.

There is an opportunity to explore the role of other tools to catalyze consumer change. These tools range from strict regulations that drive a specific behaviors such as mandated recycling (often referred to as sticks), to more creative incentives and a more enabling environment for consumers and citizens to be rewarded for making decisions that ultimately use fewer resources such as a reward scheme for increased recycling (referred to as carrots).

One tends to assume that the power of carrots and sticks lies in the hands of policymakers and governments, but this need not be the case. Companies can also engage consumer behaviors. Indeed, retailers and manufacturers do just that every day. A retailer who stops selling a product like incandescent light bulbs (a process known as choice editing) is effectively having the same impact as a government regulation that bans their sale. Meanwhile in-store promotions can send price signals to the consumer to change buying habits.

It is now increasingly common that influence consumer behavior. A nudge is a policy or small incentive that can cause a bigger change in consumer behavior. If we think of our simple system above, how might carrots, sticks and nudges encourage consumers to use less energy and water?

A stick approach might cap the energy use of any given household, or more likely, employ a tiered pricing model for both electricity and water to encourage consumers to use less of both. In this case, a designated amount of water and electricity required for everyday living can be offered cheaply, subsidized by higher prices paid by those who want to consume more over a certain threshold. Such an approach would require measurement of water and energy use so that the consumer can have feedback on their use and adjust accordingly.

There would also need to be educative campaigns put in place to explain the new system. The nudging part would be offering more information to households in a digestible way. People may not know what a kilowatt-hour is, but if they are consuming more electricity than their neighbor, they will redouble efforts to reduce their consumption.

Across each of these changes, technology would play an increasingly important role. Using smart meters and communications with citizens, it becomes ever easier to provide feedback to consumers. Smart phones and apps can provide this information and suggested behavior changes in real time.

Personal technology also enables us to go beyond efficiencies of our existing system to explore new business models that might need far fewer resources. One new business model making waves is that of "collaborative consumption" or fractional ownership. Citizens do not own a product outright but use it when they need it. While this may not make sense for a phone, it certainly does for a car, which might only be required once a month. Car sharing platforms such as Zipcar, enabled by connective technologies, allow cars parked around a city to be unlocked and used by subscribers.

Some retailers are getting into the game of leasing white goods, so you never need to own the latest refrigerator that will soon be outdated. Instead, one can lease the latest model and have it upgraded when a more efficient one comes out. The old refrigerator can then be redistributed or retired by the retailer who may be working with the utility to reduce electricity consumption.

Some retailers are increasing their efficiency by getting rid of the store altogether. While Internet shopping is no longer new, it was Tesco that pioneered the idea of a subway supermarket in Seoul, giving shoppers the benefits of a familiar shopping experience and the visual cues they like with the simplicity of home delivery. Through its subway shopping system with a custom smart phone app, Tesco has made shopping easier for commuters while delivering goods directly to homes to increase convenience. Meanwhile, the retailer saves money on energy, logistics and eventually retail space while increasing consumer loyalty - the aspiration for any retailer.

Putting it together

The World Economic Forum has been working with businesses, NGOs and experts to explore the sustainable consumption issue for the past four years. At the Annual Meeting in Davos in January 2012, it was agreed by consumer industry CEOs that a fruitful area of focus would be the juncture between consumers, new social media, emerging cognitive and behavioral work on consumer behavior, and sustainability.

Several general levers through which citizens are influenced on sustainable consumption can be identified:

- Pricing: Honest price signals, pricing the costs of pollution and constraining use of natural resources are foci
- Education : Needs to be a significant effort to combat extrinsic

consumption messaging
- Metrics: Measurement of consumer products impacts and simple communication of this information
- Choice Editing: Regulation of harmful products by companies or policies and standards
- Aspiration Tuning: Shaping cultural norms and desires with marketing and cognitive science
- New Business Models: Moving beyond efficiency from volume to value, from products to services

Collectively, these levers have the potential to change consumer behaviors across the full systems of water, food, energy and climate.

A new project at the World Economic Forum exploring how to engage "Tomorrow's Consumer" has been kicked off to explore this interconnected area. The project will bring together Chief Marketing Officers, Chief Sustainability Officers and other executives from media and communications, technology, and consumer industries. Working with psychologists, cognitive scientists and sustainability experts, the new project will explore how to close the intention-action gap to take us one step closer to sustainable consumption.

Consequences of climate change on oceans

Climate Institute

One of the most pronounced effects of climate change has been the melting of ice masses around the world. Glaciers and ice sheets are large, slow-moving assemblages of ice that cover about 10 percent of the world's land area and exist on every continent except Australia. They are the world's largest reservoir of fresh water, holding approximately 75 percent of the earth's supply.

Over the past century, most of the world's mountain glaciers as well as the ice sheets in both Greenland and Antarctica have lost mass. Retreating of this ice occurs when the mass balance (the difference between accumulation of ice in the winter versus ablation or melting in the summer) is negative such that more ice melts each year than is replaced.

By affecting the temperature and precipitation of a particular area, both key factors in the ability of a glacier to replenish its volume of ice, climate change affects the mass balance of glaciers and ice sheets. When the temperature exceeds a particular level or warm temperatures last long enough, and/or there is insufficient precipitation, glaciers and ice sheets lose mass.

One of the best-documented examples of glacial retreat has been on Mount Kilimanjaro in Africa. It is the tallest peak on the continent, and so, despite being located in the tropics, it is high enough that glacial ice has been present for many centuries. However, over the past century, the volume of Mount Kilimanjaro's glacial ice has decreased by about 80 percent. If this rate of loss continues, its glaciers will likely disappear within the next decade. Similar glacial melting is occurring in Alaska, the Himalayas, and the Andes.

Glacial melting

When researching glacial melting, scientists must consider not only how much ice is being lost, but also how quickly. Recent studies show that the movement of ice toward the oceans from both of the major ice sheets has

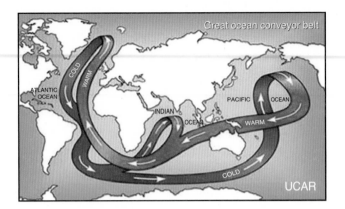

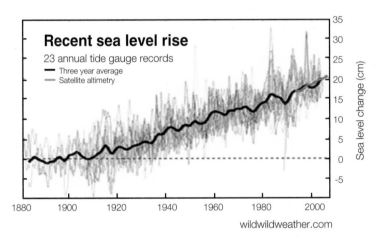

Recent sea level rise

23 annual tide gauge records
— Three year average
— Satellite altimetry

Sea level change (cm)

wildwildweather.com

Trend of sea level change (1993-2008)

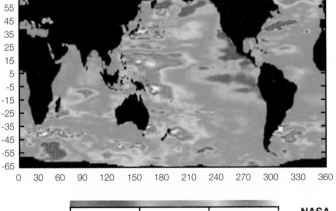

-5   0   mm/year   5   10   **NASA**

increased significantly.

As the speed increases, the ice streams flow more rapidly into the ocean, too quickly to be replenished by snowfall near their heads. The speed of movement of some of the ice streams draining the Greenland Ice Sheet, for example, has doubled in just a few years.

Using various methods to estimate how much ice is being lost (such as creating a "before and after" image of the ice sheet to estimate the change in shape and therefore volume, or using satellites to "weigh" the ice sheet by computing its gravitational pull), scientists have discovered that the mass balance of the Greenland Ice Sheet has become negative over the past few years. Estimates put the net loss of ice at anywhere between 82 and 224 cubic kilometers per year.

In Antarctica, recent estimates show a sharp contrast between what is occurring in the East and West Antarctic Ice Sheets. The acceleration of ice loss from the West Antarctic Ice Sheet has doubled in recent years, which is similar to what has happened in Greenland. In West Antarctica, as well as in Greenland, the main reason for this increase is the quickening pace at which glacial streams are flowing into the ocean. Scientists estimate the loss of ice from the West Antarctic ice sheet to be from 47 to 148 cubic kilometers per year.

On the other hand, recent measurements indicate that the East Antarctic ice sheet (which is much larger than the West) is gaining mass because of increased precipitation.

However, it must be noted that this gain in mass by the East Antarctic ice sheet is nowhere near equal to the loss from the West Antarctic ice sheet. Therefore, the mass balance of the entire Antarctic Ice Sheet is negative.

Sea level rise

Most of the world's coastal cities were established over the last few millennia, a period when global sea levels have been nearly constant. Since the mid-19th century, however, sea levels have been rising, primarily as a result of human-induced climate change.

During the 20th century, sea levels rose about 15-20 centimeters (roughly 1.5 to 2.0 mm/year), with rates at the end of the century greater than those occurring at its beginning. Satellite measurements taken over the past decade, however, indicate that the rate of increase has jumped to about 3.1 mm/year, which is significantly higher than the average rate for the 20th century. Projections suggest that the rate of sea level rise is likely to increase during the 21st century, although there is considerable controversy about the likely size of the increase.

This controversy arises mainly due to uncertainties about the contributions to expect from the three main processes responsible for sea level increases: thermal expansion, the melting of glaciers and ice caps, and the loss of ice from the Greenland and West Antarctic ice sheets.

Causes of sea level increase

Before describing the major factors contributing to climate change, it should be understood that the melting back of sea ice (e.g., in the Arctic and the floating ice shelves) will not directly contribute to rising sea levels because this ice is already floating on the ocean (and so already displacing its mass of water). However, the melting back of this ice can lead to indirect contributions to rising sea levels.

For example, the melting back of sea ice leads to a reduction in albedo (surface reflectivity) and allows for greater absorption of solar radiation. More solar radiation being absorbed accelerates warming, thus increasing the melting back of snow and ice on land. In addition, ongoing breakup of the floating ice shelves allows a faster flow of ice from land into the oceans, thereby providing an additional contribution to rising sea levels.

There are three major processes by which human-induced climate change directly affects sea levels. First, like air and other fluids, water expands as its temperatures increase (i.e., its density goes down as temperatures rise).

As climate change increases ocean temperatures, initially at the surface and over centuries at depth, the water expands, contributing to rising sea levels because of thermal expansion. Thermal expansion is likely to have contributed to about 2.5 cm of sea level rise during the second half of the 20th century, with the rate of rise due to this term having increased to about three times this rate during the early 21st century.

Because this contribution to rising sea levels depends mainly on the temperature of the ocean, projecting the increase in ocean temperatures provides an estimate of future growth. Over the 21st century, the IPCC's (Intergovernmental Panel on Climate Change) Fourth Assessment projected that thermal expansion will lead to sea level increases of about 17-28 cm (plus or minus about 50 percent). That this estimate is less than would occur from a linear extrapolation of the rate during the first decade of the 21st century, when all model projections indicate ongoing ocean warming, has led to concerns that the IPCC estimate may be too low.

A second, and less certain, contributor to sea level increases is the melting of glaciers and ice caps. IPCC's Fourth Assessment estimated that during the second half of the 20th century, melting of mountain glaciers and ice caps led to about a 2.5 cm rise in sea levels.

This is a higher amount than was caused by the loss of ice from the Greenland and Antarctic ice sheets, which added about 1 cm to sea levels. For the 21st century, IPCC's Fourth Assessment projected that melting of glaciers and ice caps will contribute roughly 10-12cm to sea levels, with an uncertainty of roughly a third. This would represent a melting of about a quarter of the total amount of ice tied up in mountain glaciers and small ice caps.

The third process that can cause sea levels to rise is the loss of ice mass from Greenland and Antarctica. Were all the ice on Greenland to melt, a process that would likely take many centuries to millennia, sea levels would go up by roughly seven meters. The West Antarctic ice sheet holds about five meters of sea level equivalent and is particularly vulnerable, as much of it is grounded below sea level; the East Antarctic ice sheet, which is less vulnerable, holds about 55 meters of sea level equivalent. The models used to estimate potential changes in ice mass are, so far, only capable of estimating the changes in mass due to surface processes leading to evaporation/sublimation and snowfall and conversion to ice.

Impacts of sea level rise

In summarizing the results of model simulations for the 21st century, IPCC reported that central estimates project Greenland would induce about a 2cm rise in sea levels, whereas Antarctica would, because of increased snow accumulation, induce about a 2cm fall in sea levels.

However, there are problems with these estimates, as has become clear with recent satellite observations indicating that both Greenland and Antarctica are currently losing ice mass, and we are only in the first decade of a century that is projected to become much warmer over its course.

While there are obviously many challenges to projecting future sea level increases, even a seemingly small increase can have a dramatic impact on coastal environments. Over 600 million people live in coastal areas that are less than 10 meters above sea level, and two-thirds of the world's cities with populations over five million are located in these at-risk areas.

With sea levels projected to rise at an accelerated rate for at least several centuries, very large numbers of people in vulnerable locations are going to be forced to relocate. If relocation is delayed or if populations do not evacuate during times when the areas are inundated by storm surges, very large numbers of environmental refugees are likely to result.

According to IPCC, even the best-case scenarios indicate that rising sea levels would have a wide range of impacts on coastal environments and infrastructure. Effects are likely to include coastal erosion, wetland and coastal plain flooding, salinization of aquifers and soils, and a loss of habitats for fish, birds, and other wildlife and plants.

More land would be lost

The U.S. Environmental Protection Agency estimates that 26,000 square kilometers of land would be lost should sea levels rise by 0.66 meters, while the IPCC notes that as much as 33 percent of coastal land and wetland habitats are likely to be lost in the next hundred years if ocean levels continue to rise at their present rate. Even more land would be lost if the increase is significantly greater, and this is quite possible.

As a result, very large numbers of wetland and swamp species are likely at serious risk. In addition, species that rely upon the existence of the sea ice to survive are likely to be especially impacted as the retreat accelerates, posing the threat of extinction for polar bears, seals, and some breeds of penguins.

Unfortunately, many of the nations most vulnerable to rising sea levels do not have the resources to prepare. Low-lying coastal regions in developing countries such as Bangladesh, Vietnam, India, and China have large populations living in at-risk coastal areas such as deltas, where river systems enter the ocean. Large island nations such as the Philippines and Indonesia and smaller nations such as Tuvalu and Vanuatu are at severe risk because they do not have enough land at higher elevations to support displaced coastal populations.

For some island nations, another possibility is the danger of losing fresh-water supplies as sea levels push saltwater into aquifers. For this reason, those living on several small island nations (including the Maldives in the Indian Ocean and the Marshall Islands in the Pacific) could be forced to evacuate during the 21st century.

Problematic issues

As CO_2 emissions and climate change continue, risks to the health of the oceans will become a more prominent concern. With accelerated melting back of glaciers and ice sheets and the subsequent rise in sea levels, and with further decreases in oceanic pH and deceleration of thermohaline circulation, the delicate balance of ocean dynamics and ecosystems is being put at risk.

These factors, combined with the uncertainty in predicting exactly how their impacts will interact, are a increasingly problematic issue for future generations.

World needs better alternatives to oil

Martin Kruse

Exploration and production of crude oil is briskly underway around the world, like off the eastern coasts of Vietnam (pictured) but there is increasing need for the development of more alternative energy sources. *Korea Times file*

It is hard to understate the importance of petroleum production for the 20th century. Oil formed the backbone of our society. Without oil, the world's largest industry, the tourist industry, would not have existed as we know it today. The process of globalization would have been limited and many of the 100 million lifted into the global middle class would have remained in poverty.

Oil is unlike every other energy source. It permeates the global economy:

transport, military, construction and manufacturing depend on it. It is used in the pharmaceutical industry, in agriculture and to produce plastic. It is an ingredient in products as different as pharmaceutical drugs, DVDs and asphalt. Oil lubricates the gears of the world's economy. It is at the heart of manufacturing. Without it, the free movement of goods as we know it would grind to a halt.

It is easy to pick on fossil fuels in these climate-changing times, but we must also recognize that without them society would have been radically

World investment in clean energy 2009 ($bil.)

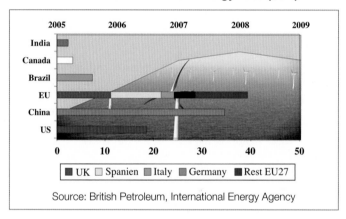

Source: British Petroleum, International Energy Agency

Oil prices ($) & production (mil. bpd)

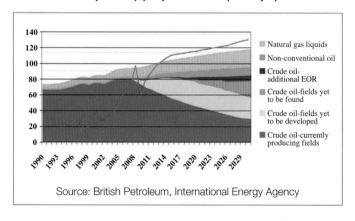

Source: British Petroleum, International Energy Agency

different. But that is precisely why it is a challenge to switch to other types of fuel. Over 95 percent of national transport systems are dependent on oil in one form or another. One of the advantages of oil in the transport sector is its high-energy value. Oil will be difficult to replace as many alternatives do not have sufficiently high-energy value.

Glimpse of possible future

A lack of oil is the worst thing imaginable. So maybe that is why we have been warned time and time again of a shortage since the 1970s, without actually experiencing one. However with the 2008 spike in prices where oil hit $147 a barrel, suddenly we had a first glimpse of a possible future.

Are things changing? Many petroleum geologists think so, and increasingly, whistleblowers from inside the International Energy Agency (IEA) have called the IEA's estimates for future oil production unrealistic. A continued write-down of the IEA's productions estimates has not helped. So what is going on?

Books and documentaries such as "The Coming Oil Crisis" and "The End of Suburbia" have conjured up a somber picture of the future when oil production peaks. "Peak oil" refers to the moment when oil production peaks, not when oil runs out. As Sheikh Zaki Yamani, the Saudi oil minister, said three decades ago, "The Stone Age did not end for lack of stone, and the Oil Age will end long before the world runs out of oil." What he referred to is the violent price increases that will occur when oil resources are reduced. There is no disagreement whether peak oil will happen, only when.

But when is not an absolute point in time; it depends on investment. What differentiates oil production of the near future from that of the 1970s is not just the amount of oil but also the type of oil fields from which it is extracted. We are not running out of oil, but we are running out of cheap, easy-to find oil. Earlier, we had access to large fields with high-quality oil, which were relatively new, since the largest ones had been discovered before 1970. Today, many of these fields are aging. In other words, they are approaching or have passed production maximum. Because of geological conditions, oil production becomes increasingly expensive after half of a field's reserves are extracted. Thus, new fields must be found to meet increasing demand or new technology must be put in place to extract more oil. However, these technologies are expensive, and the new fields being discovered are smaller than those discovered many years ago

Security of supply

Peak oil is not a future catastrophic event, as in when oil will hit $200 a barrel or more. Peak oil is now. Peak oil discussion often overlooks the fact that increased oil prices make increased oil investment and thus enhanced oil recovery possible. Worldwide, the average recovery rate from oil fields is 35 percent, yet in some places on the Norwegian shelf, it's between 50-67 percent, one of the highest in the world. For every one percent we manage to increase the global recovery rate, we delay peak oil by six years

IEA has time and time again pointed to the need for more investment in oil in order to avert a supply crunch. However, there are nations, most notably Russia and several OPEC countries, that have incentives to maintain high oil prices so as to finance their state budgets. In other words, the oil prices hikes we see are a question of strong demand from developing countries, but that has just as much to do with a lack of investment, creating a tight market for oil.

Security of supply is a major problem for the future political situation. Countries are committed domestically but also internationally, such as those of the European Union, to withstand a short stop in supplies. The crisis of the 1970s showed with all clarity how much power resource rich countries may have over resource-poor nations.

The increase in prices we witnessed between 2006 and 2008, which culminated with an oil price of $147 a barrel, has been a contributing factor to putting oil dependence on the agenda. Nearly 80 percent of the expected increase in production of both oil and gas is expected to come from national companies, primarily from the Middle East.

The oil price increase alone during the 2005-2008 price hike meant that the United States had to transfer $100 billion extra to the Middle East. That is more than half of the first stimulus package put in place in 2008 to put the U.S. economy back on its feet.

That is money the United States has an interest in keeping within its borders, especially considering its economy and the fact that the Middle East regimes aren't the most stable. The same goes for the European Union, which has a strong interest in minimizing energy supplies from Russia. Since Russia has repeatedly shown its willingness to use energy supplies as a political weapon, Korea, a resource poor country, has the same issues and needs to adopt policies that make it less dependent on foreign countries' energy supply.

Special role of China

The developing world is moving into an industrialization phase of ever-increasing GDP, and with this comes a higher need for commodities, especially energy. Dependent on how you measure this, China entered this phase ten years ago and has seen its GDP double four times faster than the United Kingdom saw during its industrialization phase. In this decade, India will follow. These developments will create an insatiable need for commodities of all kinds, fueling frustration and possibly contributing to riots and revolutions like those witnessed in the Middle East or fueling military conflict and a less secure world.

China has become the world's biggest emitter of carbon dioxide, which is a serious problem if we are to curb greenhouse gases. Indeed, as more companies outsource productions to low-wage countries, we see a decline in carbon dioxide intensity in the production sector in various Western countries, yet a strong increase in output, primarily in China. Since China's carbon dioxide emissions per $1,000 GDP created are roughly double the average of OECD nations, the world's total output from production is increasing. Scandinavian countries like Denmark and Norway are looking to employ measures to decrease emissions by as much as 30 percent, but in the great scheme of thing it means nothing. China's monthly carbon dioxide emission increases roughly equal those of Norway for a whole year.

China alone uses more coal than the United States, Europe and Japan combined, so even though it has the world's third biggest coal reserves, it will suffer from coal depletion in the future. With 16 of the 20 most polluted cities in the world located in China, with acid rain in 50 percent of the cities and 17 percent of rivers not meeting the lowest standards for irrigation, health problems related to air pollution are on the rise. China is aware of her problems. It will suffocate in pollution, and economic growth will decline.

But all it not lost. Chinese demand for oil has been elevating world prices. As oil prices go up, so does the market for renewable energy. China has now passed the United States in government spending on clean technology research and development. The Chinese green powerhouse has meant a rapid fall in solar cell prices, and China has heavily invested in wind and other renewable energies; countries like Korea and India have joined in. Prices of renewable energy are falling rapidly, so even though in many respects China in particular seems to be the problem, it is where we can increasingly look for solutions as well.

Oil as dominant energy

Sheikh Zaki Yamani was right when three decades ago he said, "The Oil Age will end long before the world runs out of oil." It will end when renewable alternatives fall to a level where oil cannot compete. And that time is approaching fast. Nonetheless, oil will be with us for a long time, particularly in the transport sector, because the demand for energy for cars will grow some 3 percent a year in non-OECD countries. Already in 2009, the Chinese car market overtook the U.S. in the number of vehicle sales. Today transport accounts for 20 percent of the world's energy consumption and 15 percent of carbon dioxide emissions, a figure expected to increase to 60 percent by 2030 in the "business as usual" scenario. However, the reduction potential when using renewable energy is 31 percent, and unlike many other areas, we can save money in the long run by investing in an efficient fleet of vehicles and infrastructure.

As renewable energy enters the market and replaces oil, either in the form of electricity created by renewable sources or nuclear power, or in the form of biofuels, oil prices will fall and a new price equilibrium will appear. Cars will still be on the road 20 years from now consuming oil, but they will use only a fraction of what cars do today. This will mark the end of an era for oil as the dominant source of energy and a new era where green alternatives will thrive.

Taking advantage of urbanization

Martin Kruse

Urbanization is inevitable as society develops and seeks better living environment as has been the case in the Gangnam district in Seoul. But research has proven that such development does not have to be detrimental to human life. *Yonhap*

Urbanization in the modern sense characterizes the shift that happens when a society moves from being agrarian to becoming industrial and knowledge-based. This trend reached a historic milestone in 2008, the first year in human history when more people lived in cities than in the countryside. This trend is also seen in developing countries. By 2025, more than half of the population in developing countries will live in cities. This is an increase of about 10 percent since 2007. By 2050, the trend will result in 70 percent of the world's population living in cities, an increase of 40.5 percent in 100 years, the greatest migration in world history.

In developed countries, the discussion of urbanization is in some an almost finished chapter, while in others it still plays an important role in relation to national politics and in particular how tax revenue is moved around, how the housing market develops, and how the growth of a knowledge society and experience economy will attract talent. Fewer children are born in European countries, more young people move to cities, and there is associated depopulation in large rural areas, strongly supported by a general tendency to settle where a critical mass is present. In other words, people move to where other innovative and creative people live, where job prospects in specialized industries are better, and where one can become a part of the innovative knowledge elite to take part in "experience consumption."

Urbanization in developing countries

If we look at developing countries, urbanization is basically an expression of people's desire to fill the basic need of employment. The city is a framework for the dream of a better future and functions as a magnet for rural population. According to the World Bank, China only had 69 cities in the 1940s. Today, the number is 670, 89 of which house a million or more people. By comparison, the United States has 37 cities of a million or more. In 1980, China's urban population was about 191 million people, in 2007, 594 million, and within 20 years the number of people moving to growing Chinese cities will surpass the entire population of the U.S. Such a migration implies major challenges for city planning, renovation and infrastructure.

In China, the urbanization process has caused other problems. Over 43 percent of rivers are affected by eutrophication, and approximately one in five cities doesn't meet China's urban air quality standards, which are lower than those recommended by the World Health Organization. Acid rain has been observed in over 50 percent of Chinese cities. For China, the environmental issues related to urbanization are becoming more important. China tries to limit internal strife in this situation and generally, so it is crucial that the growth of wealth continues unabated. The horror scenario would be one of widespread urban poverty destroying urban cohesion from within. In trying to accommodate the massive increase in urbanization, China may, like many other developing countries, learn from the mistakes made in the West.

Cities in the West have gone through different stages. In the industrialization phase, smog caused by large amounts of spent coal created air pollution. Later after coal burning was banned in cities, smog was caused again by vehicle emissions from internal combustion engines and industrial fumes.

Green urban transport

Today, while many Western countries fight air pollution, many initiatives are changing them. In Copenhagen, people now bathe in the midst of the city, something unthinkable just 15 years ago. For cities of the developing world, the hope is that hard learned experiences of the West will enable other nations to leapfrog the development stage and create new and green or smart cities. Cities can envision integrated intelligent systems utilizing low-carbon urban transport solutions, water/waste networks that function in a sustainable manner, and renewable energy sources as part of urban building design.

Considering future challenges in transportation and infrastructure and the great climate challenges that follow growing energy consumption, work is already being accomplished with extensive metro systems. To prevent urban sprawl, cities are extended upwards rather than outwards. This lesson comes not least from Atlanta in the U.S. This is a city 160 km wide, meaning that its inhabitants drive an average of 106 km every day to get to work and get around town. Traffic congestion is one of the major problems for cities today. According to the Official Journal of the European Union, annual congestion in urban areas costs the EU economy 1 percent of GDP. An effective transport system is crucial since transport systems all over the world are significantly under stress, no more so than in developing countries where we will continue to see a significant increase in the number of vehicles.

If congestion problems aren't slowed, a dramatic increase in CO_2 emissions will occur. In response, a number of national strategies have been developed to expand public transport and reduce citizens' dependence on private motoring. By and large, these strategies have met with only limited success, partly because privately owned vehicles provide much greater flexibility and privacy than public transport. What is needed is even better public transport and greener car transport.

More than 20 years ago, an idea known as the RUF system was put forth in Denmark. The idea was based on combining cars and trains. The concept involves motorists leaving their homes as normal, but when they reach the motorway they link up with other cars on a monorail.

The benefits of this approach are that it reduces air resistance, increases safety, and cuts fuel consumption. However, the RUF concept never really stood a chance due to high infrastructure costs. Nevertheless, the idea behind the RUF may well come to life in new smart cities of the future.

More technology

More and more car models today feature sensors that "read" the car's immediate surroundings and warn passengers of impending danger; these sensors may soon be able to take control and steer the vehicle.

Initially, this technology was created to make cars safer; however, the next step is to introduce even more intelligent systems, utilizing GPS, short-distance 24 GHz radar and automatic communication between vehicles and traffic control systems so that a car can "drive itself."

This form of transport for the future may well lead to a wide range of vehicles in which the driver can sit and work, eat breakfast and do pretty much anything apart from actually driving. This would create a much more effective transport system. What is more, this development would not be affected by whether the vehicles of the future operate on gas, electricity, hydrogen or biomass, or whether an advanced, petrol-powered internal combustion engine powers them. The infrastructure will not present any obstacles, a significant advantage.

Green urban buildings

In OECD countries, buildings account for approximately 40 percent of energy consumption. The problem with the building sector is a slow renewal rate. The buildings' mass renewal rate is only one percent per year, meaning that half of all buildings in the world today will still be around in the year 2050. For the OECD, the number is closer to 2/3. Consequently the biggest potential for CO_2 reduction in OECD countries is through retrofitting and renovating the building mass.

By 2050, energy consumption in households will have increased 67 percent. According to IEA baseline scenarios, however, the reduction potential is 83%. This would require a meager five percent growth from 2007 to 2050: a great challenge, but not an impossible one.

The good news is that many of the necessary measures actually would save us money in the long run. A Danish Building Evaluation Centre study on international building projects showed that over a 20-year lifetime, the extra cost of constructing a sustainable building is paid back 10-20 times through savings in energy, operation and health. Generally, up-front building expenditures account for only 15 percent of a building's life cycle expenditures, while operations account for 85 percent. Heating, water and electricity appliances alone account for some 60 percent.

Better utilization of insulation, ventilation, lighting and energy efficient appliances, coupled with an intelligent energy infrastructure, are some ways to bring down CO_2 and at the same time create a healthier environment. The smart green city of the future will utilize roof gardens to reduce heating and energy consumption as well as cooling needs. Green buildings collect and reuse rainwater, and biological waste is used for biofuel. Buildings are becoming sustainable, as cement made from magnesium silicate demands less heating and absorbs 100 kg of CO_2 during curing. The possibilities that new green cities give us are almost endless, and if we are to accommodate the many hundreds of millions of people moving to the cities, greening them is the only way to go.

Chapter 4

Government
(Executive and Legislature)

Green growth is a revolutionary paradigm shift

A new way to meet the environment

People, nature converge at 4 major rivers

Why I work in shorts and sandals

Are environmental conflicts all bad?

In pursuit of low-carbon growth

Achieving shared growth through green ODA

Environmental governance in NE Asia

Geopolitics of energy and Korea's choice

Can policies prevent environmental accidents?

Yeosu Declaration to bring life to ocean

Green growth is a revolutionary paradigm shift

Seung-soo Han

This is an experimental hybrid wind-solar power facility which can run 24 hours a day. It is operated by Sahwa Energy Control as part of the Korean government's initiative to promote green growth. *Korea Times file*

What follows is the full text of an interview with former Prime Minister Seung-soo Han. - ED.

The Korea Times : What in your perception is green growth?

Seung-soo Han : Green growth is a new growth paradigm different from traditional quantity-oriented fossil fuel-dependent growth. So it has to be initiated directly by the government. For this growth paradigm shift, the government has to lead, while the private sector is a follower. Once the government sets the strategy in motion, then there will be incentives for the private sector to join in.

Green growth is a revolutionary paradigm shift, but a revolution of this kind does not take place in the market. The government needs to take the initiative to lead the green revolution. Green growth cannot be achieved if the national and global economy is left to the free market. So the government needs to play a role in providing economic incentives and disincentives, subsidies, regulations and other macroeconomic planning tools, especially in developing countries.

KT : What, in your opinion, is Korea's position on the global stage in terms of green growth?

Han : Korea is the first country to implement a green growth strategy. Green growth is Korea's response to the challenge of climate change. Most countries are trying to respond to climate change, but unless you change the system, you will not be able to solve the fundamental problems. Climate change is one of the best examples of externality on a global scale. What we are trying to do in Korea is to internalize it by endorsing climate change as a domestic variable in the policy planning equation.

Korea is the first country to implement green growth policies since January 2009. We have initiated several institutional frameworks. The Presidential Committee on Green Growth was established and the National Assembly has passed a Framework Act on Low Carbon Green Growth, the first of its kind in the world. We are in the third year of the First Five-Year Green Growth Plan (2009-13). There is no other country pursuing this kind of system change at this moment.

Three years ago when I was the prime minister and served as chairman of the 2009 OECD Ministerial Council Meeting, I was able to garner unanimous support of the participating ministers to adopt the Declaration on Green Growth. Based on that resolution, the OECD Secretariat began to study green growth, producing this year a very important document entitled "Towards Green Growth."

KT : It is commonly said that green technology is a luxury of the rich. It is the luxury of countries that have already achieved everything and now can care about such things as the environment. What is your response to such an idea?

Han : That is exactly the problem facing us when we want to emphasize the need for a growth paradigm shift. I think the paradigm shift is facilitated because of the rapid advancement of information and communications technology. Many developing countries are beginning to benefit from development in this way. Green growth is not a luxury that can only be afforded in developed countries but a necessity for any country that wants to grow and at the same time enhance environmental sustainability.

KT : What are your worries about the future of the world and your hopes, as far as green issues are concerned?

Han : I believe that mitigation alone will not solve the problem of climate change and that in order to change the system, the new paradigm of growth, i.e. green growth, must be adopted globally. That's why Korea's green growth strategy is timely and why this new paradigm will be able to fundamentally solve the problem. The Global Green Growth Institute (GGGI) was created to share Korea's knowledge and experience on green growth with developing countries.

KT : What is the role of the government in promoting green growth?

Han : Green growth cannot be achieved if the national and global economy is left to the free market. The government needs to provide economic incentives and disincentives, subsidies, regulations and other macroeconomic planning tools, especially in a developing economy.

Traditional, quantity-oriented growth models cannot solve the problem of climate change. Since the First Industrial Revolution, the world has grown by means of electricity, steam and mass production - physical power.

This will change. From now on, mental capacity will be the driving force of a Third Industrial Revolution. Climate change is a slow phenomenon. As people do not feel an urgent need for change, they tend to maintain the status quo.

KT : Can you talk about the journey for you and major achievements of the Institute?

Han : Although GGGI is headquartered in Seoul, it is an international institute. We also have offices in Copenhagen, Abu Dhabi and London. President Myung-bak Lee also went to Denmark and concluded an agreement with Prime Minister Rasmussen to form a green growth alliance, the first of its kind in the world.

We hope to expand this alliance to include other countries interested in observing as well as promoting green growth within and outside their boundaries. The GGGI is still very young.

I think there is a great demand for knowledge about green growth all over the world, and we will continue to promote this new model of economic growth and development through cooperation with partner countries and partner institutions.

KT : How is it financed? To what extend is GGGI connected with the government?

Han : GGGI has received financial support and encouragement from Australia, Denmark, Germany, Japan, Korea, the UAE and the U.K. It is partnering with Brazil, Ethiopia, Indonesia, Cambodia, Kazakhstan and the UAE in the development of green growth economic development plans.

KT : Are you looking to convert it into an international organization?

Han : The adoption of the Establishment Agreement was held at the Global Green Growth Summit on May 10, 2012. GGGI is expected to hold the IO Conversion Signing Ceremony on the occasion of the Rio+20 conference in Rio de Janeiro, Brazil in June. Also in late October, GGGI will be converted into an international organization on the occasion of the pre-COP Ministerial Meeting.

KT : On which criteria does GGGI select countries for cooperation?

Han : GGGI provides analytical and institutional support to developing countries that wish to develop green growth strategies aligned with other national economic goals.

A typical GGGI country program consists of green growth plan (GGP) analysis and design, domestic capacity building, and public-private partnerships to support GGP implementation.

The institute provides support for the development of GGPs when it receives a high-level request from a developing or emerging market government. The precise scope of work in each country depends on the starting conditions and specific challenges.

KT : Why was the institute founded?

Han : I think that unless we change the past paradigm of the earth, we won't be able to solve the problem of climate change, which is what the future of humanity basically depends on. Until now, the growth paradigm of the world for economic progress has used labor and capital as its main factors of production and highly depends on fossil fuels for energy, emitting immense amounts of carbon into the atmosphere. Because of these carbon emissions, the average temperature of the earth over the past 10,000 years has increased by 1 degree centigrade.

What we are trying to do is change the so-called growth paradigm of the past century from high-carbon to low-carbon. GGGI was created only a year ago but has been affecting many countries already. We hope to continue sharing the experience and knowledge of green growth with developing countries where domestic capacity is lacking.

KT : What are the goals of GGGI?

Han : GGGI focuses on three primary areas: green growth planning, research, and public-private cooperation. To date, our most developed platform is green growth planning. This involves partnering with developing countries jointly to arrive at local, environmentally sustainable methods of economic development.

Currently, GGGI is active in Ethiopia, Indonesia, Kazakhstan, the United Arab Emirates, and Cambodia, with plans to expand to a number of other countries. Together with other partner countries, we are assisting these nations on specific green growth projects ranging from household irrigation to deforestation.

As of now, a large portion of GGGI's operating budget is dedicated to these kinds of projects. The remainder funds research and public-private cooperation. These ratios will change as we evolve and grow as an organization.

KT : What are your future plans? What is your vision? How can Korea and your institute play a leading role in the adoption of green growth technology?

Han : Our ultimate vision is for the world to emulate what Korea is trying to do in tackling the fundamental problem of climate change. GGGI was created only a year ago but has had an impact on many countries already. We want to continue sharing our experience and knowledge on green growth with developing countries where domestic capacity is lacking. Developed countries will not have any problem emulating what we have been doing.

As the main factor of production in green growth is new ideas, transformational innovations and state of the art technology, GGGI has to do its best in promoting green technology.

KT : What is your role as Chairman of the Board of Directors of GGGI?

Han : My role is to make strategic decisions in encouraging governments, private institutions and academics of the world to move toward economic and industrial policies that decrease emissions of greenhouse gases.

Countries with advanced economies can easily emulate others' green-growth policies because they have the capacity. Therefore, the main role of GGGI is to share ideas for green growth with developing economies.

A new way to meet the environment

Young-sook Yoo

Seagulls make another return to Upo Wetland

Every winter, Upo Wetland of Changnyeong County, located in the southeastern part of the Republic of Korea, is crowded with special guests. They are no other than the migratory birds that have escaped the harsh cold weather of Siberia. Some of the migratory birds wintering in Upo Wetland are worldwide-endangered species such as the Eurasian Spoonbill and Whooper Swan. A spectacular view of thousands of migratory birds nesting there is more than enough to attract numerous tourists every year.

Upo Wetland, also known as "a paradise of migratory birds," is the largest undisturbed wetlands in the country. Not only migratory birds but also many kinds of plants, trees, insects, fish and humans inhabit this benevolent land and enjoy the gift from nature. Also called "a museum of ecosystem," Upo Wetland was designated as a wetland with international importance in 1998 by the Ramsar Convention, an international treaty for the conservation of wetlands. Millions of people at home and abroad are attracted by the seasonal changes and visit Upo Wetland annually. The accumulated economic value is said to reach tens of billions of won. Thanks to the endeavors of the municipal government and the local people who chose to coexist with nature over development, nature is conserved.

Ecotourism attraction

This is not a story confined to Upo Wetland. Suncheon Bay, the widest reed bed in Korea and one of the world's top-five coastal wetlands, has long been in the limelight as a most successful ecotourism attraction. About two million tourists visit Suncheon Bay annually and significantly contribute to the local economy. Such a success story was made possible due to continuous endeavors by the local people, who made a radical decision to remove 300 telephone poles around Suncheon Bay, as well as by the local farmers who gave up farming in winter. In fact, during winter, they fill up the rice paddies with water for migratory birds to bathe in.

These success stories tell us that we can achieve both environmental conservation and economic development by invigorating ecotourism. Ecological travel can create a virtuous circle of environmental conservation and economic development, and it can serve as a model for low-carbon green growth. The current generation is amplifying rather than reducing the outstanding ecological and cultural value of ecotourism, so that the next generation also can enjoy what we have now. Such considerate actions make the future very hopeful.

Sustainable development

In the 21st century, where climate change and environmental crises are threatening our existence and where each one of us struggles to find a way to coexist with nature, sustainable development is an issue of keen interest. To this end, many countries across the world are opting out of conventional expansionist-centered development and are eagerly searching for ways to harmoniously live with nature and achieve sustainable development.

Tourism is no exception. The beautiful nature of Southeast Asia is famous for tourism. Nevertheless, natural disasters like tsunamis caused by climate change, coastal erosion and reckless development have destroyed many invaluable assets of the region and even have damaged the habitat of indigenous people whose livelihood is heavily dependent on natural resources and tourism. The substantial threat of climate change to humans has never been greater. We even hear of gloomy forecasts that the Maldives, an island nation in the Indian Sea, might be inundated completely if the sea level keeps rising at the current speed. It is no wonder that people have started to realize the ultimate way to continue the tourism industry is by conserving nature. Recently, ecotourism has gained popularity in the sense that it can be an option for sustainable tourism.

New experience

Ecotourism enables travelers to experience nature and interact with it. Ecological tourism has humanistic and philosophical aspects as well, since it affords visitors the chance to reflect while marveling at the breath-taking scenery nature provides. In 1990, the International Ecotourism Society (TIES) defined ecotourism as "responsible travel to natural areas that conserves the environment and improves the well-being of local people." As such, ecotourism is a win-win journey to take for both the environment and the economy.

Ecotourism has characteristics that distinguish it from conventional tourism. First of all, it holds plenty of stories on indigenous forests, mud flats, plants and animals. It gives great meaning to know the original stories and true nature of the area. As tourists grasp the name of various plants and flowers along the paths, their minds are enriched with stories of nature.

Another distinctive aspect of ecotourism is a limit on the number of tourists. The environment is easily damaged and disrupted with concentrated numbers of tourists in one place. Ecotourism regulates the number of people who travel to a site that protects the natural resources. This ultimately allows a small group of tourists to enjoy quality time with a more pleasant and meaningful visit.

Ecotourism does not stop at amplifying the value of natural resources; it can even change the paradigm of local economic cycles. Conventional tourism too often is driven by conglomerates that construct hotels and other infrastructure, and only the investors with money benefit from the development. On the other hand, ecotourism encourages indigenous people to participate in programs and share the benefits with local communities. The Ministry of Environment is taking the lead, and all governmental organizations have made efforts to vitalize ecotourism.

Moreover, it can be said that ecotourism has significantly changed the public perspective on protecting nature. The Korea National Park Service surveyed ecological tour participants in 2010. According to the survey, 98 percent of the respondents said they were satisfied with the ecological tour they participated in, and 97 percent responded that they grew more interested in the protection of nature after the tour. World Research also conducted a survey of the general public in Korea with a similar theme. Approximately 67 percent of the respondents said they believed ecotourism could develop local communities and boost the economic value of natural resources.

Local community

It is remarkable that more local communities demand to be designated as an environmental conservation area. The Ministry of Environment has designated six spots as environmental conservation areas since 2010, and all six of the local communities voluntarily requested this status. For instance, the owner and local residents of wetlands in Gonggeumji, Sangju, eagerly wanted their wetlands to be designated as an environmental conservation area in order to draw more eco-tourists to their community. This clearly shows that the public now has a different perspective toward the designation of environmental conservation areas. The public used to think that the designation of environmental conservation areas would affect the community negatively, but now an increasing number of people believe that a well-protected ecosystem can contribute to the local economy. It is no exaggeration to say that ecotourism is a frontrunner of sustainable development.

Partnership symposium

This year, the Ministry of Environment and the United Nations Environmental Program (UNEP) co-host the "UNEP Global Partnership for Sustainable Tourism Symposium and the Second Annual Conference" in Seoul. It is a remarkable event where one can observe global trends and learn about other countries' experiences in sustainable tourism, which conserves the environment and revitalizes local economies by creating green jobs.

One aspect of the "UNEP Global Partnership for Sustainable Tourism Symposium and the Second Annual Conference" worth noting is that the attendees will take an ecology field trip to the Demilitarized Zone (DMZ). The DMZ is a strip of land running across the Korean Peninsula. It has served as a buffer zone between South and North Korea ever since the ceasefire agreement for the Korean War. The DMZ has not been developed because of the landmines in the area. Recognizing the ecological value of the DMZ, the United Nations Educational, Scientific and Cultural Organization (UNESCO) decided to designate it as a UNESCO Biosphere Reserve in July this year. The designation of a UNESCO Biosphere Reserve will turn the tragic history of the DMZ into something meaningful.

Visiting the DMZ will be a rare chance to gain a glimpse of sustainable ecotourism in Korea in the future. It is hoped that the DMZ will turn into a tourist hotspot symbolizing peace and ecology, and become even more popular than Upo Wetland and Suncheon Bay when the UNESCO Biosphere Reserve designation is completed in July. Hosting the "UNEP Global Partnership for Sustainable Tourism Symposium and the Second Annual Conference" will bring Korea one step closer to realizing sustainable ecotourism, which is comprised of an ideal triangle: environmental conservation, efficient utilization of nature and economic value generation. It is hoped that this event will serve as a stepping-stone for Korea to be a powerful driving force of green growth.

People, nature converge at 4 major rivers

Do-youp Kwon

This is a photo of the Ipo Bridge in Yeoju, Gyeonggi Province which has been transformed into an avenue for cyclists as part of the restoration of the nation's four major rivers. The bridge is located in the southern segment of the Han River. *Korea Times file*

The number of people visiting areas around the country's four major rivers up to early July crossed the 7 million mark, less than eight months after restoration of them was completed last October.

This figure compares with the 7.78 million people who saw Transformers 3, the biggest hit in the movie industry last year and more than the 6.81 million fans who headed to baseball parks to watch professional games.

It is also more than double the 3.03 million people who flocked to professional soccer matches and more than the 6.57 million who visited the Everland amusement park in Yongin, Gyeonggi Provine, and the 5.78 million crowding Lotte World in southern Seoul last year.

In the case of the four major rivers, namely the Han, Naktong, Kum and Yongsan, the number of visitors is expected to increase dramatically as the country heads into the summer vacation season. The popularity of facilities in and around them has been unexpectedly high only eight months after their "reopening."

Nature and livelihood

What drives the popularity of the four major rivers? The main reason is the combination of nature and people's livelihoods and how these fit comfortably with the changes and flow of the times.

This becomes more evident when you use search websites like Naver and Daum which immediately introduce facilities located around the four major rivers.

Among them are camping sites, cycling paths, fitness facilities and the availability of water sports which are most popular with visitors and sports enthusiasts.

You can jog along while enjoying the view of the blue waters of the rivers; dine while watching the sunset and wake up to the lovely mists of the early morning.

There are ecological parks that stretch over a total area of 130 square kilometers and 18 large-scale camping sites, helping to fill some of the shortages of cultural and recreational space. In fact, many will agree that these facilities help to improve the quality of life to a considerable extent.

There are cycling paths that extend over a total course of 1,757 kilometers along the four major rivers which is a symbolic and cultural part of what has been called the "Four Major Rivers Restoration Project."

And while people indulge in nature, there are also important considerations about the environment. They are often sensitive to environmental values and are willing to participate in preserving the ecology.

Environmental implications

In many ways, visits to the four major rivers encourage people to share their personal experiences, particularly from the environmental perspective.

In the early stages of the restoration project, there were concerns about environmental implications but there is ample evidence that it has in fact played a vital role in Korea's efforts toward green growth.

As part of the project, 33,313 greenhouse plots over a space of 6,791 hectares, which had been regarded as major sources of water pollution, were completely refurbished.

More than 3.9 trillion won was invested in water quality improvement projects, including the construction of wastewater treatment facilities.

Among the highlights of the project is the installation of natural water paths - taking into consideration the distinctive characteristics of each area - which has been key to preserving eight varieties of fish in danger of becoming extinct.

The environmental value of the four major rivers restoration does not stop at merely restoring the ecology of the areas surrounding them.

Small-scale hydropower facilities were constructed to generate 270 million kilowatt electricity every year, sufficient to satisfy the needs of a city of 250,000 residents.

This environmentally-friendly generation of electricity substitutes for the import of 450,000 barrels of crude oil worth 60 billion won.

It also equates to a reduction of 180,000 tons of carbon dioxide, thus contributing, at least in a small way, to the prevention of global warming.

Minimizing flood damage

Moreover, the restoration of the rivers has proven to have played an important role in minimizing flood damage last summer when there were unprecedented amounts of rainfall.

Farmers active around the four major rivers, who constantly fall victim to flooding, saw their damage drop to just one tenth of what had previously been the annual average.

Even during this spring, when there was an unexpectedly serious drought, the water level at the rivers actually increased by 1.8 meters, making it possible to maintain a stable supply of water.

Prior to the restoration of the four major rivers, quality control had been primitive at best. Over the past 10 years (2001-2010), damage from floods totaled 1,482 billion won with rehabilitation costs hitting 2.4 trillion won.

In fact, rehabilitation costs far exceeded preventive investments, testifying to the reality that the management of rivers took a backseat in the overall land development.

Compared to the investment of 77.9 trillion won spent on road pavement and 36.4 trillion won for the construction of railways between 2001 and 2010, the comparable figure for river management remained at 8.8 trillion won.

Looking at it from this perspective, the restoration project has created a whole new paradigm in terms of river management

'New Green Deal'

The ambitious project has presented fundamental solutions to droughts and flooding while preserving the ecological environment and culture while helping to revive regional economies.

It is a Korean "Green New Deal" that has been an important part of keeping the country developing even as the global financial "crisis" continues.

Perhaps for this reason, there are numerous accolades for the achievements of the restoration project. It is deemed as a timely project, particularly in view of the climate change gripping the attention of the world.

Achim Steiner, secretary general of the United Nations Environment Programme (UNEP), has said the project was truly an example of green investment which secures a stable supply of water while battling climate change.

Julia Marton-Lefevre, secretary general of the International Union for Conservation of Nature and Natural Resources (IUCN), complemented the restoration effort as a rational one.

She observed that many rivers in Europe were too contaminated for fishing or swimming but respective governments introduced determined programs to revive them.

Also, Angel Gurria, secretary general of the Organization for Economic Cooperation and Development, emphasized the outstanding example that Korea has set in terms of resolving problems related to water.

During a visit to Korea in spring this year, Thai Prime Minister Yingluck Shinawatra visited some of the sites along the four major rivers and made emotional comments about the results of the restoration project.

Just some time ago, it was a source of envy to see people in the large cities of Europe swimming and fishing in rivers and to witness the dramatic changes that they have brought about.

But this is no longer the case. The tables have turned and Europeans are expressing their surprise at the accomplishments Korea has made in terms of reviving its rivers. There are ample reasons to take pride in the ecological evolution that has taken place right here at home.

Why I work in shorts and sandals

Won-soon Park

Establish and operate an 10 energy foundation

01 Make Seoul a city of sunlight where the entire city is a PV plant(320 MW)

Create citizen lifestyle with 09 energy-saving actions

02 Ensure energy self-sufficiency of core facilities by fuel cells(230MW)

Create 40,000 green 08 jobs in energy sector

「One Less Nuclear Power Plant」
10 Key Action Plans

03 Improve energy efficiency of buildings (houses, commercial buildings, schools, etc.)

Secure 150,000 memberships 07 for car-sharing scheme

04 Realize a city of smart lights by LED(dissemination of 8 million LED units)

Reinforce design standards for 06 new buildings by introducing energy cap and other measures

05 Launch '2030 City Master Plan' with a view to energy-efficient urban structure

The "One Less Nuclear Power Plant" is a large–scale initiative with the total budget amounting to 3.24 trillion won. This campaign will bring a groundbreaking change to Seoul's energy consumption paradigm. The campaign will take a multi–faceted approach, consisting of 78 specific projects in 6 policy categories, which can be re–categorized in 10 key action plans.

"It would be okay to wear blue jeans in the office if they were neat. / It would be cool if we wore shorts as school uniforms in summer. / Please don't worry about the other people around you." Do you remember these lyrics? They are from the song "Dance with DJ DOC" by popular group DJ DOC. Just like in the song, I am wearing shorts to the office this summer.

I heard my initiative on wearing shorts to the office had become a controversial issue among the civil servants. In fact, I felt a bit shy about wearing shorts and hesitated several times.

Truth be told, my "bold" fashion statement was an effort to save energy. People can untie their neckties and wear sandals and shorts to feel less hot in summer, which helps save energy on air conditioning.

I know I am hopeless when it comes to fashion but I bravely decided to wear shorts because one of my goals as Seoul Mayor is to try to facilitate "One Less Nuclear Power Plant" during my service.

It is widely known that greenhouse gases are mainly responsible for global warming. About 90 percent of greenhouse gas emission is attributable to energy consumption.

With the demand for energy always growing, the amount of greenhouse gases emitted is also ever increasing. As a result, a variety of unusual weather conditions have been observed around the world, including floods, droughts and heavy snow, which result in enormous human and property damage.

In the wake of the tragic accident at the Fukushima Nuclear Power Plant in Japan in March 2011, and the large scale blackout in Seoul last September, a social consensus has been formed on the necessity for a reduction in energy consumption and the importance of the production of sustainable, environment friendly sources of natural energy.

Renewable energy

Seoul City took a set of initiatives in April of this year to pool the wisdom of citizens in saving an amount of energy equivalent to the power generated by one nuclear power plant and expanding the production of new renewable energy.

These initiatives are aimed at making Seoul a global climate and environment capital by raising its electricity self-sufficiency rate to 8 percent by 2014 and 20 percent by 2020.

More specifically, the city plans to save 2 million TOE (tons of oil equivalent) of energy by 2014, which is equivalent to the power generated by one nuclear power plant.

To realize this goal, 10 major projects were chosen in six fields, including the expansion of new renewable energy production, the improvement of energy efficiency in buildings, the construction of an eco-friendly transportation system with higher energy efficiency, the creation of more jobs in the energy industry, the establishment of a low-energy compact city structure, and the promotion of an everyday energy-saving lifestyle for citizens.

The city government is concentrating its resources on these projects, through which the city's energy consumption paradigm is expected to undergo a drastic change.

By 2014, Seoul will have transformed into a "city of sunlight." Solar power generators with 290MW electricity generation capacity will be built on the rooftops of about 10,000 public buildings, schools, houses and office towers.

Energy self-sufficiency

At major city facilities such as subways, hospitals and water supply and sewage systems, hydrogen fuel cell power plants and hydro power plants will be built for their energy self-sufficiency, which will allow the smooth operation of basic city facilities during power failures.

The city will also drastically improve the energy efficiency of buildings, which account for 58 percent of the total energy consumption. Newly-constructed buildings will be subject to strict energy consumption regulations. They will also be subject to stringent energy-saving standards from the design stage.

The city will replace indoor light bulbs at such public facilities as public office buildings, roads, subways, underground shopping centers, large-scale business buildings and department stores with LED (light-emitting diode) lights with higher energy efficiency by 2014 to make Seoul a "City of Smart Lights." What is most important for the success of the "One Less Nuclear Power Plant" campaign, however, is the participation of citizens.

In Dongjak-gu, a southwestern district of the city, you will find the Seongdaegol Children's Library.

The library was built and is operated by villagers. These villagers have developed a community around the library.

The nuclear disaster in Fukushima, Japan, last year, left the villagers in agony.

They inquired of several NGOs (nongovernmental organizations) to find out what they could do to avoid such a disaster.

They also asked these organizations to provide lectures for them at their library. After repeated requests over about a month and a half, Green Korea United finally responded. Officials began offering lectures for children and their parents at the Seongdaegol library.

The lectures bore fruit in their new practices

The villagers decided to hold a campaign with the goal of promoting "One Less Nuclear Power Plant." They chose 10 "good energy custodians" to visit the members of the library, hold discussions, explain the dangers of nuclear power plants and teach them what to do to realize "One Less Nuclear Power Plant." Thirty-four families out of the 200 members of the library participated in the campaign. They turned off television sets and wore more underwear in winter.

Some families even flushed toilets after several uses to save water. They saved 140KW of electricity in this way, which amounts to the total electricity consumed by 18 people for a month. Pretty cool, right?

Switching off TV

In addition to the reduction of electricity bills, which is helpful for the family economy, the campaign brought about many happy stories around the village.

Some say that their children read more books after turning off the TV.

Relations among family members have become more amicable since they slept holding each other in rooms with reduced heating. Some say that their children didn't catch cold after wearing underwear and staying in rooms with an optimal indoor temperature.

These stories spread by word of mouth and more families are joining the campaign to contribute to "One Less Nuclear Power Plant." Recently, the villagers went beyond the simple reduction of energy consumption and built a power plant of their own.

Since the nuclear explosion in Fukushima, Japan has become a scene of tragedy. Among Japan's intellectuals, a pessimistic view is prevailing that the country may never return to the peaceful state before the nuclear explosion.

Wouldn't it be most unfortunate if we, who live nearest the neighboring country of Japan, fail to learn a lesson from the nuclear explosion in Fukushima? "One Less Nuclear Power Plant" will be the best gift from our generation to future generations.

Are environmental conflicts all bad?

Kyoo-yong Lee

Major national projects like the development of Saemangeum in North Jeolla Province cause severe environmental conflicts among residents and interest parties but also provide related parties an opportunity to reach viable solutions. *Korea Times file*

Conflicts occur in every society. Some disagreements concerning environmental problems are coupled with development projects, stretching from which end of the water resources residents are in and involving numerous interested parties.

Conflicts happen all over the world, no matter what the size and depth of the problems are in terms of economic and media considerations. Owing to the fact that the adverse effects of environmental conflicts tend to be communicated to the public, there is a deep-rooted social stigma that conflicts must and should be prevented at any cost. But are conflicts really and only destructive in nature?

Traditionally, Korean people have lived in a culture that stresses the importance of harmonious coexistence, and this is well reflected in the education system. Accordingly, it is generally understood that environmental conflicts result in heavy economic and social costs as well as social disruptions. However, the reality is that there are both positive and negative functions of environmental conflict, just as with other forms of social confrontation.

The basic element of environmental conflicts is a function of maintaining the balance between development and preservation. While most environmental disagreements are causes of waste in budgetary and other expenses, they also tend to serve the purpose of preventing financial waste by helping to terminate or modify unnecessary development projects.

Unavoidable confrontations

Certainly, there are instances when these occurrences bring about confrontations and disputes among parties of interest, but the same can be said for the fact that they sometimes prevent further escalations in disagreements.

Such conflicts often provide the opportunity for the parties involved to coordinate their differences. There are naturally instances when they serve the opposite purpose. One thing for certain is that they put the spotlight on important issues for which discussion and debate are desperately needed.

Consequently, it would not be appropriate to attempt to avoid environmental conflicts simply because of their positive or negative implications. In a diverse and modern society, such conflicts are, in many ways, unavoidable. The point would be to sidestep the undesirable impact of such confrontations to allow rational functions to take their course.

In Korea, and in any developing country, environmental conflicts are bound to occur. The pace of development speeds up with economic prosperity, and the side effects of such major developments are to be expected, thus bringing about clashes in interests.

In many instances, political considerations and efficiency tend to override environmental and economic viabilities. More often than not, the interests of residents and civic organizations are not well reflected in pursuing major development projects.

The problems are further aggravated by the absence of objective measurements on the economic benefits and the practicality of such development projects and the environmental impact they could have on future generations.

For instance, differences can be resolved if there is a way of putting accurate financial value on, say, the quality of air that current and future generations of people enjoy.

In other cases, conflicts arising from contrasting interests and understandings are relatively easy to address.

Contrasting interests

Take the case of Paldang Lake, which provides water to more than 25 million people living in and around the capital district and the related need to preserve the quality of water on the Nakdong River.

By introducing different pollution quotas and water charges depending on the locality, that is the upper or lower reaches of the water resources, residents can be persuaded to accept the rationale of regulations and impositions in a spirit of coexistence.

On the other hand, when conflicts in understanding collide with financial considerations, disputes become more difficult to resolve. Major cases in point are the construction of the Tonggang Dam and the development of the Saemangeum region that have long been enveloped in confrontations.

In the case of the Tonggang Dam, considerations include the economic benefits of its construction and safety in addition to the ecological and cultural damage. Also posing as a serious problem is the breakup of the residential community. These combine to create a situation of severe conflict in terms of both the respective interests and the economic implications.

Owing to the complexity of the elements involved, it is difficult to form a platform for seeking a solution through dialogue, and political decisions are needed to either terminate or push ahead with the project.

Difficult challenges

While the details of cases tend to differ in terms of their fundamental characteristics, conflicts surrounding environmental considerations exist in every country, and they certainly pose difficult challenges.

However, as a person who has spent most of his career in government dealing with environmental policies, this writer would like to stress that while challenging, there are viable ways to activate elementary functional methods of minimizing conflicts.

Simply put, it is vital that strong public consensus be realized through ensuring the rationality of projects and policies in question and by always observing proper procedures.

Detailed economic feasibility work will have to be undertaken and all environmental aspects, including environmental impact assessments, should be comprehensively initiated.

Such efforts are particularly important in pursuing major development projects such as the installation of a circular road around Mt. Sapae and the Seoul-Busan bullet railway network through the Mt. Cheonseong Tunnel.

For government officials involved in such projects, it is vital they equip themselves with viable alternatives and act with sincerity in seeking cooperation among the parties involved.

In showing commitment and conviction and by engaging in dialogue, this writer has experienced that there is always a workable solution within reach.

Confrontations resulting from differences in the views of residents in the upper and lower reaches of rivers have arisen concerning the implementation of a special law for the refurbishment of the nation's four major rivers. Others have occurred concerning the construction of a landfill in the capital area.

There was also a major dispute among lawmakers, the media and protesting parties that required open and public debates surrounding the selection of one of 12 options for the route of the circular road around Mt. Sapae.

At the same time, there is a need to provide proper compensation for residents who must make sacrifices in terms of environmental damage and emotional and psychological suffering.

In the case of the special law for the refurbishment of the four major rivers, tough regulations were imposed for the upper reaches of the tributaries, while an additional water charge was introduced for the lower reaches.

As for the construction of the landfill in the capital area, ten percent of the revenue from its operations was provided to residents living in the surrounding area.

Role of expert groups

On the other hand, the importance of the role of the media, expert groups and opinion leaders cannot be overemphasized for ensuring objectivity and neutrality.

More often than not, there are instances when conflicts are aggravated or ignored with the involved parties choosing an easy way out. It is during such cases that rational decisions are sought and sincere opinions are needed the most.

In the middle of the 1990s, there was a severe conflict over water sources between Yeongwol and Jaecheon. In this circumstance, undisputable reports of shortages from related experts were crucial in resolving the differences.

Environmental conflicts have a tendency to leave deep scars when not properly addressed and resolved, but they also provide opportunities for settling differences.

Consequently, rather than avoid environmental conflicts from the simple perspective of their being positive or negative, it is critical that the fact they are unavoidable be accepted and that wisdom is exercised to realize rational solutions.

In pursuit of low-carbon growth

Soo-gil Young

Shown are symbols of new energy sources as presented by Hyundai Engineering and Construction at its headquarters in Seoul to highlight the potentials of new energy. *Korea Times file*

The following is a presentation made during the Global Green Growth Summit held in Seoul May 10-11, 2012.

My father was a lawyer, so I did not learn much about green growth from him. But I have been learning a lot since President Myung-bak Lee declared low-carbon growth as Korea's vision for development for the next 60 years.

    Environmental consciousness found its way into Korean policies in the early 1990s. But we have also been pursuing policies under basic energy planning along the lines of low-carbon strategy since about four years ago.

That was the beginning of Korea's "green growth" big bang. And this vision is a long-term one. It represents a complete economic approach to the concept of green growth. The core components are environmental protection, energy efficiency and the introduction of renewable energy sources.

Every economic activity is based on some kind of energy, ranging from agriculture to forestry, fisheries, manufacturing and services. Our aim is to change the entire base of the energy economy in activities. This in essence is a new paradigm for economic development.

The first thing we did was to create a presidential commission on green growth that involves 14 ministries. That number of ministries represents the scope of Korea's green growth policies. The 14 organizations include the Prime Minister's Office. The green growth committee consists of 13 ministers and the Prime Minister, plus high-level participation from the private sector.

Role of private sector

Why do we include the private sector? Because pursuing policies effectively requires public-private sector consultation. We created a pan-national coordinating body, and we have been meeting once every two months in the presence of President Myung-bak Lee.

Whatever has been agreed to is given to ministries for implementation. The proposals are brought back to Cabinet-level meetings where they become formal policies.

In order to guide the deliberations, we discuss and pursue policies arising from the national green growth strategy that provides ten policy directions for the development of individual policies. Below the directions, we have 50 specific policy tasks, and it is the implementation of these tasks that constitutes the process of pursing green growth.

We have adopted the long-term vision of becoming one of the five ranking green economies by 2015. This provides a sense of destination and inspiration.

The strategy also comprises three strategic objectives: go for low carbon, reduce greenhouse gases and invest in green technologies, commercializing them in industries.

All of the foregoing implies changes for our lifestyles. We have to change them. What about land-use planning and urban transportation planning? They are to be guided by the principle goals assigned to individual sectors.

Yet another component is adapting to climate change, something bound to happen to some extent, whatever the world is doing about global warming.

There also is an adaptation component. For example, we have been rehabilitating our four main rivers, a typical adaptation project.

Over the past three years, we have been examining three sectors covered by each strategy. We have a five-year plan leading up to 2013 for the implementation of the long-term strategy.

In this way, we have laid the institutional foundation including a framework act on low-carbon green growth, which enables and authorizes the government to intervene in the market with regulations on the one hand and supportive measures on the other.

The priority goal has been to implement the greenhouse gas reduction target for the period up to 2020, in order to implement what we call the Greenhouse Gas Target Management System.

We have identified 470 or so emitters and assigned them greenhouse gas emission targets for next year. In another year, the targets will be increased and so forth.

In that way, we already are moving to bring down the emission of greenhouse gases but this is a primitive form, a precursor to the greenhouse emission trading scheme to be introduced in 2015.

It has not been politically easy to pass this legislation, but the National Assembly somehow passed this bill recently with unanimous support.

We also have been taking measures to develop and deploy renewable energy. Right now, renewable energy accounts for 2.5 percent of the total in the primary energy mix, and our goal is to increase this to the 11 percent level or more by 2030.

We now have a portfolio standard RPS, and power producers are striving to meet their own targets in this regard.

Probably more important are our efforts to improve the efficiency of energy use, considering energy efficiency the fifth source, as we call it.

New growth engine

In order to secure leverage for all these goals to create new growth engines, we have been investing in research and development of green technologies and their commercialization.

We have managed to improve our level of technological competence since 2007. Our goal is to join the top-tier countries by 2030. We have been making pretty good progress.

Major businesses have been investing in so-called new and renewable energy sectors as a matter of the highest priority. As a result, the amount of investment by big businesses has been increasing at a rate of nearly 80 percent for the first three years (since 2007). It has slowed down a little bit now.

We believe that we have made good progress in terms of the actual outcome in the development of green technologies, and I think we have joined the ranks of the top 10 countries in this area.

We have the largest electrical vehicle carrier in the world. We have installed the largest tidal power plant, and we are second in bringing electrical vehicles to the market.

As a result, there has been a very rapid increase in the production and supply of renewable energies, although it is from a very low basis.

The number of firms involved with new and renewable energy doubled during the first three years with sales increasing seven-fold.

Energy efficiency

The outcome has been pretty good except that we still find ourselves not so efficient in the use of energy. Energy efficiency at the macro level is below the average level for OECD countries (Organization for Economic Cooperation and Development).

Our businesses are at the micro level in energy efficiency, like steel maker POSCO. The problem is that our economy, too industrial compared to services and manufacturing, is highly energy-intensive.

Consequently, we have to shift our industry structure. The problem is that this takes time, a challenge we are facing now but not something that we can achieve over a few years.

We are trying to bring in all kinds of measures to improve energy efficiency in the industrial sector and in the household sector this year; this is proving to be tough challenge.

Environment Info
Ocean pollution

Energy recycling is the recovery process of utilizing energy that would normally be wasted, usually by converting it into electricity or thermal energy.

Undertaken at manufacturing facilities, power plants, and large institutions such as hospitals and universities, it significantly increases efficiency, thereby reducing energy costs and greenhouse gas pollution simultaneously.

The process is noted for its potential to mitigate global warming profitably. The work usually occurs in the form of combined heat and power (also called cogeneration) or waste heat recovery.

Waste heat recovery is a process that captures excess heat that would normally be discharged at

manufacturing facilities and converts it into electricity and steam, or returns energy to the manufacturing process in the form of heated air, water, glycol, or oil.

A waste heat recovery boiler contains a series of water-filled tubes placed throughout the area where heat is released. When high-temperature heat meets the boiler, steam is produced, which in turn powers a turbine that creates electricity.

Achieving shared growth through green ODA

Dae-won Park

Dozens of government and organization officials from 13 countries view the windmills at the Sihwa Lake in Hwaseong, Gyeonggi Province as part of the East Asia Climate Partnership program organized by KOICA. *Korea Times file*

Green economics is drawing greater attention from the international community. The UN Conference on Sustainable Development (UNCSD), more commonly known as Rio+20, which runs from June 20 to 22, 2012 in Brazil, will discuss ways of making the transition to a green economy.

In order to take global measures to achieve a green economy while following the principle of the UN Framework Convention on Climate Change (UNFCCC), namely to carry out "common but differentiated responsibilities and respective capabilities and their social and economic conditions," what is needed is the financial and technical support of developed countries to bring developing countries into the "green movement."

Most people think that aid activities put a priority on poverty eradication in countries that are unable to meet basic human needs. There is likely to be some degree of skepticism about the idea of raising environmental issues in these countries.

Natural disasters

However, it seems that such a well-worn viewpoint may need to be re-thought in the face of overwhelming evidence in the form of frequent weather changes and natural disasters that are becoming more widespread these days. Developed countries, with relatively abundant resources and sophisticated technologies, are capable of preventing and recovering from the damage caused by natural disasters. Developing countries, however, lack the resources to do so and thus have no choice but to suffer the most from drastic climate change and environmental degradation. With ill-equipped infrastructure, even the strike of a single natural disaster may leave them vulnerable to massive loss of life, crops and buildings. Lacking resources, restoration efforts often seem to take forever. It is not surprising that 70 percent of the deaths caused by natural disasters occur in developing countries.

The Korean government has chosen "low carbon, green growth" as a national vision and, in line with this concept, it has conducted "green Official Development Assistance (ODA). To be specific, it has launched the East Asia Climate Partnership (EACP) program, which represents the government's effort to support climate change mitigation projects in developing countries. Initiated by the Korean government during the 2008 G8 Extended Summit, it is a special fund set up to combat climate change and support green growth in developing countries.

The main beneficiaries of EACP are East Asian countries, which, while continuing to undergo a period of drastic industrialization, have become vulnerable to climate change due to having insufficient infrastructure in place. Since 2008, the Korean government has carried out a five-year EACP program and has offered help in five priority areas: water management, low-carbon energy, low-carbon cities, waste management, and forestation. With a total budget of $200 million, the government has conducted bilateral and multilateral environmental projects, invited government officials for training in Korea, and pursued research in green growth for developing countries.

The Korea International Cooperation Agency (KOICA), the main grant aid channel of the Korean government, was put in charge of the EACP program and has sought to expand it ever since. After accepting project requests from 31 countries and conducting feasibility studies on the requests, it selected 20 projects and has implemented them in 10 countries. The projects are to be completed by the end of this year in line with the Korean government's commitment made in 2008 toward the international community.

Water management

Water management is one of EACP's leading support programs. As its goal is to help developing countries deal with water shortages, the program includes forming master plans for water resources management and the provision of necessary facilities such as water supply and sewage treatment systems. However, the ultimate goal of water management lies in achieving overall improvement in living conditions by preventing floods and droughts, ensuring a stable supply of drinking water, and improving water quality, which will lead to an increase in agricultural productivity. "Water Landmark Project" water management programs are operating in Mongolia, the Philippines, and Azerbaijan, with a combined budget of $70 million.

Making use of renewable energy resources, such as solar energy, is also included in the EACP program. In Cambodia, KOICA provided a solar-powered electricity facility for a village where war-veterans live. In Mongolia, it presented a high-tech heat system, which reduces air pollution. In the South Pacific, where countries are threatened by rising sea levels, KOICA focuses on strengthening the capacity to utilize renewable energy sources.

In addition, Korea's forestation techniques have become valuable assets to countries such as Indonesia and the Philippines that are threatened by rapid deforestation. Recently, the Korean government handed over a satellite reception and analysis ground system to Sri Lanka, which will make possible weather forecasts and preventive measures based on data transmitted from Korea's meteorological satellite "Chollian."

To share the spirit of Green ODA, EACP is working with international organizations such as the WHO, IMO and World Bank to identify mosquito-borne diseases as climate change issues and seek solutions for the illnesses. In addition, it is involved with international academic research aimed at developing eco-friendly ship technology.

Such efforts on the part of the Korean government have not been in vain: some 100 government officials from partner countries have shown great interest in Korea's rapid economic growth and its leading role in green growth discussions. Considering that Korea survived the aftermath of the Korean War and has succeeded in combating poverty, there is the unanimous opinion that Korea's training programs are more motivating than those provided by other aid agencies around the world.

Effects of climate change

The effects of climate change are not limited to a particular state or region. Therefore, the international society must stand together to deal with this problem, realizing that environmental issues decide whether the world achieves sustainable development. Accordingly, the "Green Economy" system that will be discussed in the upcoming Rio+20 Summit can only be realized when developed countries provide active support for developing countries and the latter's participation in achieving the green economy. Now is the time to focus our energy on implementing Green ODA, not just for the survival of developing countries but also for shared growth and sustainable development of the entire international community.

The EACP program is now in its final stage, but it will remain as the best practice of Korea's green growth initiative and is set to become the foundation for expanding the percentage of Korea's Green ODA by 30 percent. Based on expertise and experience acquired through the five-year program of EACP, Korea will strive to spread Green ODA around the world, eradicate poverty in developing countries and mitigate the side effects of climate change.

KOICA and the Ministry of Public Works of the Republic of Indonesia recently held a workshop on "Master Planning and Feasibility Study of Karian Dam-Serpong Water Conveyance and Supply System" at the Marriott Hotel in Jakarta, with one hundred stakeholders from the Korean embassy, KOICA and EDCF, and the Indonesian government present.

The main goals of this study were to establish the master plan for water conveyance and treatment plants and plan a PPP (public private partnership) scheme in order to stabilize the supply of water from Karian Dam to the Jabotabek (Jakarta, Bogor, Tangrang, and Bekasi) area, where water shortage has been severe. This study commenced in July 2010 and was completed in June 2011 with KOICA's technical assistance.

Since 2006, KOICA has continuously wrestled with the water shortage of Jabotabek area in cooperation with the Government of Indonesia, under the title of "Feasibility Study and Detailed Design for the Karian Dam Project." Successful implementation of the water conveyance and supply system will enhance the lives of approximately four million people in the Jabotabek area.

At present, consultation is in progress between both governments to prepare the implementation of Karian Dam Construction that will be financed by both the EDCF of Korea and the Government of Indonesia. With the completion of this study in June 2011, efficient financing and development scheme soon will be proposed for the construction of water conveyance and water treatment plants.

Recently, water shortages have become an urgent global issue due to climate change. With the successful implementation of this model, business opportunities in Indonesia for Korean enterprises will increase, especially in water-related sectors.

In Sri Lanka, a solar power plant has been completed at Hambantota with the assistance of the Korean government and KOICA.

The Korean government has set its "Low Carbon, Green Growth" strategy as a national goal and initiated a five-year plan. As a part of the plan, KOICA established the East Asia Climate Partnership (EACP) to share Korea's knowhow and technology in the area of renewable energy, energy efficiency and sustainability with developing countries through ODA projects.

Under EACP, KOICA has invested $3 million for the construction of a 500kw solar power plant that will be connected to the national grid system. This power plant will be equipped with solar panel modules, inverters, transformers and a computerized monitoring system by LG CNS. It currently generates an average of 2 kW per day and provides electricity to more than 300 rural households in the region. The plant is expected to solve the power shortage problem in rural areas and also to strengthen the relationship in terms of renewable energy between Korea and Sri Lanka.

Environmental governance in NE Asia

Mi-ae Choo

Yellow dust blowing in from China and Mongolia creates a smog-like atmosphere as seen from the top of Mt. Nam in central Seoul. Experts say such phenomenon makes it necessary for a new order in regional environmental governance. *Korea Times file*

As can be seen in the transport of yellow dust from China and the crisis last year over the nuclear disaster at Fukushima in Japan, there are significant geographical implications arising from the environment. In the Northeast Asian region, in particular, there are no national boundaries when it comes to the impact that environmental problems can have. There are consequent issues of enormous environmental significance that have to be addressed at the regional level.

The yellow dust and other air-polluting materials that originate from the deserts of China and Mongolia affect people not only in Korea and Japan but also in Pacific region countries, resulting in respiratory problems and conjunctivitis, Making matters worse, the transportation of micro dust particles from the areas are believed to cause acid rain and severe problems for livestock.

According to a recent report from the Organization for Economic Cooperation and Development (OECD), the number of people dying prematurely due to microdust is expected to reach 36 million a year by 2050. Owing to the fact that the phenomenon is proven to affect elderly citizens by a two- to three-fold margin, this development will have particularly severe implications for Korea and Japan where aging is more significant than in other countries.

Environmental accidents

The earthquake last year in Japan, followed by a massive tsunami, caused radiation to spread not only in Japan but also into the East Sea and the Okhotsk region, threatening ecology across a wide-ranging area. Owing to the seriousness of radioactive penetration in the region, Korea and Russia have been working together to monitor the situation and ongoing developments.

There also are efforts to prevent the infiltration of radioactive food materials from Japan in various countries as a primary preventive measure against the spread of radioactive pollution. The implications from what happened pointed to the need to establish comprehensive environmental governance in order to cover health, food safety and proper regulation in economic activities and trade.

In other words, there must be more than NOWPAP (Northwest Pacific Action Plan) of the UNEP (United Nations Environmental Programme) to deal with the wide variety of issues that we face. From health issues and food safety to trade regulations there must be multispectral environmental governance to address the range of problems.

Unfortunately, the reality is that environmental governance in the Northeast Asian region is not yet as effective as in other regions of the world. According to scholars and academicians, the main reason for this is political diversity among affected countries and different levels of economic development. There also are uncomfortable truths pertaining to historical experiences and the simple fact that civil societies in these countries have not reached a level of maturity.

The specific nature of the political, economic and historical past makes it difficult to create a common platform for environmental coexistence.

FTAs and the environment

From another perspective, the order of the Free Trade Agreement, which basically puts the United States in the central role, makes it even more difficult to find common ground for environmental governance in Northeast Asia.

In the 1990s, the World Trade Organization (WTO) played a critical role in bringing about a conclusion to the negotiations of the Uruguay Round for free multilateral trade activities. The United States was apparently disappointed in not being able to promote its interest and thus provide better conditions for developing countries. As a result, Washington avoided multilateral negotiations and engaged more aggressively in exclusive agreements such as free trade accords.

The main purpose of pursuing bilateral negotiations can be seen as targeting its role in the regional existence of the Northeast Asian region, the result of which has been the FTA with the United States and the projected conclusion of a similar agreement between Korea and China.

In most cases, FTAs are focused on cutting trade tariffs and removing barriers for the movement of goods and services among the countries concerned; there usually are not many environmental implications. However, in the case of the Korea-U.S. FTA, there have been in-depth discussions about the impact the agreement will have on the environment. The agreement was designed to protect environmental laws and make the process transparent so that anything occurring through the FTA would be within the confines of environmental regulations. All issues pertaining to the environment involving the implementation of the FTA are to be closely examined for any violation. Similarly, issues such as environmental implications and intellectual property rights will have to be taken seriously, as with the joint development of resources.

There are common areas of concern, including pollution in the western coastal areas, the transportation of yellow dust and the possibility of accidents at nuclear power plants. The Korean government is determined that these environmental issues be addressed in a proper manner when discussing free trade and other related issues.

But environmental considerations go beyond national boundaries, so that greater efforts must be made to pursue common values. From this perspective, there are limits to pursuing free trade agreements, and these limitations will continue to exist as we seek ways to improve bilateral trade relations.

Environmental implications

From this perspective, environmental governance in the European Union is a model to be emulated. The European Union established a pan-European environmental body in August 1994 to pursue the development of environmentally-friendly technologies. At the same time, the European Union set up the European Environmental Agency (EEA) in Denmark to engage in close cooperation with international environmental organizations.

In particular, the European Union introduced the Environmental Information and Observation Network (EIONET) in 1993 that was specifically designed to reduce ineffective environmental policies.

Where environmental policies are concerned, there is nothing more important than bilateral and international cooperation. And this is what the European Union is doing well.

In addressing the issue of coexistence, we must accept the fact that preventive steps have to be taken and that damage from environmental pollution must be paid by the polluters. In this argument, the establishment of environmental governance is important, from establishing preventive measures to discussing the necessity for polluters to take responsibility.

During a meeting of environment ministers in Japan in 2010, a ten-step cooperative initiative was adopted for environmental government in the Northeast Asian region. According to officials of the Environment Ministry of Korea, the initiative was under study for implementation, although there is no specific timeline.

However, it is high time that stronger steps be taken to prepare against natural disasters and present preventive measures for protecting food safety and health by assuming a leading role in introducing effective and relevant environmental governance in Northeast Asia.

Geopolitics of energy and Korea's choice

Hee-bong Chae

This is the nuclear repository in Postmark in Sweden which is a testament that atomic energy can be developed and used safely around the world. Korea has also been working on finding a suitable location for a nuclear repository. *Korea Times file*

There are several forthcoming and important changes in the geopolitics of world energy and climate change issues that require attention. First, China's presence in the global energy market will be evident in the next three decades. Already ranked first in the world in terms of total energy consumption, China is forecasted to account for around 40 percent of the increase in world oil consumption over the next three decades.

Prominently increasing China's presence in the world energy market will certainly bring some significant changes to world energy geopolitics. Already scrambling for oil and gas in Africa and the Middle East to satisfy its explosive oil demand, China's robust demand will function as a main factor driving up international oil and gas prices for at least the next three decades.

China also will try to increase its political and military capability to improve energy security because of its relative vulnerability to sudden interruptions in the supply of oil, especially in terms of sea-lane transportation. About 85 percent of oil imports pass through the Malacca Straits and the Indian Ocean, and any blockade of these transportation choke points could prove disastrous for China's oil security. The building of its first aircraft carrier on the unfinished Soviet carrier Varyag shows Beijing's anxiety over oil security and its determination to develop as a naval power to protect oil transportation sea lanes, challenging U.S. maritime supremacy.

There also is an energy motive behind China's move to claim its sovereignty of the Paracel Islands (Xisha Islands in Chinese) and Spratly Islands (Nansha Islands): they are rich in oil and natural gas reserves.

China's rise in the energy sector will bring significant changes to Sino-U.S. relations and the geopolitics of world energy.

Fierce competition between the United States and China to secure limited oil and natural gas supplies may cause political and military tensions. Before China became a net oil importer in 1993, these two countries were joined at the hip because there were not rivals in terms of scrambling for oil.

Outward policy

After China became a net importer, it adopted three important strategies to secure oil. The first is to diversify its sources of oil imports beyond the Middle East. This strategy reflects China's perception that the United States could easily use Middle Eastern oil as a weapon against China if the two nations have conflicts. China's sources of oil imports have extended to regions other than the Middle East, such as Sudan, Iran and Venezuela.

Second is to boost the proportion of oil imports through inland transportation. This is the reason why China is trying to import oil from Kazakhstan by building an oil pipeline that passes through Atyrau in Kazakhstan and Xinjiang.

China's third strategy is to take advantage of state-owned enterprises (SOEs) like China National Petroleum Corporation (CNPC), PetroChina and China National Offshore Oil Corporation (CNOOC) to secure equities in foreign oil and gas fields. This outward policy also has encouraged China's oil SOEs to make bold investments in oil-producing countries.

Forthcoming developments that we need to monitor closely are related to Iran's nuclear development. Iran has consistently denied allegations that it is seeking to develop a nuclear bomb. It maintains that nuclear facilities are being built for the purpose of power generation and that it has the legitimate right to do so. However, the United States and Israel suspect that Iran is concealing its intention to develop nuclear arms.

Israel is anxious about Iran's nuclear arms development because it will pose a serious threat to its safety. Saudi Arabia, which historically has competed for the status of regional power in the Middle East, has also expressed doubts about Iran's nuclear development, judging the move as a covert military strategy to rise to the fore in the Middle East.

The United States is trying to thwart Iran's nuclear ambition with sanctions aimed at reducing its allies' oil imports from Iran. In response to this development, Iran is threatening to block the Strait of Hormuz through which 40 percent of the world's oil trade passes. Increasing military tensions between Israel and Iran also could cause military clashes that might lead to another war in the Middle East. This would cause serious upward volatility in world oil prices, rising to over $200 per barrel under this eventuality.

Last but not least, there are forthcoming developments in terms of climate change. Climate change is a result of the use of energy and demands the human race to change how it produces and uses energy. The Intergovernmental Panel on Climate Change (IPCC) said the maximum temperature increase that the world can sustain by 2050 without causing irreparable damage is about 2.5 degrees centigrade.

Even though the Copenhagen Climate Change Conference failed to reach a concrete and fruitful agreement with legally binding emission reduction targets at the global level, individual country's efforts to reduce carbon dioxide emissions will be stepped up and implemented at a national level.

Nonetheless, expanding the role of low-carbon energy in each country will be politically difficult. To reduce carbon dioxide emissions, the use of renewable energy and nuclear power, along with efficient use of energy through conservation, should be promoted. The price of renewable sources such as solar photovoltaic energy or wind power is relatively high when compared to conventional fossil fuels like coal and oil. Consumers of electricity must shoulder additional costs when power generation companies increase the portion of renewable energy in their energy mix by following renewable portfolio standards regulating the minimum portion of renewable energy in their total generation amounts.

In the case of nuclear power generation, it appears its popularity as an effective way to reduce the level of carbon dioxide emissions is waning following the Fukushima nuclear disaster of March 11 last year. The disaster has prompted fierce political debate in Japan and Germany and has led many countries to question the safety of nuclear power generation.

Energy and climate change

What will be the major implications of future developments in the geopolitics of energy and climate change, and what do they mean for Korea?

First, higher oil prices will be inevitable, considering China's energy demands and the increased use of renewable energy. China's light-duty vehicles are likely to increase from roughly 25 million to nearly 230 million by 2030.

Oil use for transportation in China is predicted to rise five-fold by 2030. The burgeoning number of its middle class and strong demand for oil will be main drivers of high oil prices.

High oil prices also will cause domestic conflict in Korea, as it is heavily dependent on oil and gas. The oil intensity in primary energy use was 40 percent in 2010. Steep hikes in oil prices will affect a significant number of people across various economic sectors. including transportation, residential and industrial sectors. Low-income families that use a higher proportion of their income to pay for energy will be most severely damaged by oil price increases, considering the fact that Korea's social programs to protect low-income families from such hikes are very limited.

Second, political instability in the Middle East also will function as a main factor increasing the volatility of oil prices. In particular, volatility arises from the poorly regulated crude oil derivatives market that provides profit only from price changes expanded. When compared to the Iraq War, a U.S.-Israel confrontation with Iran would have a much bigger impact on oil prices considering the Iran's military capability and a possible blockade of the Strait of Hormuz. Along with the financing of oil markets, political instability in the Middle East would increase the overall volatility of oil prices.

Third, political instability and resulting disruptions in world oil security might pose a serious threat to Korea. Currently, Korea imports 80 percent of its oil from the Middle East, and in 2010, it imported 10 percent of its oil from Iran. If military clashes between the U.S. and Israel and Iran break out in the Middle East, and if Saudi Arabia fails to function as a swing producer, Korea's oil security will be in peril.

Fourth, Korea will come to realize the difficulty of securing equity and stakes in foreign oil and gas fields because of the U.S.-China rivalry in competing for foreign oil. The United States has maintained a strong presence in the Middle East, especially in Saudi Arabia. China is scrambling for oil and gas in Africa and Central Asia to meet its exploding energy demands.

Oil-producing countries already reinforce their control over profits in oil and gas fields. It is already rare to find concession agreements or product sharing in oil and gas contracts that are favorable to foreign participants. A growing number of oil-producing countries are taking advantage of their national oil companies to maximize profits.

The Korea National Oil Corporation (KNOC) still lacks the technical capability to act as a main operator in oil projects even though it has aggressively invested in foreign oil fields with the help of government money.

Energy strategy in the 21st century

In order to address energy challenges and climate change issues in the 21st century, it is essential for Korea to adopt three strategies for energy policies: transition to a low-carbon economy; integrating energy infrastructure with North Korea and Northeast Asia; and rising to a major global player in the world energy market.

First, it is important for Korea to transform into a low-carbon economy. The government should take bold measures to increase the use of renewable energy. In the case of broadband networks in information technology industries, the nation has succeeded in building extensive high-speed Internet infrastructure by making aggressive investments. The expansion of renewable energy has been relatively sluggish because of the fear of rising energy costs. The Korean government should persuade consumers to accept the increasing role of renewable energy and corresponding burden of increased energy costs. In this process, a social program to alleviate the burden on low-income families should be expanded.

The role of electric vehicles should also be expanded in order to reduce carbon dioxide emissions. Electric vehicles will be crucial not only in transforming the transportation sector into an environmentally-friendly one in terms of carbon dioxide emissions but also in reshaping the competitive structure of the world automobile industry. Buyers of electric vehicles should be given strong incentives, including procurement subsidies and tax breaks.

In the case of nuclear power generation, Korea should decide which model to follow between the French and German variants. The French model emphasizing the role of nuclear power in its energy mix dates back to

Geopolitics of energy and Korea's choice

Charles de Gaulle. De Gaulle, the French statesman famous for his politics of grandeur, held the view that France should continue to pursue a course to become a major global power and should not rely on other nations for its national security and prosperity. During his first term as French president, he tried to secure a full nuclear cycle and nuclear capability as a strategy for being a regional power in Europe and the world.

In contrast to France, Germany, which was not permitted to have nuclear arms capabilities and utilized nuclear power only for peaceful purposes, has decided to phase out all 17 nuclear reactors by 2022 while stepping up efforts to increase the capacity of renewable energy in its energy mix.

A growing number of Korean people, especially from liberal blocs, are strongly opposed to extending the operation of old nuclear power plants and the construction of new units in the wake of the Fukushima nuclear disaster. Proponents of atomic power, mainly conservatives, maintain that nuclear generation should be promoted as an effective way to reduce carbon dioxide emissions. Some conservatives also argue that Korea should have the right to reprocess spent nuclear fuel, forbidden under the Korea-U.S. Nuclear Agreement.

Second, more substantial efforts to link South Korea's energy system with that of North Korea and Northeast Asia should be made to increase the South's access to vast energy resources in Russia. Russia ranks first in terms of natural gas reserves and eighth in terms of oil reserves. In this regard, importing Russian natural gas through the pipeline that passes through the North is vital for the South's energy future. The project will enable South Korea to import relatively cheap Russian gas. South Korea currently imports all its natural gas in the form of expensive liquefied natural gas (LNG).

Natural gas can also function as a bridge fuel in changing from oil to renewable energy. Increasing imports of natural gas will help Korea reduce carbon dioxide emissions in the energy sector.

Many barriers should be removed in order to finalize the Russia-North Korea-South Korea natural gas pipeline. Solving the issues of Pyongyang's nuclear missile program might be a prerequisite condition before Seoul makes a final decision on the natural gas contract with Russia. When an agreement on North Korea's nuclear issues is reached, related countries' cooperative mechanisms, such as the Northeast Energy Development Bank, may be needed to help build energy infrastructure in North Korea.

Third, Korea should rise to become a major global player in the world energy market. Unlike the semiconductor or shipbuilding industries, Korea has not succeeded in becoming a key player in the world energy market. In the age of Capitalism 4.0, energy is a very important factor in overcoming resource restraints and expanding the frontiers of capitalism. The role of state-owned enterprises like KNOC and Korea Gas Corporation (KOGAS) should be promoted as we have seen in the case of Chinese SOEs like CNPC.

Currently KNOC (oil) and KOGAS (gas) are operated separately, even though the separation of oil from the natural gas business is rare. Putting these two firms under the umbrella of a holding company or merging them could produce a synergy effect.

In tackling the above-mentioned energy and climate issues and Korea's energy strategies, presidential leadership is very important. Energy security is crucial for Korea's security, and a president's ability to persuade people is crucial in the process of setting a course in energy policies.

Can policies prevent environmental accidents?

Kyoo-yong Lee

Scores of whooper swans, designated as natural monument No. 201, grace the lower reaches of the Nakdong River as an indication of the improvement in the quality of the river. *Korea Times file*

Environmental policies in Korea, particularly those relating to water pollution, have a significant impact on reducing the incidence of accidents and other matters of concern regarding water supplies.

Accelerated economic growth has meant that the importance of environmental policies took a backseat during the 1980s and 90. This imposed a major obstacle for establishing methods of preventing "accidents."

This was encouraged by the conservative policies of budget agencies and complaints from residents, as well as by powerful lobbying from corporations to ease environmental regulations.

More than 100 water quality-related incidents occurred in the 1990s, but this number contracted to around 50 in the 2000s, most of which have been associated with leaks of hazardous materials and the extinction of fish in some areas.

Clean-water policies

In 1989, metallic substances, bacteria, ammonia and abnormal levels of nitrogen were found in tap water, triggering a public service announcement from the then Ministry of Construction and Transportation. This immediately resulted in public distrust about the safety of tap water. The government proceeded to introduce an integrated plan to secure clean water in September of that year.

Under this plan, the government invested 2.2 trillion won during 1996 for the upgrading of wastewater and other basic water-related facilities. Paldang and Daechong Lakes were designated as an area for special monitoring. However, the designation of the lakes for special monitoring triggered strong resistance, not only from the Home Ministry but also from provincial governments and residents.

It was only in June 1990 when the Board of Audit and Inspection reported the presence of cancer-causing substances in tap water to the National Assembly that a plan for special protection of the regions, which supply water to some 30 million residents, was legislated. Subsequently, compensation funds were established for victims of water pollution, and a permanent budget for basic environmental facilities was set up in 1990.

Phenol incident

In March 1991, the leakage of phenol into the Nakdong River rang additional alarm bells about the safety of our drinking water and served as a trigger for the introduction of tougher water management regulations. In fact, it caused the single most important drive to advance investment in basic water management facilities throughout the 1990s and beyond.

Following the first water pollution incident, the government devised the Four River Water Quality Upgrading Plan, and following a second incident that occurred a few months later, it developed the Pan-National Water Purification Plan.

These plans increased manpower deployed to manage water quality in the upper reaches of rivers and sparked a crackdown on companies that dispose of harmful chemicals in streams. Environment Management Committees were established for regions along the four rivers - Nakdong, Han, Geum and Yongsan - to resolve water quality problems. More of the federal budget was earmarked for wastewater treatment and other water-related facilities in the provinces under the control of the then Ministry of Home Affairs (now Ministry of Public Administration and Security).

As a result of these dangerous incidents, the government also introduced an integrated five-year plan in July 1993 for the supply of clean water throughout the country, injecting 15.9 trillion won in 31 projects. A total of eight ministries, including the Environment and then-Construction Ministries were charged with working together in a pan-national effort to improve the safety of water.

More incidents

Then in January 1993, another incident occurred in which oil waste was leaked into the Nakdong River, causing a stench and a shortage of drinking water in the Busan and South Gyeongsang Province areas.

This led to a statement from the Environment Minister who said that cancer-causing agents, including benzene and toluene, had been detected in the river and used oil had been leaked illegally into the upper reaches of the Nakdong River. These revelations created enormous distrust among residents of the region, and the government saw the need to bring about fundamental changes to water management policies.

Such was the case not only along the Nakdong River but also for the upper reaches of the Yongsan River, where pollution created a foul odor in tap water in the Mokpo region.

Between 1996 and 2005, a total of 27 trillion won was injected into the upgrading of 597 water treatment facilities, including 287 wastewater treatment plants, as part of an expansive program to clean up the water supply around the country.

Owing to the importance and intensity of the issue, then-Prime Minister Lee Hoi-chang personally revealed the nature and details of the program. As part of the initiative, all aspects of water management that had been split up among different government agencies such as the Ministry of Home Affairs were streamlined into the Environment Ministry, and its status was elevated to the highest level of government agencies. At the same time, water quality checking stations were set up at the four major rivers, and regulations concerning the upper reaches of rivers were introduced as part of plans to protect the quality of tap water.

Preventive measures

In 1998, the worsening of water quality in the Paldang Lake triggered need for another revision of laws governing the management of the four major rivers. This included control over leakage of hazardous materials into the rivers as well as levies imposed for the use of river water.

Looking at the details and why this was necessary, the BOD (biochemical oxygen demand) at Paldang Lake dropped to 2.0 ppm (parts per million) due to drought, just when the quality of water was reaching Grade 1. This created major concerns among residents in the metropolitan area and called for implementing more specific measures to protect the quality of water in the upper reaches.

By undertaking this task, it came to light that the liberalization of land use regulation for real estate development was also a major source of the problem. Subsequently, a water quality improvement task force was formed under the Prime Minister's Office, and more than 420 public hearings and discussions were held among experts, residents and provincial officials to put together a master plan for protecting the quality of water in the upper reaches of the major rivers.

A special law governing the management of the four major rivers was introduced under the win-win spirit of sharing our resources and looking back at faults committed in the past. This uncovered the fact that residents living in the upper reaches of rivers were confined to strict regulations and made all the sacrifices, while the rest reaped the benefits of clean water.

There was a need to change the system through which a spirit of co-existence could come into being along with policies for protecting water quality, while schemes to alleviate some market control of real estate in the areas also were put in place.

While accidents and incidents affecting the quality of water should not occur, the fact they do has brought about fundamental changes to environmental policies, certainly for the better.

Through these efforts, Korea's water management policies have received accolades from the Organization for Economic Cooperation and Development and the World Economic Forum.

Nonetheless, the reality is that however effective post-accident programs may be, it is critical that realistic preventive programs are put in place.

Damage from water pollution cannot be entirely calculated in numbers, from the difficulties residents have to suffer to the impact it has on industrial activities. Some people say that the solution may be to use only mineral water, but then the reality would be that households and restaurants cannot feasibly use cook and clean dishes.

In conclusion, the clear and simple answer lies in the prevention of water pollution.

Yeosu Declaration to bring life to ocean

Do-soo Jang

Brilliant fireworks are underway at the site of the 2012 Yeosu Expo in the South Jeolla Province on the first day of the Year of the Dragon, celebrating the onset of the event that kicks off next week. *Korea Times file*

As the opening date for Expo 2012 Yeosu Korea approaches, Yeosu, a beautiful southern coastal city vibrant with life, is making final preparations. Many features of the international fair such as Beluga whales, the Big O - an innovative circular venue - and the 73-meter tall Sky Tower have already created a media buzz.

But the real objective of the Expo is to promote a vision of "green growth from the sea," a spirit of harmony between the ocean and people encapsulated in the Yeosu Declaration.

Essence of the Yeosu Declaration

The Yeosu Declaration aims to promote greater stewardship of the marine environment, sharing knowledge and understanding of how oceans and coastal resources can be enjoyed in a sustainable manner for present and future generations. One of its key messages to the global community is the importance of marine resources to a new green economy. Resources on land are becoming scarce, and long term provision of extra food is an issue of concern. The Expo aims to foster innovative industries and technologies that use marine resources and energy in a sustainable, environmentally friendly way.

The year 2012 is excellent timing for the Yeosu Declaration, which will be published exactly four decades after the Stockholm Declaration on the Human Environment was officially announced in 1972, followed by the Nairobi Declaration of the United Nations Environment Program Governing Council on the State of the Worldwide Environment in 1982, the Rio Declaration on Environment and Development in 1992, and the Johannesburg Declaration on Sustainable Development in 2002.

The Yeosu Declaration is a highly relevant and timely endeavor, streamlining reciprocity with the above listed declarations.

Moreover, the Expo is the first international exposition whose main theme is focusing on the ocean, coasts and islands in international recognition of their role. Millions of people will visit alongside reporters and the press, allowing the expo to have a greater impact on education and outreach to the world about oceanic issues.

As an intellectual legacy, the declaration will draw unimaginable attention from ocean and non-ocean communities, children and adults, and scientists and non-scientists.

When it comes to credibility as ocean memorabilia, it is a significant milestone for the Expo, the Bureau International des Expositions (BIE), and for all participants who recognize and value the ocean and coasts.

In order to strengthen technical expertise and to reinforce international recognition of professional knowledge about issues related to the sea, the Declaration is being developed by the Drafting and Review Committee, comprised of 53 chartered marine experts from home and abroad, including officials from specialized international organizations such as the FAO, GEF, IMO, IOC/UNESCO, OECD, UNDP and UNEP.

Committee members have been deeply involved for about three years, sharing their expertise in oceanography. The Yeosu Declaration has been reviewed through a number of international and domestic symposiums and forums.

The Declaration proceeds from a three-fold overview of humanity's relationship with the marine world: 1) the ocean is a planetary treasury but remains mysterious; 2) the oceans are under pressure due to human needs; 3) the oceans must be kept healthy for future generations.

Keywords of the Yeosu Declaration

The first point emphasizes the importance of the ocean to the Earth's ecosystem as a source of food and income to billions of people who depend on marine ecosystems for their livelihoods. Furthermore, it underlines the ocean as a conduit for trade and exchange. However, as economies grow and coastal areas become increasingly populated, the ocean and coasts are under increasing stress and demand for more space, not only in coastal areas but also on and below the surface of the seas. In addition, because of human influence, climate change is causing sea levels to rise, and glaciers to melt. This might increase extreme weather patterns, thereby posing serious threats to the health of the ocean and the socio-economic well-being of the people who depend on it.

The Yeosu Declaration calls for urgent international cooperation in scientific and technological research and for expanding global ocean observation to find ways of reducing natural disasters. Special attention is given to the needs of developing nations, including small islands, to help address the ocean-related challenges they face.

In this respect, the Yeosu Project, supporting capacity building in developing countries, is also a major step forward.

At the center of the Expo are practical ideas for efficient management and conservation of marine resources such as the invention and implementation of technology for the maintenance of biodiversity and restoration of coastal wetlands. Other main issues being explored at the Expo include finding effective responses to marine pollution, research on technology for handling oil spills in oceans, measures to cut shipping-related greenhouse gas emissions, and ways to deal with marine environmental pollution.

Expo organizers, participating countries and international organizations, including specialized agencies, 53 drafting and review committee members, and the supporters who agreed to join through SNS and onsite promotion events, which start from the opening to the closing of the event, are joining and supporting the Yeosu Declaration. Though it is non-binding, the wording used could become universally acceptable.

Concrete action

The Yeosu Declaration will be read at the Yeosu Declaration Forum scheduled for August 12. It will be held at the Expo Hall, International Pavilion C in the expo site right before the closing ceremony. The forum will be attended by UN Secretary-General Ki-moon Ban, the Prime Minister of the Republic of Korea, the Prime Minister of Tuvalu, and a general audience of over 700, including national commissioners, drafting and review committee members, marine experts and scientists, students and children, NGOs, and general citizens.

During the forum, there will be a panel discussion about the expectations and measures to translate the spirit of the Yeosu Declaration into concrete action. The panel includes experts from international organization such as UNESCO, UNEP, IMO, and the OECD. The outcomes of the Yeosu Declaration Forum will be disseminated worldwide to relevant recipients. The original copy of the proceedings will be documented by the BIE.

Environment most vital part of Expo

Expo 2012 Yeosu, Korea seeks to make its contribution to the cause of the environment, particularly in the marine area.

In this exercise, what is important is understanding and gaining the support of the international community. The Yeosu Declaration and the Yeosu Project, in a nutshell, aim to enhance public awareness of the challenges of environmental changes, present ideas and technology for meeting the challenges, and reaffirm international cooperation for dealing with the grand task through concrete and concerted actions.

Planned projects

At the center of the Expo are practical ideas for efficient management and conservation of marine resources such as the discovery and implementation of technology for the maintenance of biodiversity and restoration of coastal wetlands. Here are some other main issues being explored at the Expo:

Response to marine pollution: research on technology for handling oil spills in oceans, measures to cut shipping-related greenhouse gas emissions, and ways to deal with marine environmental pollution.

Marine environment exploration: observation of climate and

environmental changes and how technology can be used to handle these problems to improve overall management of the coastal environment.

Marine safety measures: development of a real-time coastal marine observation system, early disaster alarm system, and technology for the prevention of harbor-related disasters.

Marine technologies

Practical use of fisheries resources: development of deep sea water, utilization of underwater ground water and desalination, and prevention of saline intrusion into ground water.

Development of marine biological resources: research on new materials and marine medicine and the reduction of greenhouse gas emissions using sea algae.

Utilization of marine mineral resources: feasibility studies on offshore oil and gas development and underwater CO_2 storage technology.

Preservation of fisheries resources: implementation of technologies for the restoration of biodiversity and the conservation of marine resources, including eco-friendly ecological aquaculture technology and floating aquaculture technology.

Advancement of fisheries technology: development of Smart Fish Aggregating Device (Smart FAD), research on changes in fisheries in relation to rising sea temperatures, and promotion of fisheries technologies and port logistics technologies.

Chapter 5

World Governments

Pricing, partnerships key to green growth
Addressing challenges with integrated policy
The failure of disaster diplomacy
Green energy growing in Arab World

Pricing, partnerships key to green growth

Christian Friis Bach

The windmills are in operation along the coasts of Denmark, playing a major role in the supply of electricity. *Korea Times file*

The following is a presentation made during the Global Green Growth Summit held in Seoul May 10-11, 2012.

When I was a teenager in Denmark, and that is of course a few years back, my father erected one of the new windmills at that time with a capacity of 55 kilowatts. Today, the 40 windmills that the company is running each generates more than a hundred times that amount of electricity.

I say this to point out that we have experienced a technological revolution in terms of renewable energy over the past 20 or 30 years.

How did this come about in Denmark? What happened? How were these windmills developed? We did so through a lot of research and a lot of support through partnerships between civil society, companies, universities and government institutions.

But foremost, it was a matter of prices and a unique price structure. I remember my father doing the calculations to determine if it made sense to construct the windmills; all of it had to do with prices.

Taxes and subsidies

The price structure involved a unique combination of taxes on fossil fuels and energies and subsidies to the renewable electricity coming from the windmills that created a market for investors. And I say that to emphasize how important prices are.

We have a big challenge right now in the world because if we want to achieve sustainable energy and we want to increase the share of renewable energy sources, we also want to increase energy efficiency and need a quite unique set of prices. This is because in order to increase energy access for everybody, we need low prices that even the poor should be able to afford.

If we want energy efficiency to increase, we need higher prices. Only then will companies find new and innovative solutions to save energy. Likewise, if we want renewable sources to increase, we need the prices to be right. We need the right combination.

You need cheap prices to allow for access and high prices to allow for efficiency and right prices to allow for renewable sources to really come into our production system. That is absolutely critical to promote the market.

In Denmark today, we just approved a new energy plan to cut consumption and total emissions of greenhouse gases by 40 percent compared to 1990 levels in 2020. This is one of the most ambitious targets in the world. The plan is then to phase all fossil fuels in our heating systems by 2035 and become carbon neutral by 2050.

The surprising thing is that companies in Denmark heavily support the program, and this is because companies know exactly what is going to happen.

Bipartisan agreement

We have a bipartisan agreement in parliament, and all major parties are part of it. There is a clear plan for the next 20 to 30 years, and companies know exactly what is going to happen. They can plan and invest accordingly, which is critical to travel along the green growth pathway.

All of this is part of prices and planning, and long-term planning is what the industry needs to invest and create green growth. It is becoming an important part of the Danish industry.

If you take into consideration the large proportion of green export companies in Denmark, you realize the impact that our plan has had thus far.

(The Crown Prince of Denmark, Frederik, led the largest-ever business delegation of 76 companies to Seoul during the Global Green Growth Summit last week.)

And why did we come to South Korea? South Korea is a big and important market, but still I believe that many came here because South Korea has decided to pursue a green growth strategy and long-term green growth planning.

And that is why Danish companies producing energy-efficient water pumps, windmills, insulation materials, and green growth technologies are coming to South Korea.

I say this along the lines of how important it is to have green growth planning and technologies for South Korea and especially for a small country like Denmark. For us, it is about prices and planning.

Green Growth Forum

On the macro side, Denmark is continuing to seek opportunities to share our experiences with other countries, which is absolutely critical, and the Green Growth Forum, which will take place in Copenhagen.

I can say from the experience I have with the South Korean government and organizations like the Global Green Growth Institute, sharing practical experiences with companies, universities and governments that come together to do specific planning and the sharing of ideas develops strong partnerships. This is central to green growth: partnerships, planning and pricing.

Cambodia's green growth plan well under way

GGGI signed a memorandum of understanding with the Government of Cambodia to develop a National Green Growth Master Plan (NGGMP) for the country to achieve continued rapid economic development while preserving its environmental integrity.

Cambodia has experienced significant economic expansion in recent years; however, this growth has been unbalanced and has largely occurred in industrial sectors such as construction, textiles, agriculture and tourism.

This has placed a significant burden on the country's natural environment and a heavy strain on its natural resources. Furthermore, the benefits of this growth have gone proportionately to Cambodia's urban population while most of the people continue to live in rural areas, often at subsistence levels.

In order to address these disparities and alleviate the strain placed on the environment and natural resources, the Cambodian government has committed to pursue a more sustainable model of growth. To that end, the government worked with the United Nations Economic and Social Commission for Asia and the Pacific (UNESCAP) to draw up a National Green Growth Roadmap, which serves as a broad foundational structure to integrate existing ideas and initiatives for green growth into the country's economic development strategy.

Drawing upon the fundamentals of the roadmap, GGGI is assisting the Cambodian Green Growth Secretariat and the Ministry of Environment in establishing a National Committee on Green Growth (NCGG) to help oversee and implement the NGGMP. GGGI is partnering with the Korea Institute for International Economic Policy (KIEP), the Korea Legislative Research Institute (KLRI), UNESCAP, Kwangwoon and Jeju Halla universities in South Korea, and EN3, an environmental engineering company.

The NGGMP is focused on five major areas: economic analysis, institutional analysis, sustainable forestry, waste management, and green job creation.

GGGI's fundamental objective is to help Cambodia meet its goals in developing the national economy, spurring job creation and identifying new opportunities for economic growth. As such, its country program for Cambodia includes both a top-down and bottom-up approach.

The top-down dimension entails performing economic and institutional analyses, including economic analysis of the aforementioned NGGMP, which is to be integrated with Cambodia's broader economic strategy, and the establishment of the NCGG, which is tasked with shepherding and supervising the implementation of the master plan.

The top-down aspect also encompasses establishing a legal framework to institutionalize green growth strategies, tailoring specific policies designed to help Cambodia achieve its millennium development goals and the government's own Updated National Strategic Development Plan, thus raising awareness of green growth amongst the population in general.

The bottom-up efforts are more local and sector-oriented, although still, of course, within the scope of the broader GGMP.

Addressing challenges with integrated policy

Torbjørn Holthe

This is a photo of a polar bear on the ice flow at the Ukkusiksaik National Park in Canada, much like those which inhabit the coastal areas of Norway. Norway is taking environmental issues into close account in developing its transport system to prevent the extinction of polar bears due to pollution and melting ice glaciers. *Photo by Ansgar Walk*

Climate change affects all areas of the globe, some parts more than others. The Arctic is one such area. Problems must be dealt with, and there might also be opportunities to seize. Norway has developed an integrated policy for the Arctic, using resources in a sustainable way to further the international legal order and international co-operation.

The High North is Norway's number one foreign policy priority. On

November 18, 2011, a White Paper, The High North-Vision and policy instruments, was released. The Norwegian government's High North policy is coherent, long-term, and based on four overriding objectives listed below:

- *Ensuring peace, stability and predictability*
- *Ensuring integrated, ecosystem-based management and sustainable use of resources*
- *Strengthening international cooperation and the international legal order*
- *Strengthening the basis for employment, value creation and welfare throughout the county*

Previously, there were few countries or major economic actors outside the region engaged in Arctic areas. This is changing. We now see that an increasing number of non-Arctic actors - North American, European and Asian - are interested in new transport routes, access to resources and knowledge about climate change, the melting ice and changes in the marine environment. They also are focusing on building expertise and capacity in those fields.

Norway is facing challenges as well as opportunities when it comes to safeguarding its own interests and taking part in developing the future of the High North and the Arctic. This article touches upon a few topics related to the High North policy of the Norwegian government.

The Arctic Council

The Arctic Council was established in 1996 as a forum for circumpolar cooperation throughout the Arctic. Initially it was a forum for environmental cooperation and has since been expanded to include sustainable development.

This cooperation is increasingly focusing on climate change and the serious impacts it may have in the Arctic. Today, cooperation with the Arctic Council encompasses shipping, integrated management of resources, oil and gas, tourism, education, research, health, economic and cultural issues in addition to climate change and the environment. The Arctic Council is the only circumpolar body and the leading political body for Arctic issues.

Norway has systematically sought to maintain and further develop ties with countries outside the Arctic region through a series of High North dialogues. Korea has been an ad hoc observer since 2008 and is now actively seeking to be a permanent member along with Japan, China and the

European Union.

Norway expressed its support for Korea's application for permanent status to the Arctic Council during the first bilateral consultation on the High North held in Seoul on May 9, 2012. Final approval will occur at the council's ministerial meeting in May 2013.

Law of the Sea

In recent decades, important issues concerning and affecting Norway's jurisdiction in the Norwegian Sea, the Barents Sea, and the Arctic Ocean have been clarified.

For all practical purposes, the outstanding issues concerning maritime delimitation of areas under Norwegian jurisdiction have been resolved. Norway is the first of the Arctic states to have had the outer limits of its continental shelf clarified in accordance with the UN Convention on the Law of the Sea.

The emphasis on the applicability of the Law of the Sea in the Arctic Ocean lays the foundation for orderly, predictable relations between coastal states and has corrected the notion that the Arctic was an unregulated area where open conflict over resources could be expected. At the same time, it signals to the rest of the world that the coastal states are taking their responsibility seriously. One of Norway's primary aims has been to play a part in bringing about this clarification.

A new energy province

The Barents Sea will become an important European energy province. How rapidly it will develop and how important it will become depends on market conditions, technological developments, the size of commercially viable discoveries of oil and gas, and how fast renewable energy sources are developed.

The development of oil and gas activities must also be weighed against considerations of other industries and interests within the framework of integrated, ecosystem-based management.

Oil and gas delivered from this region can improve European energy security and make an important contribution to global energy supplies while at the same time providing a basis for developing industry and services in North Norway. This has important economic and foreign policy implications.

In Norway's contacts with other states and foreign commercial interests, issues related to access to energy and energy security will become increasingly important both in themselves and as part of foreign and security policy.

Environmental standards, technology, the protection of particularly valuable areas, and emergency response systems will be especially important, as will opportunities and challenges related to the development of technology for Arctic waters.

New Sailing Routes

At some point in the future, ice may no longer be a barrier to transport between Asia, North America and Europe through the Arctic Ocean. There is no immediate prospect of year-round shipping in these waters where harsh weather and ice continue to cause difficulties.

But even today, merchant ships operating under normal commercial conditions are using the Northeast Passage to cut travel times and costs. There is reason to believe that the volume of shipping will increase. Russia will face a number of challenges in connection with traffic along a coastline where little infrastructure has been developed.

Norway will have to deal with the risks involved in increased traffic along its coast but will also have opportunities to provide services for these ships.

In the near future, however, transport to and from Russia and petroleum-related activities are expected to account for most of the increase in transport volume. Increasing activity will make it necessary to develop cooperation between Norway and Russia to improve the safety and efficiency of maritime activities.

These developments will have geopolitical consequences. Countries such as China, Japan, Korea and Singapore are showing interest in the possibilities of using Arctic sea routes, and a new window of opportunity is opening up for cooperation and exchange with them. This will extend considerable room for developing expertise, infrastructure, and networks that make spin-off effects in Norway more likely. Shorter transport distances and lower prices may improve the competitive position of Norwegian actors in Asian markets while reducing environmental pollution and easing access to European markets for Asian actors.

Strategic importance

All these trends combined will increase the strategic importance of Norway's coastline and port capacity. Growing activity may increase the need for regulation in the northern sea areas due to related impacts, including environmental considerations, and may have implications for search and rescue capacity and oil pollution emergency response.

In conclusion, Norway is taking a leading role in the field of knowledge and as a responsible actor and partner will continue to develop Norwegian centers of expertise in key strategic areas, demonstrating to the world that Norway is a preferred and responsible partner in the North.

More importantly, Norway will continue to exercise sovereignty in a consistent and predictable manner and ensure compliance with fundamental principles of international law and respect for the special rights and responsibilities of coastal states while taking environmental risks into full consideration.

The failure of disaster diplomacy

Ilan Kelman and JC Gaillard

Volunteers of the Disaster Relief Foundation paint drawings on the walls of a house refurbished after a major flooding in Sunchang, North Jeolla Province. *Korea Times file*

Earlier this year, hope emerged for North Korea. The United States, China, North Korea and others reached an agreement that Pyongyang would receive food aid in exchange for progress on nuclear and missile talks.

This is a classic case of disaster diplomacy, one where a disaster - here, leading to humanitarian aid - is used to move forward with diplomacy. It also represents a classic case of disaster diplomacy by following the same pattern as every single other disaster diplomacy case study that has been examined in detail: it failed.

Exactly one month after the landmark deal was hailed in February, the U.S. government stopped aid to North Korea due to a missile test. Even China was irate at the North's actions.

This pattern is not new. Since 1995, North Korea has been suffering from a series of floods, droughts, and famines. Some estimates suggest that over a million people have died.

The disasters occur mainly due to North Korea's own agricultural mismanagement. That illustrates how weather variability leading to floods and droughts can become disasters when society treats the environment poorly. It is not extreme weather that has caused the disasters but rather North Korea's own actions in terms of inappropriate environmental management and food production. One consequence has been continual international food aid.

North Korea has also long been trying to avoid international scrutiny regarding its nuclear and military ambitions. Linking humanitarian aid to increased international access to the country yields disaster diplomacy.

Each time, the same cycle has recurred. North Korea reaches a deal for food aid, and even receives some in exchange for military and access concessions. As soon as possible afterward, it reneges on the deal, and aid stops.

That was the same following April 22, 2004, when a massive train explosion rocked North Korea. Aid was delivered, but soon afterwards, the country closed off again. North Korea represents typical disaster diplomacy failure, supported by in-depth analyses of dozens of other instances.

What is disaster diplomacy?

Disaster diplomacy research investigates how and why disaster-related activities do and do not influence conflict and cooperation. The key phrase is "disaster-related activities."

Post-disaster actions such as response, recovery, and reconstruction are included. Pre-disaster efforts are also covered, including prevention and mitigation.

Deforestation, constructing improper sea walls that reduce coastal sedimentation, and poor farming practices that augment rainfall runoff all contribute to augmented environmental hazards. Cooperation across borders is often essential to tackling these challenges.

Disaster diplomacy is not just about what happens when a volcano erupts in a war zone or when political enemies deliver humanitarian aid. It also is about what happens before a disaster and how setting up a warning system might bring together antagonistic parties, or how vaccinations might lead to permanent ceasefires. Yet that does not happen.

Two main types of disaster diplomacy scenarios have been examined: first, a specific country or region that experiences disaster, such as North Korea, and second, a specific disaster event or type of disaster. Earthquakes in Iran have had potential for improving U.S.-Iran relations but have never done so.

Dealing with disasters entails dealing with the environment, by understanding and building for different types of earthquake faults and floodplains. We all live in the environment and need to live with its characteristics, trends, and extremes-such as intense ground shaking or rainfall.

It seems reasonable to expect that enemies could find some common ground and move toward reconciliation as part of living within the same environment. That rarely happens.

Catalyze peace

All evidence so far suggests that while disaster-related activities do not create fresh diplomatic opportunities, they sometimes catalyze peace. But only in the short term, not in the long term.

In the short term — on the order of weeks and months — disaster-related activities can but do not always impact diplomacy. They influence it, they spur it on, and they affect it, as long as a pre-existing basis exists for that impact. The pre-existing basis might be cultural connections, trade links, or secret negotiations.

On December 26, 2004, tsunamis raced across the Indian Ocean, with the two hardest hit areas being Sri Lanka and the Indonesian province of Aceh. Both locations lost tens of thousands of people. Each had a long-running conflict that had been particularly violent over the previous 30 years.

In Aceh, a peace deal was reached months after the tsunami. So far, it has held. The peace deal was based on secret negotiations that started just two days before the tsunami. It did not create the peace, but it did help the ongoing peace process succeed. The parties involved wanted peace and used the tsunami as an excuse to reach it.

In Sri Lanka, the humanitarian emergency and international aid exacerbated the conflict. Within a few years, Sri Lanka's military had won. The parties involved had reasons for continuing the conflict and used the tsunami as one excuse to avoid peace.

That shows how the potential effect of disaster-related activities for achieving diplomacy does not always appear. When it does happen, it works only in the short-term.

Over the long-term — in terms of years — non-disaster factors take over. Examples are leadership change, distrust, the belief that an historical conflict or grievance should take precedence over present-day humanitarian needs, and priorities for action other than conflict resolution and diplomatic dividends.

Why does disaster diplomacy fail?

Many reasons explain why disaster-related activities sometimes have less diplomatic influence than might be expected or hoped for. Reconciliation is not necessarily an important objective, irrespective of saving lives in a disaster. The United States and Iran illustrate this point.

Inertial prejudice, misgivings, and distrust can overcome disaster diplomacy efforts. The United States initially did not respond to Iran's aid offers following Hurricane Katrina in 2005.

Additionally, lack of political forethought and media hype can derail good intentions. That was the case when the American government tried to send a high-profile emissary with aid supplies to Bam, Iran following the 2003 earthquake disaster. Iran firmly stated that humanitarian relief was acceptable but not political intentions.

Denying that international assistance is needed allows countries to avoid accepting external help from enemies. Then, no basis exists for even attempting disaster diplomacy.

With lingering memories of the failed Bam-related earthquake diplomacy, Iran declined an American offer of aid following the February 2005 earthquake disaster in the southern part of the country. Iran stated that they could handle the disaster domestically. Yet aid was accepted from several other countries and international organizations.

Too often, politics can be higher priority, even when political goodwill is present. Should more efforts be made to force disasters to support peace and diplomacy? Opposing answers emerge.

Some say "absolutely not." Extensive effort occurs to divorce disasters and politics. New mechanisms for linking them are not wanted. Instead, encouraging further separation would be preferable.

Others state, "Of course, yes." Disasters are inherently political events, and trying to separate disasters and politics is naive. The more positive the outcomes that can be fostered from disasters the better. Such outcomes should be actively pursued.

Disaster diplomacy in the Philippines

The Philippines illustrates the inextricable links between disasters and politics. In November and December 2004, four typhoons struck Quezon province, killing over 1,000 people through floods and mudslides in areas with a long-standing guerrilla conflict led by the New People's Army (NPA).

Illegal logging was quickly identified as one of the causes of the devastating slope failures and floods. Such environmental degradation has long been associated with exacerbating the impacts of many forms of disaster. The Filipino government promptly associated the illegal logging with the NPA.

The government could have grasped the opportunity to tackle the long-standing conflict and illegal logging simultaneously. That would be part of long-term disaster reduction, environmental management, peace and development. Instead, the government sought to shift blame and to inflame the public against the NPA.

Fanning the NPA conflict occurred even though a parallel conflict with religious separatists in the south had cooled down. Was the government determined to seek a conflict somewhere? Perhaps so in order to bury the opposition's claims of new evidence for governmental corruption and incompetence?

The opposition blamed the government for not tracking down the loggers and for contributing to the environmental damage in disaster-affected areas. The opposition even suggested the death penalty for the loggers.

All sides had media allies promoting their arguments vociferously. Instead of disaster diplomacy, the events became politically constructed by everyone according to pre-conceived narratives that conveniently blamed one another.

Since then, several typhoons and volcanic eruptions have struck conflict-prone areas of the Philippines. All saw similar characteristics regarding the political construction of the disaster and the lack of disaster diplomacy.

Sometimes, firefights occurred between guerrillas and government soldiers during relief operations. Sometimes, various parties declared unilateral ceasefires during the disaster and then took up arms again after the major crisis had dissipated.

There was never much scope for longer-term peace. Disasters have sometimes produced short-term, but never long-term diplomatic dividends.

Any hope for disaster diplomacy?

Rather than giving hope for peace, disaster diplomacy can distract from it. It can raise expectations that cannot be met immediately. That creates disillusionment, impatience, and ammunition for contrarians.

Furthermore, disaster diplomacy seeks a quick fix to long-standing, fundamental causes of enmity and disaster vulnerability. Short-term peace-making solutions tend to fail in the long-term, as do short-term measures, to reduce disaster vulnerability.

Even stopping illegal logging, which would reduce flood damage in places such as Pakistan as well as the Philippines, is not enough. Measures are needed to examine why people devastate the environment around them, increasing their own disaster vulnerability. Ultimately, it is usually because they have inadequate livelihood choices and no prospects for improvement.

In fact, all peace and disaster reduction activities require long-term commitments, not a one-off approach expected to solve all disaster and diplomacy problems right away. These peace and disaster reduction activities need to be linked to how people use environmental resources around them to achieve their livelihoods.

Should we lose all hope for disaster diplomacy? A successful example of new, lasting diplomacy based on only disaster-related activities may yet emerge. In particular, parties involved could make the active choice to seek long-term solutions using nothing but short-term disaster diplomacy.

So far, that has not been unambiguously witnessed. As with North Korea, active decisions are usually made to scuttle any hope of disaster diplomacy. Without more commitment from all those involved in disaster and diplomacy efforts, disaster diplomacy is doomed to failure.

Green energy growing in Arab World

Thani Al-Zeyoudi

Despite the recent accident in Fukushima,Japan, nuclear energy remains one of the most viable sources of energy in the world. This photo show the New Gori Nuclear Power Plant, which uses the Advanced Power Reactor (APR1400) technology, four units of which KEPCO is helping to build in the United Arab Emirates. *Korea Times file*

In the United Arab Emirates, we believe in realizing our potential. This belief is why we're striving to become one of the best countries in the world, part of our national UAE Vision 2021 strategy. It's also the driving force behind our pioneering efforts to build a green economy.

In achieving this sustainable development, both environmentally and economically, the UAE is facing unique challenges. Our harsh desert climate means heavy energy usage for air-conditioning and water desalinization, which we rely upon for 99 percent of our fresh water consumption. And given our exponential population growth, national electricity demand has risen 500 percent over the last twenty years. Also, our industrial structure and production capacities are very energy intensive. We have to build roads, bridges and infrastructure, elements that are already in place in other developed nations.

Nonetheless, we find inspiration in the challenges we've overcome and in the potential that lies ahead. That is precisely why the UAE is transitioning from a resource-based to a knowledge-based economy, bringing to life new ideas that test, build, and scale the diverse energy mix necessary for a sustainable society.

We believe economic diversification is the surest path to sustainable development in a future less reliant on oil.

Sustainable development

While the UAE is indeed blessed with tremendous energy reserves, our founding father Sheikh Zayed bin Sultan Al Nahyan instilled upon us the responsibility of preserving our natural resources. And it is the benefits of these oil and natural gas reserves that we are now leveraging in order to bring about the additional resources the world will need to meet future demand.

We see renewable energy as a natural extension of our existing energy expertise, a logical step forward in maintaining prosperity and safeguarding our environment. Here in the UAE, we're implementing a long-term approach to ensure sustainable national development.

The northern Emirates have an urban planning strategy in place for 2030. And in our major cities, among the most advanced in the world, we have strict efficiency codes for new buildings, public lighting, air conditioners, and water usage. Additionally, new energy-efficient technologies will harness the UAE's pioneering role in the green revolution and reduce its carbon footprint.

The UAE is recognized as a leader in the energy sector, and leadership entails responsibility. As part of a growing, international movement, we're collaborating with other like-minded nations to continuously learn, build upon our progress, and create a sustainable future for all.

Through our commitment to UN Secretary-General Ki-moon Ban's Sustainable Energy for All initiative, the UAE is improving clean energy access through projects in Afghanistan and Tonga. Also, our country's commercially-driven enterprise, Masdar, is helping build the UK's London Array, the world's biggest offshore wind farm, eventually reducing carbon emissions by 1.4-million tons each year. And our partnership in Torresol Energy is creating ground-breaking renewable energy storage in Spain, solar plants that are able to run at capacity even at night.

Also, the UAE is a participant in the Clean Energy Ministerial, a high-level global forum promoting policies and programs that advance clean energy technology. Through these meetings and discussions, we're better able to share lessons learned and best practices, more effectively encouraging the transition to a global clean energy economy. Ideas and initiatives like these are helping the UAE bring game-changing innovations to life through our international partnerships.

Renewable energy

While our country does possess vast energy reserves, we recognize that we can't rely on an endless supply of hydrocarbons. So we're positioning our economy to capture developing trends and adapt to changing global realities, investing in measurable goals to achieve sustainability objectives with real-world impact.

Our capital city, Abu Dhabi, has set a seven percent renewable energy target for 2020, and Dubai, our international business hub, a five percent renewable energy target by 2030. To achieve these goals, we're now finalizing the installation of Shams 1, the first utility-scale commercial solar power project in the Middle East. And next year, the first stage of the 1,000-MW Mohammed bin Rashid Al Maktoum Solar Park will be complete. The UAE's extreme climate conditions present unique challenges to widespread solar deployment, but we're taking active steps to improve its use and identify the technologies that best meet our needs.

Additionally, we are driving the clean energy sector through leadership to forge international partnerships. The Global Green Growth Initiative, led by South Korea, selected Abu Dhabi as home for its regional office, driving green growth across the Middle East and North Africa.

The UAE also houses the global headquarters of the International Renewable Energy Agency (IRENA). Through this alliance, our contribution to the agency's Global Solar and Wind Atlas is serving as a model for developing countries and for those with similar climatic conditions to design clean energy polices and procure financing and partners.

Falling renewable energy technology prices mean that renewable energy is becoming the financially rational choice for global power generation. The

UAE is using our energy expertise as a foundation for innovating and advancing clean technologies. In our country, wind energy has already achieved grid parity in the northern emirates, and solar energy is close on its heels. When you factor in the opportunity costs of consuming valuable hydrocarbons domestically instead of exporting them, the case for clean energy becomes even more compelling.

Looking forward, it's clear that the revenue potential for renewable energy technology is vast. Our country is investing extensively in clean energy technologies to safeguard the economy and environment.

Energy Security

While the UAE is a major oil-and-gas producing nation, we do not have an endless supply.

Our nation has been among the fastest-growing in the world over the last ten years; the UAE population has more than tripled since 1995. And just like any country, the UAE takes very seriously its commitment to raise public awareness about responsible energy consumption, continually educating citizens about their role in initiating sustainable change.

Energy-tariff reform has resulted in lower consumption rates. But because almost all of our new electricity demand is fueled by natural gas, cleaner-burning than oil or coal, this remarkable growth has transformed us into a net importer of natural gas. We realize that a sustainable range of energy resources must fuel balanced growth.

Along with our commitment to relying more heavily on solar energy in the years to come, the UAE is striving to diversify our generation mix and improve energy security. To achieve this, we are relying, in part, on South Korea.

Through our partnership with KEPCO, the UAE will deploy 5,600MW of safe and secure nuclear capacity between 2017 and 2020, enough electricity to meet about 25% of national demand. Our nuclear program is uniquely international, as it doesn't require fuel enrichment or processing. We will have validation from international organizations and governments, and the International Atomic Energy Agency will monitor it.

Without rivers for hydroelectricity or seismic activity for geothermal energy, peaceful nuclear energy is among the most viable, carbon-free base-load energy sources available to our nation as we try to minimize the current environmental impact of our growing cities.

A Green Economy

As you can see, the UAE is using its energy expertise as a foundation for innovating and advancing clean technologies.

Our Green Growth Plan will implement policies in energy, agriculture, investment, and transport to build an economy that protects the environment, supports economic growth and enhances our global competitiveness. Through game-changing clean technology innovations, international partnerships, and investments in measurable sustainability goals, the UAE is already making great progress toward a green economy.

All of these actions are proof of the UAE's proactive role in ensuring a sustainable future for all.

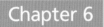

Chapter 6

National Think Tank

Making perpetrators pay the price

Climate change, resource depletion trigger
dramatic global change

Mt. Baekdu eruption's impact on NE Asia

Risk governance in age of uncertainty

Environmental for Future Generations

Making perpetrators pay the price

Chin-keun Park

People participate in a campaign for protecting the quality and supply of water along Cheonggye Stream in downtown Seoul. The government and civic groups have been active in the protection of water supply in recent years. *Korea Times file*

The following is an article compiled by Korea Times reporter Bo-eun Kim based on an interview with Park Chin-keun, chairman of the National Research Council for Economics, Humanities and Social Sciences (NRCS). - ED.

Identifying and assessing the costs incurred to save the environment carry enormous importance from an economic standpoint. Environmental problems such as climate change, depletion of natural resources, and pollution of the environment are not only dangers that we face today but also are factors that deteriorate the quality of our lives.

In trying to overcome these problems, we have no choice but to pay for them, but the cost incurred is another factor that complicates the issue at hand.

It is important that we assess whether the nation can cope with the costs. Being able to determine whether the costs are at an optimal level is not an easy task, but fortunately, research is currently being conducted on this matter.

First, an indicator (either a composite or brand new one) that shows how "green" a nation is should be developed. Then, based on the indicator, one can determine where a nation stands in terms of being committed to conserving the environment. In turn, the optimal level of costs the nation should bear is calculated. Finally, one can examine whether those costs are adequate in relation to the nation's economy.

Paying the price

The dominant principle in a market economy is that when a certain activity incurs social costs, the subject of the activity must pay the price. This is according to the principle of external diseconomies, and a violation of this principle leads to market failure.

External diseconomies are factors that increase the long-run average costs of production, one of which is environmental pollution. When external diseconomies arise, the responsible company should bear the costs.

In the United States, in certain areas where pollution is concentrated with levels of ozone and carbon monoxide that exceed permissible levels, the government has mandated that individuals owning more than a certain number of cars who wish to purchase a new one must purchase a certain percentage of vehicles that use cleaner fuel.

This is an example of a government requiring the perpetrator to take responsibility for the damage caused. However, it is problematic since in most cases, other companies, the victims of these negative factors, end up paying for them. When this happens, production costs of those companies inevitably rise, leading to market distortions. One reason is the inadequate distribution of human resources. But the problem also lies in the fact that the cost structure is distorted.

In China, the price of industrial products is extremely cheap. However, we have to ask ourselves, if China were to implement a proper cost structure, would the Chinese products still be competitive in the international market?

When market failure occurs, government intervention is necessary. Economists believe that environmental problems occur because there is no prices paid for the societal losses that occur when pollutants are discharged.

So the solution that the field of economics presents regarding environmental issues is actually quite simple: it is to ensure that the perpetrator pays the price. For example, if a shoe factory in the upper reaches of a river lets out industrial waste and causes significant damage for fisheries in the lower reaches of the river, it should be the shoe factory that is held responsible.

However, if strict environmental standards were immediately imposed on all corporations in Korea, a significant number would go bankrupt. Consequently, the nation's economy would inevitably suffer.

Ultimately, finding the optimal standard is most important. Each nation is at a different level of economic development, and citizens have differing levels of awareness regarding environmental issues. Therefore, it is crucial that a balance between economic development and environmental pollution be identified.

Ethical Consumerism

In the past, when purchasing goods the main criterion for consumers was price or function. However, today, consumers have started to look into whether the product and its production process are environmentally friendly. We refer to this as ethical consumerism.

Ethical consumerism is the practice of purchasing products and services that minimize social and environmental damage, and of avoiding products that harm society or the environment. This is seen today mainly in developed nations, especially countries in Western Europe.

In essence, ethical consumerism is a practice that heightens consumer sovereignty. And in this case, consumers are willing to pay for the extra costs that occur.

We have yet to see how long this will continue. This is because the market is essentially a system determined by price. However environmentally friendly a product may be, if it is too expensive, it will be difficult for consumers to continue spending so much for it.

International cooperation

Fortunately, human society possesses great intellectual capabilities. We should tackle environmental problems today with a willingness to address these issues through effective international cooperation.

When doing so, we must understand that environmental problems and methods for managing them differ for each and every country. Each country has varying goals, standards and degrees of regulation regarding the environment. The reason is that countries have differing natural environments, and the value that citizens place on the environment also differ.

This also is why some environmental policies favor certain countries, while for others they may be a disadvantage. This can raise the possibility of conflict between nations.

In particular, the Kyoto Protocol implemented in 2005 mandated that developed nations, consisting mostly European nations, reduce the amount of greenhouse gases emitted.

At the Copenhagen climate change conference, developed nations demanded that the greatest emitters such as the United States and China should also be subject to a heavy cut in emissions.

The post-Kyoto era, the period after 2012, when the first commitment period comes to an end, will require more nations to decrease emissions of environmentally hazardous gases.

Cutting down on emissions

Developed nations in Europe and Japan, which are mandated to reduce emissions, especially for carbon dioxide, are stepping up environmental protection in an effort to make environmental industries the breakthrough for economic growth, as growth is increasingly becoming limited.

Accordingly, environmental issues have become the new key agenda in international society today. Environmentalism can be seen in the form of environment-related standards, technology regulations and evaluation standards, and use of superior technologies by nations to protect their own industries.

Another reason international cooperation is essential is that environmental problems are not a single nation's concern. Pollutants effortlessly and inadvertently cross borders and spread to other countries. Pollutants from China easily spread throughout the Korean Peninsula. Various pollutants from China's industrial belts as well as yellow sand continue to flow into Korea's atmosphere.

The principle of the perpetrator bearing the costs of pollution applies to international environmental problems as well. In other words, the country that causes environmental damage is the one that should be held accountable. However, in an international society in which individual nations pursue their sole interests, the principle is close to impossible to adhere to.

As for international cooperation, we are currently in the stage where acceptable norms are being established. But just because we strive to cooperate doesn't mean that all issues can immediately be resolved. There are positive developments, in that research on the environment is actively being pursued around the world.

In the past, institutions would conduct individual research projects. Today, these institutions are collaborating with a common goal. With the study of international cases, there is an active exchange of knowledge occurring, which is definitely a positive sign.

Keeping in mind the fact that environmental problems are directly linked to the survival of all of humanity and not just a single country, we should steadily pursue international cooperation.

Climate change, resource depletion trigger dramatic global change

Eung-kyuk Park

One of the biggest challenges facing mankind and governments across the globe is tackling the dire consequences of climate change, pollution and the destruction of the ecosystem, and natural resource depletion due to the mindless activities of human beings. The effects of these changes are not only lethal to men but also to a vast majority of other species. By and large, the overall effects of these changes have produced natural disasters that have claimed a significant number of lives and property all over the world.

The impact of these changes also has been felt with the attendant increase in temperatures, rising sea levels, economic upheaval, shifting landscapes, and extinction of wildlife, to mention just a few. This impact has shocked the world like nothing before and, if left unchecked, could threaten fundamental biotic existence.

Therefore, it is high time that the entire world begins to realize the significance of these challenges, which have created several imbalances in Earth's life by adjusting the form and abundance of land, sea and air, the three most indispensable elements needed to survive on the planet.

Climate change is real

A number of Earth's inhabitants have complained bitterly about a surging increase in summer temperatures. Some have recounted stories of a "hot" winter, while many others face freezing landmasses. Climate change has unleashed untold havoc on our ecosystem, and the entire world feels its adverse effects.

From mammoth hurricanes in the United States to massive floods in Korea, the entire world is being fazed by the unflinching phenomena of natural disasters, resulting from unprecedented climatic change that is largely attributable to global human activities.

The abnormal change in climate has given rise to a sporadic increase in the occurrence and magnitude of natural disasters around the world, with an expected likelihood of their continuation into the future. Considering the evident rise in temperatures and sea levels, and associated unpredictable events, we do not need further signs to know that the effects of climate change are already wreaking havoc in our world today. Former President of the United States Bill Clinton noted that "the incidence of economically devastating natural disasters will accelerate around the world with the changing of the climate," which is hitting the nail on the head.

Apparently, the looming saga expected to arise from the demise of Mother Earth is more or less a myth to many people. Some have argued blindly that this is not possible, while others have concocted some support to debunk the news. Fortunately, we have passed the initial stage of disagreement, evasion and escapism about the grave effects of climate change. Scientists around the world agree that global warming is a result of the maddening pace of industrialization and anthropogenic greenhouse gases emitted into the atmosphere. Global warming results when gases in the atmosphere (such as methane, nitrous oxide, carbon dioxide and water vapor) retain the heat that the Earth is supposed to radiate back to space. Meanwhile, the quantity of these gases in the atmosphere has increased, owing to a number of human activities, including the burning of fossil fuels and industrialization among others.

A greater number of Earth's inhabitants also have embraced the discovery and have made it an obligation to pursue a way out of the precarious situation. Research conducted at sea, on land and in the air indicates that there has been unprecedented rise in temperatures over the last century and the Earth is experiencing all-time highs. According to the Intergovernmental Panel on Climate Change, "Warming of the climate system is unequivocal, as is now evident from observations of increases in global average air and ocean temperatures, widespread melting of snow and ice and rising global average sea levels."

Global warming, global change

The magnitude of changes effectuated as a result of global warming and climate change is far greater than generally perceived. We have now reached the stage of "global change," which means that the intensity of global warming has spread far beyond changes in weather and carbon emissions to include every sphere of human life: agriculture, natural resources, including water, and fertility, thereby introducing demographic changes, changes in ecosystems, endangering species, migration, and international business.

Changes in temperature, sea level and Northern Hemisphere snow cover

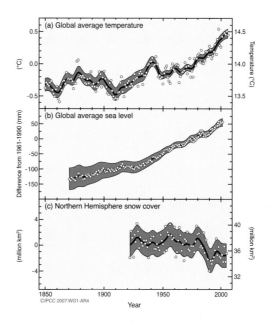

Climate change happens at a global level, but its effects are realized at the local level in all regions of the world. It is now understood that there exists a close inter-relation between global changes and their effects on the local environment. The incidence of high magnitude hurricanes and flash floods and epidemics in flora, fauna and humanity are now more rampant than ever before. Every region is affected to a varying degree - while some regions are significantly affected, making the region unsuitable for habitation, other regions may be only marginally affected. In the Northeast Asian region, China, Japan, and Korea are already highly susceptible to floods, droughts and desertification. The result is unprecedented heavy rainfalls, deforestation, and the concentration of residential and commercial activities in flood prone areas. All of these developments put people at a greater risk, but in many other areas, people face drought and a decreased supply of water from upper regions.

Climate change, resource depletion trigger dramatic global change

Resource depletion

For centuries, men have been in an unending pursuit of convenience and adaptation. They have toiled on Earth to extrude every possible resource and provide the inhabitants of this planet with a new lifestyle, which has been greatly achieved. This dynamic has resulted in more inventions and ultimately, an easier way of life. However, overuse of the planet's resources is reducing the amounts available for future generations and a tougher lifestyle is now beginning to confront the world.

Dating back to an eventful beginning, our planet has been enormously endowed with abundant natural resources. These materials are found naturally in the environment. However, due to an abnormal overstretch in this age's use of resources, the continuous existence of some is under threat. This is regrettably a result of massive exploitation at the hands of humans due to our insatiable desire. The resource depletion has been attributed to the inability to allow for the proper restoration of the materials due to an immense craving for industrialization and economic growth.

To describe the situation, Jerry Marden, an expert with the International Forum on Globalization (IFG), came up with the term "triple crisis", which highlights the prevailing social and ecological forces that are uniting to threaten the biotic existence of our planet and industrial society. The components of this "triple crisis" are (1) a rapid increase in climate disarray resulting from a vast heating up of the planet caused by the accumulation of greenhouse gases, (2) the peaking of the availability of natural gas, oil and coal, which is ushering in a regime of expensive energy, and (3) the depletion of forests, fresh water, coral reefs, wildlife, biodiversity and other natural resources.

A significant part of resource depletion is the end of cheap and abundant oil. The supply of oil on Earth is limited. After some time, we will have consumed 50 percent of the oil, which means that the remaining 50 percent will become costlier, and it will be less and less available, and finally, there will come a stage when there is no oil or when the amount of money and effort needed to recover it will make it unfeasible. The time when we would have consumed 50 percent of the oil is known as "peak oil". It is said that "peak oil" will be a reality one day, and we must prepare ourselves for it.

The rate of resource consumption is a major cause of the dangers that face the Earth. This calls urgently for the world to educate everyone how to deal with the issue of consumption. Such awareness is especially important in the developing world, which tends to imitate every move of developed countries. This awareness should be directed toward checking the uncontrolled burden

Global anthropogenic greenhouse gas emissions

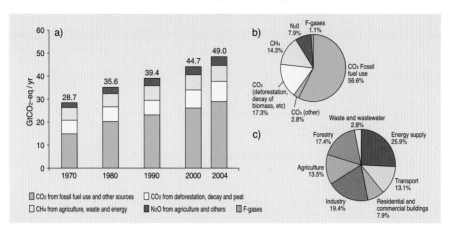

Oil production world summary

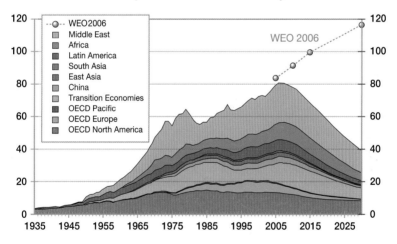

Source: Energy Watch Group: "Crude Oil Supply Outlook," 2007, p.12.

that men place on natural resources and that results in various conflicts around the world.

Destruction of the ecosystem

Pollution also has been a major contributor to the 'sick' nature of our planet. The pollution and destruction of the ecosystem at any point in time results in

Summary of observed changes in extreme events and climate anomalies in Asia

Region Heatwaves	Key trend	Reference
Russia	Heatwaves break past 22-year record in May 2005	Shein, 2006
Mongolia	Heatwave duration has increased by 8 to 18 days in last 40 years; coldwave duration has shortened by 13.3 days	Batima et al., 2005
China	Increase in frequency of short duration heatwaves in recent decade, increasing warmer days and nights in recent decades	Zhai et al., 1999; Zhai and Pan, 2003
Japan	Increasing incidences of daily maximum temperature> 35 degrees C, decrease in extremely low temperatures	Kawahara and Yamazaki, 1999; Japan Meteorological Agency, 2005
Korea	Increasing frequency of extreme maximum temperatures with higher values in the 1980s and the 1990s; decrease in frequency of record low temperatures during 1958 to 2001	Ryoo et al., 2004
India	Frequency of hot days and multiple-day heatwave has increased in past century; increase in deaths due to heat stress in recent years	De and Mukhopadhyay, 1998; Lal, 2003
Southeast Asia	Increase in hot days and warm nights and decrease in cold days and nights between 1961 and 1998	Manton et al., 2001; Cruz et al., 2006; Tran et al., 2005
Intense rains and floods		
Russia	Increase in heavy rains in western Russia and decrease in Siberia; increase in number of days with more than 10mm of rain; 50 to 70% increase in surface runoff in Siberia	Gruza et al., 1999; Izrael and Anokhin,2001; Ruosteenoja et al., 2003; Gruza and Rankova,2004
China	Increasing frequency of extreme rains in western and southern parts including Changjiang river, and decrease in northern regions; more floods in Changjiang river in past decade; more frequent floods in NortheastChina since the 1990s; more intense summer rains in East China; severe flood in 1999; seven-fold increase in frequency of floods since the 1950s	Zhai et al., 1999; Ding and Pan, 2002; Zhai and Pan, 2003; Zhai, 2004
Japan	Increasing frequency of extreme rains in past 100 years attributed to frontal systems and typhoons; serious flood in 2004 due to heavy rains brought on by 10 typhoons; increase in maximum rainfall during 1961 to 2000 based on records from 120 stations	Kawahara and Yamazaki, 1999; Isobe, 2002; Kajiwara et al., 2003; Kanai et al., 2004
South Asia	Serious and recurrent floods in Bangladesh, Nepal and northeastern states of India during 2002, 2003 and 2004; a record 944mm of rainfall in Mumbai, India July 26-27, 2005 led to loss of over 1,000 lives with loss of more than $250 million; floods in Surat, Barmer and in Srinagar during the summer monsoon season of 2006; May 17, 2003 floods in southern province of Sri Lanka were triggered by 730mm of rain	India Meteorological Department, 2002 to 2006; Dartmouth Flood Observatory,2003

Southeast Asia	Increased occurrence of extreme rains causing flash floods in Vietnam; landslides and floods in 1990 and 2004 in the Philippines, and floods in Cambodia in 2000	FAO/WFP, 2000; Environment News Service, 2002; FAO, 2004; Cruz et al., 2006; Tran et al., 2005
Droughts		
Russia	Decreasing rain and increasing temperature by over 1 degrees C have caused droughts; 27 major droughts in 20th century have been reported	Golubev and Dronin,2003; Izrael and Sirotenko, 2003
Mongolia	Increase in frequency and intensity of droughts in recent years; droughts in 1999 to 2002 affected 70% of grasslands and killed 12 million livestock	Batima, 2003; Natsagdorj et al., 2005
China	Increase in area affected by drought has exceeded 6.7 Mha since 2000 in Beijing, Hebei Province, Shanxi Province, inner Mongolia and North China; increase in dust storm affected areas	Chen et al., 2001; Yoshino, 2000, Chen et al., 2001; Yoshino, 2000,
South Asia	50% of droughts associated with El Niño; consecutive droughts in 1999 and 2000 in Pakistan and northwest India led to sharp decline in watertables; consecutive droughts between 2000 and 2002 caused crop failures, mass starvation and affected ~11 million people in Orissa; droughts in northeast India during summer monsoon of 2006	Webster et al., 1998; Lal, 2003; India Meteorological Department, 2006
Southeast Asia	Droughts normally associated with ENSO years in Myanmar, Laos, the Philippines, Indonesia and Vietnam; droughts in 1997 to 1998 caused massive crop failures and water shortages and forest fires in parts of the Philippines, Laos and Indonesia	Duong, 2000; Kelly and Adger, 2000; Glantz, 2001; PAGASA, 2001
Cyclones / typhoons		
Philippines	On an average, 20 cyclones cross the Philippines Area of Responsibility with about 8 to 9 landfall each year; with an increase of 4.2 in the frequency of cyclones entering PAR during the period 1990 to 2003	PAGASA, 2001
China	Number and intensity of strong cyclones increased since the 1950s; 21 extreme storm surges in 1950 to 2004 of which 14 occurred during 1986 to 2004	Gan and Li, 2005
South Asia	Frequency of monsoon depressions and cyclones formation in Bay of Bengal and Arabian Sea on the decline since 1970 but intensity is increasing causing severe floods in terms of damages to life and property	Lal, 2001, 2003
Japan	Number of tropical storms has two peaks, one in mid-1960s and another in the early 1990s; average after 1990 and often lower than historical average	Japan Meteorological Agency, 2005

Source: IPCC, "Working Group II Report: Impacts Adaptation and Vulnerability," Asia Chapter 10, p.47

Climate change, resource depletion trigger dramatic global change a disturbance of the natural balance and affects organisms in different ways. It is necessary to know the effect that a minute act, such as the introduction of toxic waste or sewage into a river, can have on the species of animals and plants in the region.

At last, the entire population of the world is beginning to realize the devastating effects of pollution on the ecosystem. An ecosystem is composed of plants, animals, and the different environmental conditions interacting as one in a given area. There are several ecosystems on this planet acting together with overlapping functions and interdependence. Over the years, it has been stated that the continuous viability and existence of the different ecosystems depends on the strict maintenance of a very delicate balance in their formation and composition.

In the meantime, the rate of ecosystem destruction due to the introduction of pollutants is alarming and needs to be addressed. Lead, detergent, nitrogen from fertilizers, and oil are capable of destroying the stability of the ecosystem. For example, pollution can unleash devastating effects on the ecological balance of a lake by enhancing the growth of plants while causing the death of numerous fish as a result of suffocation from oxygen deficiency. In this case, pollution stops the oxygen cycle, which renders the polluted water useless for animals that depend on the lake as a source of life and water.

Indeed, awareness of the destruction of our ecosystem is a duty for us all. The far-reaching impact of polluted water is known to be severe due to its continuous travel across many lands. This makes us understand that the destruction of an ecosystem ultimately affects other ecosystems within the environment. The overall effect of the incessant destruction of ecosystems on the planet through pollution will in turn reduce our quality of life and endanger the possibility of passing the baton of existence to future generations.

Entropy: A new worldview

With all the problems facing our world, the impending catastrophe must be averted by all means. In his famous book, "Entropy: A New World View," Jeremy Rifkin submitted that the principle of entropy entails that our present world has begun to wind down, the irrefutable result of a long-term colossal exploitation of natural ecosystems.

Although not very often, there are times when ideas come forward that modify human history. One such idea is the Entropy Law. According to this law, energy migrates inevitably from an orderly system to a disordered one and from a stable to an unstable entity. This implies that whenever there is an appearance of a created order at any point on Earth, or in the universe, the immediate environment bears the effect of the disorderliness that results. After an age-long debut in the 19th century, the world has recently felt the need to explore the maximum implication of this law.

Rifkin provided the basic re-conceptualization of entropy as it applies to the everyday life of an individual on this planet. With entropy, he was able to provide answers as to why civilization has not been able to achieve peace and order despite inventions and technology but in fact has produced the opposite results: pollution, chaos, crisis and decay. For everyone who wonders why nothing seems to work anymore and why the solving of one crisis usually begets another, often larger one, entropy has the right answers for them. It is an important concept necessary to the proper understanding of the world.

Rifkin also noted that humanity is now at the fringe of its most important experiment to date, one based on remodeling human consciousness in order to ensure the survival of human beings in the new global society, so as to live mutually with one another. Amid these and many other concerns such as waste management, deforestation, water scarcity, energy depletion and so on, the earth's population needs to be aware of the need to live in a way that is more sustainable.

Ways to save our planet

To solve the challenges posed by global change, we need to understand that they are the result of our actions and inactions. We have collectively failed to shoulder our responsibility toward Mother Earth, and we all need to do our bit to save the planet. We need to rise up to the challenges and work to save Mother Nature itself and also the vast numbers of species that form our ecosystems.

So far, mankind has developed tools to tailor environments, instead of adjusting to the environment. With technological advancements, we have tried to better our lives and gain the upper hand over nature, but in the process we have interfered with and disturbed the evolutionary process of the Earth with our mindless actions. This mad rush to move faster and faster has brought us to the point of no return, as we face severe crises on the social and environmental fronts. The need of the hour is to create a collective effort in the form of government policies that are in tandem with Mother Nature and the ecosystems.

In order to save our planet, a few steps need to be taken by everyone, and the cumulative efforts will give us a more sustained planet to pass on the baton of life. The first place to start is by conserving energy resources. This can be achieved if everyone turns off the fans, lights, televisions and every other electronic appliance whenever they are not in use. Conducting a regular servicing of household devices is also an essential part to utilize less energy, thereby reducing the menace of global warming. In addition, proper maintenance of cars and other motor devices is one of the most important steps to save this planet. Exhaust from vehicles is a major contributor to environmental pollution.

Considering the number of problems and challenges plaguing the world, the task of saving the planet is a duty we all have to accept. Think about taking a walk when it is not necessary to take the car. Doing this will boost your health, save some gas and ultimately save the planet. There are a lot of small actions that can be taken by every individual. Every inhabitant of the planet should contribute and these efforts will accumulate into all the differences we need to save the planet.

In the meantime, the most significant of all changes to be made is the modification of consciousness, which is important for the purpose of reaching out to fellow human beings. Forming resistance against this change will harm our resolution to tackle the challenges surrounding us. Moreover, as the world travels through the magnified forces of globalization, the age-long rational mode of consciousness will soon become a source of danger to all humanity. Without a doubt, the future implications that are expected to arise from the surfacing of empathetic consciousness will be profound and extensive. Therefore, the time to act is now. This is our planet. We have to save the Earth!

Mt. Baekdu eruption's impact on NE Asia

Chang-seok Park

Citing the rise of the surface temperature of Mt. Baekdu, geologists predict its eruption in a couple of years. *Korea Times file*

Yes, one! There's only one thing about which they think in the same way - the concern about a possible eruption of Mt. Baekdu. The two Koreas remain at odds about everything. But they are one in discussing how to counter the possible volcanic explosion of the highest mountain on the Korean Peninsula.

Inter-Korean anxiety is mounting, with growing apocalyptic predictions about the dormant volcano. A South Korean geological expert has warned that the volcano could erupt sometime around 2014 and 2015.

Former North Korean leader Jong-il Kim reportedly said people in some regions of Yanggang and North Hamgyeong Provinces were feeling anxiety over a volcanic eruption of Mt. Baekdu. Kim called for quick countermeasures by the North Korean authorities.

If the volcano located on the border between North Korea and China erupts, damage could be 10 to 100 times greater than that caused by the April 2010 eruptions in Iceland. Experts predict that the ashes would not only hit the neighboring area but also would damage agriculture and cause serious disruptions in industrial activities and air flights. The Korean Peninsula, China, Japan and Russia would be severely damaged.

A volcanic eruption begins when pressure in a magma chamber forces magma up through the conduit and out the volcano's vents. When the magma chamber is completely filled, the type of eruption partly depends on the amount of gas and silica in the magma. The amount of silica determines how sticky (level of viscosity) the magma; water provides the explosive potential of steam.

The 2010 Iceland eruption caused enormous disruption to air travel across Western and Northern Europe, although relatively small in size for volcanic eruptions. About 20 countries closed their airspace, and hundreds of thousands of travelers were affected. A very high proportion of flights within, to, and from Europe were cancelled, creating the highest level of air travel disruption since World War II.

Geological studies

Fears of a Mt. Baekdu eruption loom large with ensuing warnings based on a series of geological studies from experts. A growing number of scholars have not ruled out the possibility of another eruption, linking the collapse of Korea's ancient kingdom, Balhae, with the previous one.

One theory comes from Professor Hiroshi Machida of Tokyo Metropolitan University. Machida first presented his view in 1992 that the eruption of Mt. Baekdu (Mt. Changbai in Chinese) led to the fall of Balhae, which had expanded its sovereignty to the vast Manchuria territory. His theory was based on volcanic ash found in Tomakomai, a port city in southern Hokkaido, in 1981. The ash was named "Baekdu-Tomakomai volcanic ash" (B-Tm) after Mt. Baekdu and Tomakakomi city where it was found, according to So Won-ju, who wrote the book "Secret of Mt. Baekdu's Great Eruption."

Machida's theory has gained momentum as an increasing number of geologists and climate change researchers have presented views that the ash was produced in the eruption of the highest mountain on the Korean Peninsula in the 10th century. The eruption of the 2,744 meter-high mountain was billed as the largest in the history of mankind, about 50 times stronger than that of Mt. Vesuvius, Italy in 79 A.D., which led to the burying and destruction of the Roman city Pompeii.

Balhae (Bohai in Chinese) was established by Dae Jo-yeong, a former Goguryeo general, in 698 after the fall of Goguryeo. Dae Jo-yeong took the helm of Jin (Zhen in Chinese), founded by his father Dae Jung-sang in 696, and renamed the country Balhae, declaring it as the successor state of Goguryeo (37 B.C. - 668 A.D.).

Balhae's ruin

Balhae occupied the southern parts of Manchuria and Primorsky Krai (now Russia's Far East), and the northern part of the Korean Peninsula. The Khitans defeated it in 926, and most of its northern territories were absorbed into the Liao Dynasty, also known as the Khitan Empire, founded in 907, while the southern parts were absorbed into Goryeo Kingdom (918-1392).

A dominant view related to Balhae's decline had been the Khitans' 926 invasion. Some conventional historians believe that the rampancy of ethnic conflicts between the ruling Koreans and underclass Mohe (Malgal) caused its fall. But others refute these allegations, giving more weight to the catastrophic explosion of Mt. Baekdu as a primary cause for Balhae's ruin rather than Khitans' attack.

Balhae had been engaged in a war with the Khitans for about two weeks and then collapsed immediately. How could Balhae with a long 200-year history fall so easily in such a short period of time? Some historians have raised doubts about the early collapse, pointing to Mt. Baekdu as a cause for Balhae's ruin.

The massive explosion was believed to have created a tremendous amount of volcanic ash, damaging agriculture and even societal integrity. The Khitans were believed to have taken advantage of this natural disaster in putting the volcano-stricken Balhae under their complete control. The eruption might have prevented Balhae survivors from rebuilding their nation.

A variety of indicators suggested by geologists and Balhae dynasty researchers who have monitored the change of Baekdu's geographical features back a scenario of the recurrence of Mt. Baekdu eruptions. Some experts say that an eruption is imminent. Geologist Yoon Sung-hyo at Pusan National University strongly believes Mt. Baekdu could erupt anytime.

According to historical records, major activity on the mountain in the 940s created a caldera at its peak whose circumference is nearly 14 kilometers, with an average depth of 213 meters and a maximum of 384 meters. Atop the mountain is Cheonji, literally meaning "heavenly lake," the largest caldera in the world.

Volcanic ash

Volcanic ash from Mt. Baekdu eruptions has been found as far away as the southern part of Hokkaido, Japan. Geologists predict the occurrence of great Mt. Baekdu eruptions every 1,000 years and that of minor ones every 200 to 300 years. Minor eruptions were recorded in 1413, 1597, 1668 and 1702 with the last activity being recorded in 1903.

Among other indicators backing the scenario of a future eruption is the height of Mt. Baekdu, which has grown nearly 10 centimeters since 2002. Experts say an expanding magma pool, a precondition for an eruption, is gradually pushing up the height of the mountain as well as the temperature on the surface. On Oct. 1, 2006, a Russian satellite found the surface temperature of the mountain notably higher than before. The finding came just days after North Korea conducted an underground nuclear test in its northern territory, which could have been a catalyst for reactivating magma flows, according to analysts.

Mt. Baekdu has been carefully observed since 1999 when a volcanic observatory was built in China, and since 2002, there have been some symptoms of an eruption. Seismic activity near the mountain has increased dramatically, and the concentrations of hydrogen and helium emissions, both volcanic gases, have risen 10-fold. There is ample possibility that Mt. Baekdu may erupt in the near future.

If Mt. Baekdu erupts, it would no doubt bring about grave consequences for the two Koreas as well as surrounding states, including China, Japan and Russia. The biggest immediate threat is the two billion tons of water in the lake on top of the crater. An eruption would likely cause severe flood damage, engulfing roads and homes within a 30-kilometer radius in just three hours and 20 minutes, a geological report recently predicted.

Mt. Baekdu's caldera

The greatest victim of a Mt. Baekdu explosion might be North Korea, especially Yanggang and Hamgyeong Provinces. These two regions, located on the tip of the Korean Peninsula, could be covered with ash in just two hours.

In about eight hours, ash could reach Ulleungdo and Dokdo, two far eastern islands of South Korea, and in 12 hours, Tottori Prefecture, Japan. After 18 hours, volcanic ash would likely spread beyond Japan.

The National Institute for Disaster Prevention conducted a simulation in 2010 to test how far volcanic ash could spread if Mt. Baekdu erupts. According to the results, the effects could differ depending on the timing. If an eruption happens in winter, Japan is expected to be more affected due to the northwest monsoon. On the other hand, a summer eruption would affect South Korea more.

Mt. Baekdu's caldera has nearly two billion tons of water. If volcanic heat evaporates the water and is mixed suddenly with volcanic ashes, it would be strong enough to engulf even Vladivostok in Russia and Hokkaido in northern Japan, according to experts. The construction of nuclear power plants by North Korea and China in the neighborhood may certainly pose a grave threat to all Northeast Asians, given the view that Mt. Baekdu's explosion would for sure cause subsequent nuclear catastrophes, as seen in Japan's 2011 tsunami disaster. A volcanic explosion is the most terrible natural disaster that cannot be easily avoided by human wisdom and knowledge.

With unrelenting outbreaks of record-breaking natural disasters around the world, and especially in the wake of Japan's massive earthquake that is now estimated to have killed nearly 10,000, the world's eyes are drawn to Mt. Baekdu. Multinational and regional cooperative monitoring systems are needed to take preemptive measures against a possible eruption.

By all indications, Mt. Baekdu is a real danger and it's not clear how long it will stay inactive. A Mt. Baekdu eruption, if it takes place, will not be a matter for one country but a global concern to determine the future of Northeast Asian civilization.

Risk governance in age of uncertainty

Eun-sung Kim

We are now living in an age of uncertainty arising from the development of emerging technologies such as biotechnology, nanotechnology, information technology, neuroscience and their convergence. At present, many nations see emerging technologies as future growth engines and make enormous investments in research and development (R&D). However, it is still uncertain whether or not the technologies will ultimately contribute to economic growth and to sustainable development and improving the quality of life.

Genetically modified organisms are at risk of genetic pollution within an ecosystem in which their genes are transferable from species to species. In the case of nanotechnology, the U.S. Environmental Protection Agency (EPA) warned in 2006 that silver nano-particles can have an adverse impact on the liver and kidneys. But scientific evidence with regard to the benefits and risks of emerging technologies is lacking.

How does uncertainty affect our lives and the way of governing technologies? First, uncertainty enables the production of various technological futures, whether they rosy or dystopian. The uncertainty of technological futures is part of science fiction novels and many movies. Many sci-fi films like "Blade Runner," "The Matrix" and "The Island" depict and construct future societies with future imaginaries of emerging technologies such as biotechnology, nanotechnology and information technology. However, the production of futures is not confined to movies but also takes place in governmental policies and public debates in civil society.

Uncertainty and social conflict

The government tends to draw rosy futures surrounding technology policies, while civic and environmental organizations sketch dismal futures arising from social and ecological upheavals resulting from emerging technologies. Various futures of emerging technologies are in conflict between governmental and non-governmental organizations. In this sense, technological futures, whatever humans touch, are not detached from the present value and interest of stakeholders. Futures are socially constructed.

Second, uncertainty yields social conflict. It also poses an enormous challenge to scientific expertise in risk decision-making as well as in dealing with social conflicts arising from emerging technologies. Various technological futures conflict in social debate. Unfortunately, scientific knowledge is limited to dealing with uncertainty because the speed of technological development is too fast. It is hard fully to predict the multiple social, environmental effects of fast-moving technologies.

The decline of trust in scientific experts and of scientific authority in the face of uncertainty can trigger social conflict associated with emerging technologies. Alternately, social conflict increases scientific uncertainty. In other words, uncertainty is socially constructed. Uncertainty goes beyond the scope of expert knowledge and is closely tied to social interests.

Uncertainty arises not only from a lack of knowledge but also from the superfluity of knowledge. In the contemporary knowledge society, an affluence of knowledge does not mean the rise of certainty but rather the growth of uncertainty due to the production of various knowledge spaces such as newspapers, social media, and the Internet as well as knowledge producers working in these places. Given uncertainty, scientific knowledge of risk analysis reaches its limit in accordance with the decline of trust in governmental policies that depend on scientific experts. In this vein, some scholars depict the age of uncertainty as one of "post-trust societies" or as the age of "post-normal science."

Third, regulatory laws are limited in the face of uncertainty. They cannot enforce legal command and control with respect to risky technologies absent adequate scientific evidence of their risks. In the absence of scientific evidence, strong laws are of no use in dealing with emerging technologies. They have to wait until scientific evidence is forthcoming. However, the postponement of regulatory actions can result in serious consequences, since it is possible that a small amount of emerging technologies has the potential to adversely affect human health and the environment on a wide scale.

Risk management strategies

Given this limitation, what are the desirable risk management strategies for coping with the uncertainty of emerging technologies? The first strategy is trial and error. The aim of that is to learn from the experience of minor errors, as the proverb "look before you leap" warns. Trial and error learns from mistakes incrementally by phasing in policy actions rather than enforcing policies all at once. It facilitates learning from the experience of errors through building effective monitoring and feedback systems.

Can we really trust all of the new high-tech?

The second strategy is a precautionary principle. It arises from the idea of being "better safe than sorry." This principle denotes the idea that precautionary measures should be required in the absence of scientific evidence whenever the potential consequences of emerging technologies are severe and irreversible. Risk foresight and risk aversion are essential to the policy function of the precautionary principle.

Traditional risk policy is aimed at optimizing risk-by-risk benefit analysis, while the precautionary principle tries to minimize risk by predicting and avoiding risk before it occurs. It involves applying varying degrees of regulation to risk policies. It is related not only to banning and prohibiting risky materials but also to building early warning and lifecycle monitoring systems for the entire technological production process from R&D to consumption.

The third strategy is design phase intervention. It is significant to enforce risk policy at the design stage of emerging technologies. This is because it is extremely difficult to withdraw risky technologies after they are built into industrial infrastructure and embedded in consumption culture. This is the phenomenon of technological inflexibility. Technology tends to create inflexibility to policy actions, depending on the size of investment capital and the dependence of consumer life on embedded technologies.

Accordingly, risk policies for emerging technologies should be implemented at the design stage rather than after they are developed. At the stage of technological innovation, R&D policies should be combined with risk management, in order that reflexive innovation systems can be constructed.

The fourth strategy is to attain technological pluralism in the R&D of emerging technologies. Technological pluralism refers to the diversification of technological choice in the technological innovation process by developing various alternatives to replace dominant technologies. Green chemistry is an alternative to traditional chemistry that leads to environmental pollution. The development of various alternative technologies enables the reduction of social and economic shocks resulting from the phasing out of dominant technologies given that their risks are proven. How is 'alternative' alternative enough? That is subject to the interpretation of stakeholders and users. Moreover, alternative technologies can also risk yielding unpredictable consequences later. Continuous risk assessment and monitoring of alternative technologies are necessary.

Technological pluralism begins with the imagination of various technological futures. The imagination itself is not only for scientists and engineers, albeit they can materialize these futures. Rather all stakeholders, including other experts and consumers, should imagine alternative technological futures. Therefore, comprehensive interdisciplinary and social communication of technological futures is vital to technological pluralism. Technological pluralism coincides with social pluralism.

The fifth strategy is to strengthen self-regulation in research organizations and companies. In the wake of emerging technologies, bureaucratic command and control shifts to a way of self-regulation where companies and research organizations build voluntary codes of conduct for the safety management of emerging technologies. If there is an absence of external control, the self-regulation approach fails absent internal control systems or a voluntary safety culture. For example, the rate of voluntary participation of companies in self-regulation is not high in the case of nanotechnology. Small- and medium-sized companies are unwilling to comply with a voluntary code of conduct. In turn, the presence of a voluntary code of conduct should be used as an indicator of evaluation in the selection and evaluation processes of national R&D.

Moreover, it is necessary to monitor whether or not companies comply with responsible codes of conduct related to the safety management of emerging technologies.

The sixth strategy is to improve public communication and the public's right to know about emerging technologies. A new way of public communication is necessary in the age of uncertainty and "post-trust societies." Traditional public communication based on an announce-and-defense strategy is limited in the face of the uncertainty of emerging technologies. People do not trust expert arguments because they receive new risk information from new knowledge spaces such as the Internet and social media. People are not consumers of risk information but rather secondary producers of it. Therefore, it is necessary to build interactional or multidirectional channels between the government and civil society.

Participatory governance

The seventh strategy is participatory governance. The rise of emerging technologies is co-produced with the emergence of participatory governance in R&D and risk policies. This is because expert knowledge lacks public trust in the age of uncertainty. Communication between experts and citizens is vital to the governance of emerging technologies. In this vein, participatory technology assessments such as consensus conferences and citizen juries have been used in several countries. However, it is still debatable how much participatory technology assessment can affect technology innovation and technology policy as well. A recent study on the ethical, legal, and social implications of biotechnology was criticized because it was separate from the R&D of biotechnology. In the wake of this critique, a new form of technology assessment called real-time technology assessment is on the rise in the governance of nanotechnology in the United States.

Real-time technology assessment is a form of anticipatory governance that forecasts the future impacts of emerging technologies through collaboration between scientists, social scientists, and citizens. It seeks a reflexive, responsible innovation system by directly intervening in the research and development of emerging technologies. Real-time tech assessment takes place within a laboratory instead of by outside technology assessment agencies. The government should launch a new R&D plan for interdisciplinary R&D to enhance collaboration between scientists, social scientists, and citizens associated with emerging technologies.

However, alternative risk policies above are unable to remove uncertainty perfectly but rather help us to cope with it. In an age of uncertainty, we should abandon the ideal or hope of certainty. Rather, this hope increases uncertainty. Alternative risk policies must address new uncertainties.

It is not about overcoming uncertainty but rather adapting to it. On this understanding, uncertainty is not a wicked monster. It is rather more like the destiny of Sisyphus in Greek's myth. As Sisyphus rolls a rock to the top of a mountain, it again rolls down. Likewise, uncertainty is like a Sisyphean existential destiny that policymakers must face forever. The most important blessing of uncertainty is reflexivity. It leads all stakeholders, including government officials, experts, and citizens, to be humble.

Ignorance keeps people modest. Therefore, the most desirable disposition in the age of uncertainty is to affirm uncertainty and then to undertake reflexive decision-making.

Environmental for Future Generations

Yong-seok Seo

More than 4,000 elementary school students gather at Dockweiler State Beach in Playa del Rey, Calif., to create a message of protecting the ocean from litter and urban runoff June 4, 2009, at the 16th annual Kids Ocean Day. *AP-Yonhap*

The early 1970s could be described as the years of self-realization. It was during these years that the world community became aware of their responsibilities toward future generations. For the very first time, people became aware of the toll that modern technology was taking on nature and its resources. They began to realize the dire consequences it could have on ecology and the climate.

Gradually, this awareness spread as more people became aware of the finite natural resources and the vulnerability of Mother Earth. People started thinking about the future of coming generations. People began to ponder the earth's future and what legacy would we leave for future generations if we continued so-called "progress" at the current pace. They talked about our responsibilities toward future generations and the privileges that these generations might not be able to enjoy.

While talking about mankind, we refer to the existence of humans as of today and in the future. It is our duty to ensure that future generations enjoy the right to a healthy environment. Therefore, it becomes obligatory for us to conserve our environment and safeguard it for all living beings and things in the present era as well as for forthcoming generations.

This duty toward future generations is described in the theory of intergenerational justice. The theory articulates that "all members of each generation of human beings, as a species, inherit a natural and cultural patrimony from past generations, both as beneficiaries and as custodians under the duty to pass on this heritage to future generations." It implies that each generation plays a dual role, as a beneficiary to the legacy and as a custodian of this legacy to be passed on to future generations. Therefore, it becomes obligatory for each generation to use this legacy so that it passes on to future generations in the same condition it was received.

Who are the future generation? This would no doubt include unborn children and the children that will be born in the coming year; it also includes all who will be living on the earth after hundreds of years. Since these heirs would inherit our environment after hundreds of years, it is quite likely that we may not yet be according them due importance.

Our Duties toward Future Generations

The power to allow or disallow forthcoming generations from benefitting and using natural and cultural resources vests within the present generation. The 20th century experienced the mindless slaughter of natural resources. Recent generations have used natural resources such as water, air and soil as dumping grounds and exacted a heavy toll on them. As a result, future generations will be penalized with polluted and inferior water and air, causing serious harm to the planet, animals and to the health of human beings. This greed and short-sightedness of present generations has created an enormous burden and risk for future generations.

There's another major impact on the environment in the distant future. We are on the verge of a population explosion. While global population has reached a record high, the resources to meet the increasing population have not increased in the same ratio. On the contrary, we are destroying the limited resources at a rapid speed, and very soon we will have used up all the non-renewable resources totally. The increase in human activity is also posing a serious threat to renewable resources like fresh water, fish stocks, and forests; before long, these will become non-renewable! As the result of anthropogenic climate change, the Northern Hemisphere is likely to get warmer with an improvement in fertility, but most of the world is less fertile and less habitable. Besides, the production of nuclear energy could threaten the very existence of thousands of future generations if nuclear emissions are released in the atmosphere or through improper nuclear waste disposal. Millions have been rendered homeless as a result of the disastrous effects that recent generations have caused. Unless we take concrete preventive steps in this direction, the incidence and impact of these disasters will only multiply and will seriously affect the lifestyle and standard of living of future generations.

The life of future generations could be severely affected by the present generation through a population explosion, creating a biosphere imbalance, using up all the natural resources, and harming the environment through nuclear waste storage. Future generations are at the receiving end, and unless we protect them, they will have to face dire consequences because of our activity. Since future generations have no say in the choices we make, and since there is no one to represent their case in the present, or to forward their case or affect the present generation in any way, their interests are overlooked at the time of political and socioeconomic planning.

International Community's Drive to Protect Future Generations

Fortunately, over the last 40 years or so, there has been an awakening in the international community and they have realized their duties towards future generations. It is this increasing awareness that has broached the subject of intergenerational justice under the spectrum of international environmental ethics.

In 1972, the United Nations Conference was held at Stockholm to discuss the Human Environment. The first principle of the Stockholm Declaration discusses the grave responsibility of humans to preserve and better the environment for both present and future generations. Later in 1987, in the Brundtland Report on Our Common Future, the World Commission on the Environment and Development adopted the concept of "sustainable development". This simply means that developmental steps should be taken in a way so as not to harm the interests of future generations.

Later, at the Rio Earth Summit held in Brazil after a period of almost five years, the international community voiced serious concern about the quality of life anticipated for future generations. The Convention on Biological Diversity, the Convention on Climate Change, and the Rio Declaration on Environment and Development supported the idea of acknowledging our duties toward future generations. This stand was further fortified by adding that development needs must be met by keeping in view the environmental and developmental needs of both the future as well as present generations, and by keeping a healthy balance between development and preserving the environment.

The Rio Declaration has framed the manner in which state parties need to keep in view the interests of future generations. It states that the efforts of parties to protect the climate system in the interests of both present and future generations must occur according to the individual state's capacities, and must shoulder segregated responsibilities as per their capabilities. These declarations give us insight into the seriousness of the international community to protect the coming generations. The Rio Summit was crucial for charting out a detailed program that set standards for global sustainable development to ensure appropriate quality of life for future generations. It was an indication that the present generation feels one with mankind and is willing to take steps to safeguard the interests of future generations.

Moreover, the 1993 the World Conference on Human Rights adopted the Vienna Declaration and Program of Action, which also supported the idea of duties of the present to future generations. In the 29th session of UNESCO's General Conference held in Paris in November 1997, a Declaration on the Duties of the Present Generations towards Future Generations was adopted. Although this was not of a legal format, it did have a moral and ethical binding, as the declaration were the result of several years of debate and discussion among experts and member states.

Overall, the debate on providing intergenerational justice to future generations has gained momentum over the last 40 years. The focus had been around how current policies would affect future generations. However, as we have witnessed environmental extremes in recent years, it is now clearer than ever that the implications of mindless use of natural resources may be more serious than hitherto predicted. The pace at which resources are degraded and destroyed with noticeable climate change implies that we are violating the terms of intergenerational justice to our direct descendants.

Time for Action

We in the present generation should be forewarned about the damage we are inflicting on our environment and our own health. However, looking to the future, the cumulative effects of our activities that are changing the climate and depleting natural resources, will create even greater costs and damage for the future. Future generations will bear the dire consequences caused by present and recent environmental devastation. Such damage poses long-lasting threats that will diminish the health and well being of future generations. As Edith Brown Weiss notes, "We have a right to use and enjoy the system but no right to destroy its robustness and integrity for those who come after us."

It is about time that we gave thoughtful consideration to protecting future generations. The current administrative and legal system either ignores or analyzes irrationally the interests of coming generations through practices such as discounting and cost-benefit analysis. There's no provision in our culture to do something for future generations. We cannot afford only to protect our own interests, and we must learn how to speak for future generations. It is about time that we rise and speak for the interests of future generations so that they are able to live on a healthy planet.

Chapter 7

Journalist

Does Earth really need our protection?
Ocean pollution and int'l cooperation

Does Earth really need our protection?

Jake J. Nho

The quality of water in the upper reaches of the Han River has in fact been improving in recent years as is the case in many other rivers in Korea. Experts say this is the result of residents and visitors taking more care when they are in the vicinity to ensure less water pollution. *Korea Times file*

A question people have faced since at least 30 years ago is, "Why does the Earth need protecting?" Or perhaps better, "Why is there so much concern about environmental protection?"

Around the end of the 1980s, there was a continuous flow of reports in the media about a giant hole in the ozone layer as a result of the excessive carbon gas emissions. The reports made it sound as if everyone was going to die of skin cancer because the ozone layer was no longer going to be there to protect us. But do we talk about the ozone layer now? And did a majority of the Earth's population get skin cancer? Not by a long shot.

These days, there are streams of reports in the media (again) about yellow sand blowing into Korea from China. This is scientifically true. But when was the last time you had to go to hospital for exposure to yellow sand? Hard to remember, isn't it?

Global warming is another big, big issue, and many experts are convinced that the end of the world is upon us because of increasing temperatures and the consequences.

The world as we know it evolves one way or another. There are parts of the world that lack potable water, and people are suffering. There are parts of the world where people cannot dwell because of harsh climate conditions.

But the fact of the matter is that while all this would indicate the global population should be shrinking at an alarming rate, it is not. The last time I checked, the global population was increasing with absolutely no signs that we will head in the opposite direction. In fact, many people are concerned that world population is increasing too quickly. If the global environment is so terrible, why would this be happening?

There are constant reports in the media (again), supported scientifically, that ice in the Antarctic is melting, leading to sea levels rising. How does this affect the health of your family?

I am forever the optimist and am one of those people who believe that Armageddon is not upon us. The end of the world could have come many times over, but it did not.

So we come back to the question of whether or not the Earth really needs our protection, if in reality the whole thing is about scientists and the media trying to make a living by feeding fear.

We really do not know if the world is coming to an end, but if it is, it is certainly would not be because we failed to protect our environment. I checked my facts, and the Earth has the ability to protect itself.

Fact checking

Let's look at the facts. According to the National Academy of Sciences of the United States, global temperatures have increased by 0.2 degrees Celsius per decade over the past 30 years. If this is true, temperatures have increased by 0.6 degrees Celsius in 30 years.

When you ask a meteorological center what the temperature is going to be tomorrow, it will say, for example, 10 degrees Celsius, but it can turn out to be 15 degrees. That's a difference of five degrees in a single day, based on information from people who watch the weather for a living. How does that compare with 0.6 degrees in 30 years, if in fact that is correct?

That report from the National Academy of Sciences goes on to say, "We conclude that global warming of more than 1 degree, relative to 2000, will constitute dangerous climate change as judged from likely effects on sea levels and extermination of species."

Let's assume that they are intelligent people and that their assumptions are true. That change of one degree will affect the sea level and exterminate species. So what? The animal kingdom has reigned on the Earth for millions, probably billions of years, and we are still here.

There are implications arising from changes in the sea level, but time has proven that the Earth and its people can deal with them. Dangerous climate change? The climate changes every day whether or not you do anything about it.

Choices for a better environment

Many of the findings reported by scientists and the media alert the world about dangers we are facing. Interestingly enough, there are often no solutions discussed in these reports.

They talk about the need to reduce the emission of carbon gases to stop global warming as if this is going to lead to the annihilation of the Earth and everyone on it. Not true.

Leakage of all types of chemicals into rivers and seas has occurred. While this is something that must be stopped, history has shown that the planet's strength can cope with it.

Consider the earthquake and the tsunami that occurred in northeastern Japan last year and the devastation they brought to nuclear power plants in Fukushima.

There are reports of radioactive contamination resulting from the "meltdown" of the power plants, and 53 of 54 nuclear power plants in Japan have been shut down.

But how serious is the radioactive contamination? Investigations have shown that they have affected water tens of kilometers away, but the effects of the contamination remain unclear at best.

Martin Freer, a professor of nuclear physics at the University of Birmingham and director of the Birmingham Center for Nuclear Education and Research, said in a recent newspaper column: "We need to promote a much more inclusive and informed dialogue about if nuclear power is to be assessed on its genuine merits, rather than dismissed on the grounds of little

261

more than ignorance and intransigence." This is a supportive statement of the fact that politicians, government officials and virtually everyone else overreact when it comes to the environment.

Overreacting to the environment

Overreacting? This will probably raise serious arguments, but facts and history show us that we have indeed been overreacting to situations and circumstances over which we have no control.

Experts talk about global warming all the time and the need to reduce the emission of carbon gases and other hazardous chemicals into the environment. Is this happening? No. We notice that automobile companies have been developing hybrid and electric cars in an effort to reduce pollution through reducing the use of fossil fuels. This concept is actually strange since there appear to be other much more cost effective and less time consuming alternatives.

Finding alternatives

One of the propositions I make to organizations like the Ministry of Knowledge Economy, which engineers energy policies, is to increase the price of gasoline and other automotive fuels to discourage regular motorists from driving unnecessarily.

The reason is that, as reported (again) in a newspaper last week, many people drive their vehicles simply because they have them, without practical or economic thought.

For these people, gasoline should cost at least 4,000 won per liter (about double what it is now) to enlighten them about using public transport systems like buses and subways.

These buses and trains run whether or not people take them; most buses use concentrated natural gas, and subway trains operate using electricity, meaning they generate virtually no pollution.

And yet, people choose, wrongly, to drive their cars to work. This is not only a waste of time and energy, but it creates huge amounts of air and other forms of pollution, probably much more than the yellow sand from China.

Responsibility

When there is discussion about environmental pollution, we look at industrial companies, hinting that they cause air and water to become dirty. While some of these arguments are true, most leading companies like steel giant POSCO make dedicated efforts to prevent such pollution. In each of the steel mills they operate, more than one trillion won ($ 900 million) is invested to ensure that none of the water from its processing systems reaches rivers unpurified. The same is true for companies like Samsung Electronics and LG Electronics because they recognize the potential of the contribution they could make to polluting the Earth.

What this argument leads to is the following: countless companies and organizations clearly are aware of the danger of environmental pollution, and they invest significant amounts of money to prevent the consequences.

In the end, it is up to us as individuals, all six billion of us, to take the precautions needed to help preserve the environment, and this is not as hard as some people imagine.

Take the bus and the subway. It may be a little inconvenient at times, but it is a small contribution that we can make for the betterment of the planet that we live on.

Some people worry that the world we are going to leave behind for future generations is going to be hazardous. The worries stop here. Government policies are great when they work, but the small little things that we can do, if we insist that we have the responsibility for protecting the Earth and the environment, are really simple.

Ocean pollution and int'l cooperation

Yearn-hong Choi

Giant water fountains reach out to the night skies near the beach in Mokpo, South Jeollla Province, during a recent festival held to celebrate the rich resources the sea brings to humans. *Korea Times file*

The sea is one, but nations want to divide and conquer it. The ocean does not acknowledge national boundary lines, Exclusive Economic Zones (EEZs) or other political demarcations. As a matter of fact, the sea ridicules and denies the existence of human constructions.

Nations want to remake and expand their ocean territories - because they contain living and mineral resources - by inventing EEZs in and under the sea. But fish freely migrate, not to mention tsunamis, because they enjoy the freedom of currents and waves.

Nations do not always agree with each other regarding coastlines, sovereign control of waters, EEZs and where continental shelves begin and end.

Nations invest millions of dollars to exploit ocean resources and secure military power on the sea to study sea beds and justify their claims over a continental shelf.

We cannot divide the sea and draw lines on water. Water evaporates, producing clouds and rain for living things on land.

The oceans appear to ridicule the wisdom of humankind in the 21st century. Nature or the Big Bang made the sea the source of life on Earth, but nations do not appreciate the value of life.

People and nations pollute seas and oceans with more and more oil and waste, using ever more advanced science and technology.

To draw a line even demarcating the surface of land is unnecessary, but drawing a line marking territory beneath the ground is ridiculous.

The Sea, one sea, is and must be the common blue space for the hope of mankind, but it is polluted and destroyed by nationalism, greed, overfishing, tensions, wars and military confrontations, even after two World Wars and the Cold War that lasted for half a century.

How ridiculous we are!

How pathetic the nations of our world!

Desertification of the Sea

The scientific journal, Marine Policy, laments fishing operations that have in recent decades been targeting unregulated high seas after stocks near shorelines have been exhausted. Elliott Norse, President of the Marine Conservation Institute and the paper's lead author, described the open ocean as "more akin to a watery desert."

The world has turned to deep-sea fishing "out of desperation" and without realizing fish stocks there take much longer to recover. Deep-sea mining and fishing are depleting life in the sea, so much so that scientists are calling for an end to deep-sea mining and fishing.

Unfortunately, protection of continental shelves and EEZs for the common heritage of humankind has not been fully discussed, even though there has been marginal discussion in intellectual societies.

Nations do not formulate and implement sea and ocean policies for nature conservation and environmental protection. Nations that share the sea, especially narrow seas, have not sought peaceful and rational boundary delimitations. China is emerging as a new imperialist nation in the South China Sea and East China Seas.

China is trying to use the continental shelf theory from the North Sea decision to claim the vast territory of the East China and South China Seas, relying on its history of ancient Chinese civilization and neighboring nations. China threatens neighboring nations with more fleets and rising military budgets.

Conserving marine resources

Attempts to share the sea with neighboring nations are not concluded or even expressed among nations. Sharing resources and responsibility for protecting the sea while conserving marine resources should be the guiding principle of international sea policies. This will eventually bring peace on the oceans.

Limiting and dismantling continental shelf demarcations and EEZs must be the mission of intellectual society. It should be our mission to protect the oceans and the seas and conserve marine resources for humankind.

More articles in newspapers and journals should discuss environmental protection in oceans as well as the conservation of resources. The Korea Institute of Public Administration and The Korea Times are jointly exploring this space.

As far as we know, the Earth is the only planet in the universe with oceans and life. Exploitation and exploration of these resources without a sense of responsibility should not be tolerated.

Exploitation is wrong according to the values of EEZs and therefore should be banned. Wars of mass destruction should be banned from the sea because they destroy life in seas and oceans.

Nuclear ships and nuclear submarines should be relegated to museums and scuttled. The United Nations Convention on the Law of the Seas started with a legitimate conception of EEZs, but this has been misused.

We should go back to the protection of fisheries and natural resources spanning from shorelines to the high seas. This sounds like Utopian thinking, but it needs to occur. Our oceans, the last frontier on Earth, should be protected.

Protection of migratory species

Protection of migratory species and sharks, fish farming, oil spills and the restoration of environmental quality should be constantly sought. Civil and criminal charges against off-shore oil production companies in the Gulf of

Mexico in 2010 should bring justice to the seas.

One interesting article in the Wall Street Journal by Laura Bush, a former first lady of the United States, notable for advocating protection of the ocean and marine resources, is a reminder of her husband's designation of four marine national monuments in the Pacific Ocean as ocean national parks in 2006.

The Papahanaumokuakea Marine National Monument,
The Marianas Trench National Monument,
The Pacific Remote Islands and
The Rose Atoll in American Samoa.

These four monuments cover more than 330,000 square miles and amount to the largest fully protected marine area in the world, larger than the entirety of the United States national parks and wild life refuges combined. They support vast numbers of fish, breathtakingly beautiful coral habitats, and a remarkable abundance of sharks — often seen as markers of an ecosystem's health.

Protection of oceans is a mission and task for humankind for present and future generations to come. Nearly half of the world's population now lives within 60 miles of an ocean, and that percentage is set to rise as more people settle in coastal communities.

Our wild ocean frontiers are disappearing and, as in the case of Yellowstone, it is up to us to conserve the most important wild areas that remain. Doing so will preserve something that is too easy to destroy but impossible to replace: natural, undisturbed incubators of life. Overfishing and degradation of our ocean waters damages the habitats needed to sustain diverse marine populations.

Regional Cooperation

The past decade has set the stage for cautious optimism about the future. Diverse forums and programs, both governmental and non-governmental, have been launched and are being activated to support environmental cooperation across the Asian region.

The ramifications of environmental politics are bound to have a larger impact in the coming decade as environmental issues become more affected by economic development strategies and production techniques. A cooperative regime on a regional basis with a win-win strategy for all participating nations is all the more necessary, not only for effective management but also for more stable regional relations in general.

All nations should develop successful strategies for socially just and ecologically sustainable development in the Asia-Pacific region, as well as in other global regions.

Existing international organizations have not been totally effective in improving environmental protection on a global scale. The UNEP has been hindered by its limited mandate, lack of resources, and physical location. The United Nations Environmental Programme (UNEP) has sponsored intergovernmental meetings of the Northwest Pacific Action Plan (NOWPAP), a regional seas program.

The UN Commission on Sustainable Development has an overly broad mandate and no enforcement powers. Environmentally sustainable development is now considered to be one of the World Bank's fundamental objectives, but it was never intended to become the focal point of international environmental governance. There is a school of thought that regional environmental cooperation might be a better solution for international environmental issues.

The Action Plan for the Protection, Management and Development of the Marine and Coastal Environment of the Northwest Pacific Region (NOWPAP) was adopted in September 1994 as a part of the Regional Seas Programme of the United Nations Environment Programme (UNEP). Implementation of NOWPAP contributes to the Global Programme of Action for the Protection of the Marine Environment from Land-based Activities (GPA) in the Northwest Pacific region.

The Northwest Pacific region features coastal and island eco-systems that sustain spectacular marine life as well as important commercial fishing territories. The region is also one of the most densely populated parts of the world, resulting in enormous pressures and demands being placed on the environment.

The overall goal of the Northwest Pacific Action Plan is "the wise use, development and management of the coastal and marine environment so as to obtain the utmost long-term benefits for the human populations of the region, while protecting human health, ecological integrity and the region's sustainability for future generations."

The geographical scope of NOWPAP covers the marine environment and coastal zones from about 121 degrees East to 143 degrees East longitude, and from approximately 33 degrees North to 52 degrees North latitude.

There should be a regional regulatory authority to make environmental regulations and enforce their use by domestic environmental agencies.

Environmental management is basically regulating polluters. Regional environmental management is about regulating polluting nations. Therefore, regional regulatory authority should obtain maximum cooperation from each nation's regulatory authority. But who should play the regional regulator's role? The NOWPAP board of directors can and should be able to demonstrate regulatory authority. This should be a major task to produce successful regional environmental programs. The East Asian and Pacific region had an average annual GDP growth rate of 7.6 percent in the 1980s and 10.3 per cent in 1990s.

Unfortunately, Asia's economic development has been achieved at great cost to the environment. China is a good example. For example, China's SO_2 production was over 20,000,000 metric tons in 2000 - 80 percent of the region's total production. China is the fast-rising, second-ranking contributor after the United States and is likely to surpass that country in the coming decades.

China's rivers, reservoirs, and other water resources are largely befouled, causing deterioration in the Yellow Sea and other oceans. Its solid and hazardous wastes are often dumped without being treated. Serious deforestation and overuse of other natural resources have fueled economic growth but have also diminished biodiversity and endangered many forms of wildlife.

No nation or the UN can regulate a superpower nation such as China, which is reluctant to admit that it is a major environmental polluter in the region, or to commit major funding to environmental programs, even though it is just beginning to recognize the seriousness of the problem.

There should be an effective regional environmental tribunal to enforce international or regional environmental laws and regulations. A regulatory authority can make regional regulations, and the court declares the nation or nations responsible and legally culpable.

Environmental crimes are not considered as serious crimes today but will be in the future.

If environmental regulation is the bedrock of environmental affairs and sustainable development, many new policy opportunities - and urgent policy imperatives - involve going beyond compliance in a dynamic of continuous improvement leading to superior environmental performance. It is only with such superior performance that the effects of rapid pollution and waste intensity of economic activity will be drastically reduced.

Chapter 8

Entrepreneur

Smart grid for smart energy

The marvels of green construction

Learning to promote sustainability

Little things that count

Smart grid for smart energy

Joong-kyum Kim

This is part of a smart grid monitoring center on Jeju Island. The operation of smart grids has been instrumental in reducing environmental pollution across the country. *Korea Times file*

KEPCO is all about green and smart technology. It was a great privilege to receive a prize for our integrated next-generation power distribution system at the Green Energy Awards.

This acknowledged our dedicated efforts to invest and promote green energy - including renewable energy - and the contribution we will make to the development of the energy industry.

KEPCO won the award, given by the Ministry of Knowledge Economy and Korea Institute of Energy Technology Evaluation and Planning, in tough competition for its integrated next-generation smart power distribution system.

Green and smart technology

This is perhaps the result of KEPCO's relentless efforts in research and development in green and smart technology, including new recycled energy, clean energy, micro grids and smart grids. Through these research and development programs aimed at low-carbon green growth, KEPCO is securing a strong position in foreign markets, providing diversified technological solutions and creating profit-making business models.

The pursuit of new recycled energy and smart power distribution systems can certainly bring benefits to consumers, and there are significant consequences of developing the integrated operation of energy resource distribution.

All over the world, concerns abound regarding the reduction of greenhouse gas emissions, improving energy efficiency, increasing the supply of recycled energy and increasing the use of electric vehicles.

The Korean government will adopt Renewable Portfolio Standards this year, making it mandatory for public buildings to reduce the electricity usage by tend percent and increase the number of electric cars to one million by the year 2020.

Safety concerns

There is also the portion of the program that calls for the "20-20-20" plan, under which heavy investment will be made for the increase in the use of renewable energy by 20 percent by 2020.

The development and advancement of green energy are going to take the form of distributed energy resources for providing efficient sources of energy on a smaller scale. However, there are safety concerns in pursuing this project. It is high time that we abort the "fit-and-forget" principle and adopt an integrated operation for voltage-reactive power control that helps resolve power factor and power loss problems.

The integrated next-generation renewable smart power distribution system is the result of the Smart Distribution System Initiative of the central government. The initiative is leading to the development of renewable energy, energy storage devices and diversification of energy resources, their related systems, and control units so as to improve the efficiency of the power distribution network.

New era in power distribution

Utilizing these systems and devices, we will secure next-generation technology for analyzing power distribution on a real-time basis and operate a more ideal control environment in enhanced safety and stability, making it possible to reduce pollution to low levels.

This energy management system boasts not only next-generation technologies for the most efficient operation of a power distribution network, but it also is an optimal system, perhaps the most advanced in the world. Such technology is essential in an era of increasingly complicated power and resource distribution networks and in order to develop solutions for the optimal utilization of renewable energy.

The distribution energy management systems in operation combine a smart distribution management system and a home energy management system to effectively monitor and control micro grids. Distribution energy management systems not only enhance operational efficiency but also connect with T-SCADA/energy management systems to function effectively as a regional energy management system.

Environmental implications

One of the other important aspects in the operation of advanced energy management systems is the implications for the environment, since power generation is often a major source of pollution. Environmental considerations are a vital part of the development of this technology and implementation in the field. The system is currently undergoing trials at the Gochang PT Center with the aim of improving the practical capability of actual application in the field and checking its environmental implications. When the Smart DMS is active, it will be instrumental in boosting the operational efficiency of the integrated energy management system by combining distributed energy resources.

In the future, KEPCO plans to invest heavily in the supply of renewable energies in the global market, thus contributing to cleaning up the environment and improving living conditions in many corners of the world.

Carrying out environment-friendly management

KEPCO takes corporate responsibility seriously, keying on environmentally-friendly management as a company producing and providing electric power, the prime power for national competitiveness. The company will enhance its environmental capability to rank among the world's top five energy utility companies by 2020.

To achieve these aggressive goals, KEPCO is determined to pursue the following environmental policies:

First, actively carry out environment-friendly management and enhance environmental efficiency.

1. Observe environmental rules and regulations. Establish and operate an environmental management system based on the international standard. Continue to improve the system to realize sound environmental management results.

2. Execute proper education and training so that management and staff participate actively in environmental management. Strengthen the communication system with major stakeholders.

3. Reduce the environmental load by promoting resource recycling and environment-friendly product use. Contribute to realizing a resource-circulating society with high environmental efficiency. Second, make efforts to realize an environment-friendly electric power supply chain, including production, transportation, sales and the consumption of electricity.

4. Strengthen environment-friendly supply chain management and related cooperative systems to enhance society's sustainability with environment-friendly production and distribution.

5. Make efforts to construct and operate facilities that coexist in harmony with the regional community. Minimize loss of electricity through efficient operational management.

6. Execute activities for energy conservation such as load management and electricity efficiency enhancement projects. Enhance the energy use rate at a national level.

Third, understand the seriousness of global challenges to the environment, including climate change, and react responsively.

7. Show leadership by encouraging the joint efforts of electric power groups to tackle the global environmental issue of climate change.

8. Consistently reduce the amount of greenhouse gases discharged by developing and distributing environmentally-friendly energy, promoting energy conservation, and by improving equipment.

9. Actively support the reduction of greenhouse gases discharged indirectly during electricity use by systematically managing electricity demand and by improving electricity transmission and transformation.

The marvels of green construction

Keung-hwan Kim

This is an experimental home in Yongin, Gyonggi Province, which has a solar-paneled rooftop among other self-energy suppying facilities. A home like this, aside from the initial investment, pays for itself due to no electrical or heating bills. *Korea Times file*

A green home is more than a house built in an eco-friendly way that uses less energy. It is the product of a comprehensive concept that also includes eco-friendly architecture as well as maintenance for low-energy use.

The emergence of the green home era is closely related to the active eco-friendly lifestyles of residents. The advent of green homes will likely lead to the full reflection of energy-reducing habits in all aspects of daily life, including the use of automobiles, thus going beyond the architecture and housing sectors.

Green homes are no longer an option but a necessity. They are forecasted to become an indispensable factor in consumers' selection of housing, as a result of their appropriateness and economic feasibility. Companies are expected to double their efforts to assume leadership in the eco-friendly green home market.

They will likely achieve joint growth with partner companies that have eco-friendly, green home technologies. Samsung C&T Corporation is planning to unveil a low-energy model house in September 2012 that includes all aspects of an eco-friendly green home based on collaboration with partner companies.

Eco-friendly buildings

Demand for eco-friendly buildings is on the rise among order-placing organizations, in addition to strengthened regulations that encourage the construction of such buildings. In the case of buildings for which orders are placed overseas, there is need to receive a certain level of LEED certification and there has been an increase in requests for pre-construction services and increased building eco-friendliness.

In Korea as well, there is a rise in the number of projects that specify the eco-friendliness of buildings as an owner requirement. From the perspective of the order-placing organization, a building's eco-friendliness can lead to various positive effects. These include enhancement of corporate image, a reduction in operating expenses, and improvement in the productivity of building employees.

This tendency will likely become stronger. To stay one step ahead of this trend, our company will continually engage in research and development activities on eco-friendly buildings and will strive to become a leading company in eco-friendly construction.

Technologies involved with improving a building's energy efficiency can be categorized into technologies that boost energy performance of the building itself and those for new and renewable energy and water usage efficiency.

Improving buildings' energy efficiency also can be divided into residential and non-residential sectors. Most homes in Korea are apartment buildings consisting of multi-story and line-type buildings.

Energy efficiency

Even a small area touches the envelope. For this reason, apartment buildings are more energy efficient than individual houses. Koreans tend to be more sensitive to the cold weather. This is why heating energy accounts for approximately 95 percent of annual heating and cooling energy, even though the country has four distinct seasons.

Koreans also like large, extensive views. This is why windows in Korean homes have a higher area ratio than homes in the West. To increase energy efficiency in this type of home, various research programs are underway. Research is being conducted on developing new insulation materials, improving window and door performance, and building a uniquely Korean, ultra-energy reduction house that includes such materials, windows and doors.

Office buildings indicate diverse energy-consumption characteristics according to the building form, envelope composition characteristics, and purpose of use. This is why an individual approach is needed for each building.

As a basic research program aimed at improving the energy efficiency of buildings, our company analyzed the amount of energy used in buildings owned by the Samsung Group in 2006, together with the Energy Systems Research Unit (ESRU) of Britain's University of Strathclyde, Japan's Building Performance Consulting (BPC), and the Korea Institute of Construction Technology.

Energy performance evaluation

Our company also surveyed the energy-consumption status at Raemian, a brand of Samsung C&T apartments. For energy performance optimization through energy performance analyses in the housing and office design phase, we have been developing a building energy performance evaluation tool together with Britain's ESRU since 2007.

In addition, Dr. Jon Hand, a prominent expert in the field, was dispatched to our company for eight months to conduct joint work and for technology transfers. In addition, consulting is being provided to optimize energy performance for several building projects that our company is conducting.

To reduce energy use in the operation phase after construction, in addition to the design phase, we installed a BEMS (building energy management system) system at the company's headquarters and the Samsung Electronics building and are monitoring them. This research activity is aimed at energy reduction in the operation phase.

Reduction of fossil energy

We are carrying out basic research on the use of new and renewable energy for the reduction of fossil energy. We also are applying geothermal heat, photovoltaic, solar heat, and wind power systems and have relevant design, construction, and maintenance technologies. We will apply geothermal systems totaling 2,883 RT at 15 construction sites. This includes apartment complexes that have already been built - Seocho Garden Sweet, Daegu Dalseong Raemian, and Nuritkum Square. This is expected to lead to oil replacement effects of an annual 1,838 TOE (tons of oil equivalent) as well as carbon dioxide reduction effects of 5,588 TOE.

There are also activities to move forward with the application of photovoltaic and solar heat systems. We plan to apply a hot-water supply system based on solar heat at a national athletics training center that was completed in 2011 and use photovoltaic power generation, solar heat and cool tube systems at the Parc 1 site in Yeouido, a high-rise building with 72 floors above ground. This is expected to lead to oil reduction effects of an annual 14.2 TOE.

Learning to promote sustainability

Tae-won Chey

Rio+20 Corporate Sustainablity Forum is underway in Rio de Janeiro, with a keynote speech by President Myung-bak Lee, amid the attendance of government leaders and corporate executives in June. In response to such global initiatives, companies are moving to help smaller companies engage in environmentfriendly business activities. *Korea Times file*

A majority portion of this contributed article was presented at the Rio+20 Summit of the United Nations in Rio de Janeiro, June 2012.

The primary objective of a business leader is to make money and successfully build a company. But in recent years, environmental considerations increasingly coming into play. In the past, CSR (corporate social responsibility) was regarded with the level of enthusiasm students have for "homework" or as an unwanted obligation. "Responsibility" was passive.

After reviewing CSR programs, I noticed several problems: first among them was how hard it is to find committed and talented people because more people are concerned with money-making rather than looking at environmental implications. CEOs and executives don't pay enough attention, although efforts are being made to address the issue of environmental pollution with which manufacturing companies are closely associated.

I came upon an SE (social entrepreneurship) model together with impact investing as a possible solution after thinking of other ways to spend CSR money more wisely. An SE must be handled like a business, and thus we need more experience in SE. I established "Hangbok Narae" as a pilot test and developed an MBA program for social entrepreneurship at a top university in Korea.

How can everyone (SEs and corporations) benefit? Benefits to SEs include social value creation, in point of fact, ten times more social value creation than through philanthropy.

Social challenges

Large corporations can leverage their capabilities and help SEs. Job inclusion, such as by providing second opportunities for the elderly and improving their lives, rather than simply by giving away money.

So what are the challenges we face?
- Not enough incentives for corporations
- Must yield returns
- SE CEOs look for investments that will sustain their organizations
- SEs have a dual task: social and economic value creation
- Small SEs can't compete or survive against large corporations
- CEOs have to decide whether or not to create more social value or make more money without any guarantee of sustainability
- There is no social value measurement scheme
- Must evaluate both social value and financial returns, as well as create a measurement or accounting system.
- Incentives and rewards, such as a transferrable tax credit
- Must attract more talented people to the SE space
- Dream is to create a social capital market And, what then are the commitments?
- An MBA program will be launched in Korea that will be extended globally in the future
- An IT (information technology) platform with the UNGC will be

created to facilitate information exchange and increase innovation

SK supports SEs and is learning by doing: learning the characteristics of everyone involved in SE. IT support is needed because it reduces transaction fees.

Learning by doing

We must figure out how to engage and lower transaction fees. SK changed an MRO (maintenance, repair and operations) business for an SE and created a different model that uses SEs as suppliers, advises other SEs, and expands their business.

The model involves nurturing other SE skills such as finance, management and HR skills. We are currently trying to open space to help SEs through innovation. Like the technology boom, we must give them room to innovate.

There is plenty of enthusiasm and energy in business for protecting the environment in the process, from air and water pollution to oil spills. We have to focus on providing positive energy through which we can hope to make a better world. We need new and innovative solutions. We must reduce conflicts of interest and dream of a new world. Open your mind and come up with new, hybrid solutions.

Nowadays, the reality is that many nations face economic saturation coupled with various social problems like unemployment and ever-increasing wealth disparities. It is in these situations that I believe social enterprise can step in and solve such problems by establishing a new economic sector, channeling corporate systems and expertise into creating social value focused on the common good.

As one of the largest conglomerates, and as a leader in the energy and telecommunication industries in South Korea, SK is striving to lead proliferation of social enterprise models domestically and then expand onto the Asian and global stage. SK has also joined in the effort to develop the Framework for Action, sparking discussion throughout the UN on social enterprises, and even agreed to host the Social Enterprise Session at Rio+20 in Rio de Janeiro.

Spirit of community

I believe these efforts will play a meaningful role in realizing the value of the UN as a global community because social values begin with the spirit of community. We should overcome difficulties together, side by side. For this to work, we need to start by creating an eco-system for social enterprises that promotes their sustainable growth. In this regard, SK would like to propose three commitments: a "Global Action Hub," a "Social Enterprise Forum" and a "Social Enterprise MBA."

First, SK will establish a "Global Action Hub", an intermediary platform spanning all components of the Social Enterprise ecosystem. The "Global Action Hub" will go beyond a mere IT platform. It will be a domain for dialogue and information exchange where investors, specialists, and social entrepreneurs can come together to facilitate change.

UNGC (United Nations Global Compact) will be a partner for this Hub. Together with the UNGC, SK hopes the Global Action Hub can eventually develop into a major pipeline for impact investing and social capital transactions by attracting diverse partnerships and additional commitments, particularly in the area of development with environmental protection as an important focus.

Second, SK will extend its social enterprise forum, which has been limited to the Korean market so far. We want to start by including the entire Asian region, and later expanding globally, so that we can share great ideas and solutions. This will help us generate better methodologies for future social enterprises.

Finally, SK has introduced an MBA program in Korea to nurture social entrepreneurs who will be nurtured to run businesses with the environment in mind. The program will be run based on UN principles for responsible management education, which will serve as guidelines for future social entrepreneurs to realize UN values in their business activities.

These days, sustainability - always with the environment in mind - is grabbing a lot of attention as an alternative to reckless growth. It will be very challenging for social enterprises to enhance sustainability by pursuing social values and business values together. But it will also be highly rewarding.

CEOs and executives don't pay enough attention, although efforts are being made to address the issue of environmental pollution with which manufacturing companies are closely associated. We've got our work cut out for us, as we need to raise interest, passion and actual support from nations, stakeholders, and economic sectors. There is a famous quote pertinent to where we find ourselves today: "Coming together is a beginning. Keeping together is progress. Working together is success." As we embark on this challenging yet amazing journey, we have to remember that there is only one earth and that it is our responsibility to preserve the environment for future generations.

We must grow progressively to encompass issues faced by more nations across the world and by proposing truly innovative ideas that contribute to global prosperity.

Little things that count

Jean Keijdener

This is a minimized version of thatched houses that are installed in the garden of Somerset Palace Seoul in downtown Seoul where there are also a pond and lots of seasonal flowers, as well as trees. The rooftop garden also has hundreds of species of plants and trees. *Korea Times photo by Shim Hyun-chul*

At the Somerset Palace, a serviced residence in the heart of Seoul, we decided, among various adaptations towards "going green," to do away with takeout disposable cups in the Residents' Lounge.

While there were some minor comments initially, residents quickly agreed that it was for the best, since disposable cups were creating so much garbage. After about a month, no one even notices. Everyone is happy with the reusable mugs and porcelain coffee cups that we provide now. Coffee and tea taste so much better in them too!

This is just a small contribution and one way that we at The Ascott Limited try to make our environment cleaner and safer and help to save it. The Earth, our only home, has been sustaining life in a unique cycle of self-renewal for so long that we often take it for granted.

But the Earth is under severe threat. Its resources are being depleted faster than they can be replenished, and it is suffering the ravages of imprudent use and abuse. The only way we can slow down, and perhaps even reverse, the damage that has already been done is to transform our business practices and cultivate a green mindset.

The Earth needs more than just our understanding. It needs us to take action; we need to be responsible for the Earth because quite simply it is the only one we have.

Corporate responsibility

We constantly try to provide valuable information about the environment and its protection to guests because they are the ones who make a difference. Here are some information and tips on how you can take simple actions to make your life and our Earth better.

Did you know that for every ton of paper you recycle, you save 7,000 gallons of water, 380 gallons of oil, and enough electricity to power an average house for six months?

The energy saved from one recycled aluminum can operates a television for three hours. The energy saved from recycling one glass bottle will light a 100-watt light bulb for four hours.

Recycling a glass bottle causes 20 percent less air pollution and 50 percent less water pollution than when a new bottle is made from raw materials.

Recycled paper produces 73 percent less air pollution than if it were made from raw materials.

The hospitality industry is among those with a significant environmental footprint, and we believe we must act responsibly. As the world's largest international serviced residence owner-operator with a presence in over 20 countries across more than 70 cities, we believe we are uniquely positioned to play an active role in transforming business practices and employee mindsets to make them more eco-friendly.

Going green is not just an investment for the long term. With more breakthroughs in green technology and practices and more products available, we can be green while maintaining our characteristic excellent quality of service. In fact, being part of the experience makes us all direct beneficiaries of green creativity and innovation.

Going green also opens up new opportunities to work with other eco-minded associates and clients who would otherwise not have crossed our paths. This widens everyone's network and increases relationships.

Of course, being green goes perfectly with our ultimate commitment to people. We show we care for people by showing our care for the very Earth we all share.

Green vision

Climate change is happening right now, and experts agree that is a phenomenon of global concern. Global warming will affect how we live, work, play and do business.

As the leading international serviced residence owner-operator, we at Ascott believe it is our responsibility to do our part and help our hurting Earth wherever we have a presence.

We have set a target to achieve 15 percent savings in water and energy consumption by 2015, using 2008 as the base year. In 2011, Ascott consumed nine percent less water and energy compared to 2008.

To help us stay focused in implementing our green vision, Ascott has developed a five-point framework mapping out areas in which to bring about change. A set of tools also has been developed to help us move forward together as a green service residence company.

The Five-point Framework lets us track our green efforts and identifies concrete targets that can be measured so we can monitor performance in the following areas:

Ascott will incorporate green elements into all new properties to be built or renovated to create sustainable serviced residences that are both comfortable and resource and energy efficient. This includes the use of sustainable building materials or products that are locally sourced, more energy efficient, and more durable, which consequently has less impact on the environment.

At Somerset Palace Seoul, we have installed a rooftop garden that is fascinating from the perspective that it sits high in the heart of downtown Seoul. Enormous efforts were made for the creation of the garden which houses more than 300 species of plants and trees.

Our aim is to contribute to the well-being and success of the people who choose to stay with us when they live and work away from home. By incorporating green elements, we are creating sustainable residences that are both comfortable and energy efficient. These translate to cost benefits as well as resource and operational efficiencies.

Ascott has put in place comprehensive environment, health and safety (EHS) procedures for its serviced residences. EHS practices are implemented across our properties to minimize pollution and health and safety risks.

EHS is a key element in the Five-Point Framework. It is important that staff embrace these practices in their day-to-day work to minimize pollution and health and safety risks.

Water, energy, paper, waste reduction

Ascott has implemented green practices to promote the conservation of water, energy and paper as well as to reduce waste.

At the Citadines Trafalgar Square London, we have installed "Save-a-Flush" devices in our water cisterns. "Save-a-Flush" is a bag placed at the bottom of the cistern beneath the flush float.

Within six hours, the bag swells up to displace one liter of water; each time the cistern fills, it needs one liter less water. We save one liter of water per flush that usually uses eight liters. The property saves approximately 12.5 per cent of its previous yearly water consumption.

At Somerset JieFangBei Chongqing, we replaced 800 11-volt lamps with four-volt lamps in public areas. This translates to a savings of approximately over 3500 kilowatt hours per month, which can power up to 25 average-sized refrigerators.

The company as a whole is trying to go as paperless as possible. Since 2009, we developed an electronic version of the Ascottour Serviced Residence Directory and made it available for download online. This has helped us reduce the number of print copies, saving approximately 8,160kg of paper per year.

Other examples of sustainability initiatives at Ascott's properties include offering long-stay residents the option not to have daily housekeeping, the installation of water-saving devices in toilet cisterns, the use of recycling bins, and providing reusable eco-bags or shopping trolleys instead of disposable grocery bags.

Stakeholder engagement

An Ascott Earth Day is held every first Friday of the month at Ascott's offices and properties worldwide. On this day, our staff and residents are encouraged to dress down, while air-conditioning temperatures at offices and properties are turned down to conserve energy. Similarly, staff and residents in temperate countries are encouraged to wear warmer clothing as the heater temperature is reduced. Ascott's offices and properties will also switch off beacon and other non-essential lights for 10 hours from 8 p.m.

And how does this work out at the ground "roots" level, you may ask? Let's revisit our Somerset Palace Seoul and look at some of the green practices we have in place:
- Switching over from regular copy paper to "Forest Stewardship Council" paper. This is not only a commitment to preserving renewable paper sources but also a source of cost reduction in paper usage.
- Promoting electricity efficiency among residents through voluntary programs and competitions, such as: "I am switched off," whereby residents are encouraged to go green by ensuring all AC units are switched off when not in the room. In return, a monthly winner is recognized for his/her efforts and wins a special gift. Another initiative is for residents to "opt out" of daily towel replenishment and housekeeping cleaning services.
- Installation of high-grade eco-friendly amenities, such as shower gels and shampoos from wall-mounted dispensers instead of "little bottles."
- Implementing the use of eco-friendly housekeeping products, such as water-based non-hazardous and environmentally friendly degreasing and deodorizing enzyme liquids for treatment of drainage pipes and wastewater.
- Use of eco-friendly deodorization products, which enables us to clean and clear even the most stubborn odor-related issues in an apartment - effectively and quickly.

These are just a handful of initiatives to showcase, and we assure you there are definitely more to come - it will be just a matter of time before more make this list.

Chapter 9

Civil Society

Environment through the lens
Nuclear technology: to have or not to have

Environment through the lens

Yul Choi

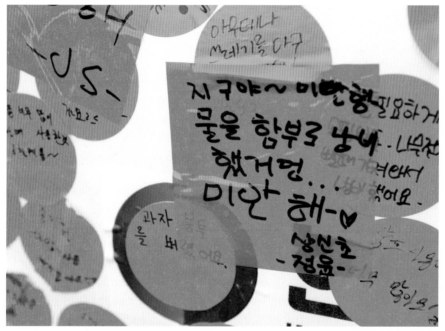

Messages from children are pasted on a window at the Seoul Green Film Festival at Samgam CGV last year, the one in front reading "Earth, I am sorry for having mindlessly wasted water," written by a Jong-yun of Sangshin Elementary School. *Courtesy of the Korea Green Foundation*

"The simplest way to approach environmental problems is through the camera. This is why I will be organizing environmental film festivals in Korea." This is what I told the World Congress of Friends of the Earth at Interlaken, Switzerland in 2002. At that time, I was Secretary General of the Korean Federation for Environmental Movement and participated in the congress to become a formal member.

This was the beginning of the Seoul Green Film Festival. In October of that year, the Korean Green Foundation was established, and two years later, in 2004, Korea's first environmental film festival was launched. Seoul Green Film Festival is now in its ninth year. There are countless numbers of film festivals in the country with different sizes and themes. Most are supported by provincial governments and participated in by local residents. But there are also numerous film events of high caliber that do not run on government funding; they treat subjects ranging from women and the environment to human rights. Seoul Green Film Festival has now grown to be one of the top three in its category in the world.

Increased entries

In the beginning, the festival received submissions from various countries, went through the reviewing process and decided which of the films would be featured, as in any other international film event. The problem was that questions arose concerning the nature and subject of some of the films, in particular whether they could be considered as related to the environment. As the years passed, the number of films submitted increased, and this year, we received more than 830 entries from 64 countries. With the increasing number of entries, there were more opportunities to select the best examples that meet our basic objectives in organizing the festival.

A film festival is an event in which people can view the interests of the world in a single location. This brings out the contrast in local and foreign films and documentaries and the level of their quality. Foreign films tend to bring reality to life in the diversity of their subjects and are wide-ranging. Local films have come a long way in the commercial category but still leave much to be desired in terms of documentaries. The main reason for this is the audience -smaller in Korea but larger in regions such as Europe.

However, there are common aspects of both local and foreign films. In both, the subject is usually a confrontation between victims and those who inflict the damage. And there are usually few national boundaries. The movie "Pipe" from Ireland, which won the grand prize during the eighth festival, depicts the conflict between residents of a peaceful village and Shell Oil Company of the United States that was trying to set up a pipeline network for natural gas through the village. Environmental problems and conflicts often have this characteristic of crossing national boundaries. Environmental challenges have no borders, indicating the reality that environmental problems require an international and shared perspective.

The themes of the Seoul Green Film Festival have drawn attention to environmental issues of concern each year. During the first festival, the theme was "Green Playground in the Heart of the City." Designed to be a non-competitive international event, we looked to focus on global environmental issues. The event also was focused on trees and resulted in entries like "Cloud in May" and "The Beautiful Life of a Tree."

The main theme of the second festival was nuclear power. It introduced "The Children of Chernobyl" by Marianne Dreo, focusing on and looking back at the biggest nuclear accident in human history. Other entries included films protesting the construction of nuclear power plants. One was "People Protecting the Plaza," telling the story of residents in Dal County who did not want the installation of a nuclear waste repository in their neighborhood.

Philosophical deliveries

When thinking about a film on the environment, it may seem easy to depict documentaries and philosophical deliveries, but this is actually not the case. There are many films, which are fun and emotional, showing complete stories. This is one of the reasons environmental films are made in the first place.

During the Third Seoul Green Film Festival, a total of 108 entries from 21 countries were presented. Those involved said the event came alive with pieces on everything from community movements to environmental science, turning it into a major "thematic film festival."

Compared to the second festival, the number of attendees doubled, and 29 of the presentations, including the opening film "Five Past Nine," were sold out. Another attraction was "Girl Riding a Bicycle," starring and produced by Yoo Ji-tae, a popular Korean actor.

The main environmental issue in 2007 was disasters caused by global warming. During the Fourth Seoul Green Film Festival, numerous entries focused on the seriousness of damage caused by climate change. Among them was "Great Warming" by Michael Taylor and narrated by the actor Keanu Reeves with singer-songwriter Alanis Morissette. It was a documentary on the reality that the effects of global warming could be turned around or made worse, as well as the need for a commitment by mankind to prevent worse disasters.

Then there was the massive oil leakage in Taean from the vessel Herbei Spirit, which completely changed the lives of residents in the region. This was the main theme of the movie "Ocean" — the cradle of Taean and its residents, during the Fifth Seoul Green Film Festival. Numerous other entries centered on oil spills around the world and the environmental devastation they cause. The number of attendees at the annual festival increased by more than 61 percent over the previous year, showing the rise in public interest in environmental developments.

The keyword for the Sixth Seoul Green Film Festival in 2009 was "Energy." The depletion of crude oil has led to a time where the price of gasoline remains extremely high, and a number of entries presented ways in which the use of energy can remain sustainable. Among them was "Burning the Future" by David Novak, which delved into the coal industry in the United States and conflicts taking place among residents of West Virginia. "A Land of Wind and Sun" was a documentary on the introduction of new-recycled energy by Indian aborigines in America.

There is also the important issue of water. More than 70 percent of the planet is covered with water. But do we have enough to supply ourselves? Following the issue of black gold, another term for oil, the seventh film festival moved on to the issue of water. The main presentation was "Blue Gold" by Sam Bozo, while other presentations looked from different perspectives at the importance of water for sustaining our basic lives.

There were numerous issues addressed during the Eighth Seoul Green Film Festival last year. Millions of cows and pigs were buried because of foot-and-mouth disease, and the earthquake -measuring an astonishing 9.0 on the Richter scale - and tsunami in Japan last March caused serious damage to the Fukushima Nuclear Power Plant, leading to radiation leakage. When critical incidents occur, public attention and interest become emphasized. The events in Fukushima immediately raised questions about the safety of nuclear power plants.

Earth Summit

"Into Eternity" by Michael Madsen is a documentary covering the world's first nuclear plant in Finland. It received the Grand Screen Prize at the Amsterdam Documentary Film Festival in 2010.

While the environment is complex, films are simpler. By watching films at the Seoul Green Film Festival, people can remain in touch with environmental issues around the world. And it is an easy way to study and learn about the environment.

There were 18,000 attendees at the First Seoul Green Film Festival, but the number has grown to nearly 80,000 as of the eighth event. People are becoming even more interested in the environment they live in and what is happening to it.

As we prepared for the Ninth Seoul Green Film Festival from May 9 to 15, 2012 we recognized that this is an opportunity to look back at the past two decades of our environment, especially with the 20th anniversary of the Earth Summit in Rio de Janeiro this year. The event presented a wide range of films that can be enjoyed by families, children and adolescents. It continues to be designed to bring environmental issues to the attention of people of all ages in a more pleasant and practical way.

The thinking should be that environmental movements are not necessarily only about activists but also are designed to help preserve nature for mankind. When we discard nature, nature discards us. By bringing elements of the environment to people in a gentle fashion, we create an avenue to better understand the world we live in and how we can help preserve it for future generations.

Nuclear technology:
to have or not to have

Jin-seng Park

Debates over the need and importance of nuclear technology linger but there is evidence, as in the case of the Wolsong Nuclear Units (left photo) in North Gyeongsang Province, there are peaceful applications without concerns of nuclear armament. *Korea Times file*

Much scientific data concerning nuclear warheads has been publicized in recent years. Research results invite a devastating realization that the number of existing nuclear warheads is critically high, and unless we reduce their number or find the means to prevent them from causing harm, all of mankind could be eradicated without warning.

Most notably, the Bulletin of the Atomic Scientists (BAS) reported this January that the Doomsday Clock was adjusted forward by one minute, and that it is now pointing at 11:55 p.m. The BAS stated during a press interview, "The clock which had been pointing to 11:54 since 2007 has been adjusted, primarily because of the rapid proliferation of nuclear weapons despite the efforts of global leaders." As the Doomsday Clock moves closer to midnight, it concomitantly brings the end of the world one step nearer.

The Doomsday Clock is not the only warning sign of possible nuclear war. Recently, one of the world's best-known theoretical physicists, Dr. Steven Hawking, claimed during an interview with the BBC that global warming and nuclear weapons could put all of humanity in a perilous situation within the next century.

Nuclear proliferation

The Nuclear Non-proliferation Treaty (NPT) officially allows nuclear warheads for only five nations: the United States, Russia, the United Kingdom, France and China. However, other non-sanctioned countries have either conducted nuclear weapons testing or have developed a sufficient degree of technology to create nuclear weapons. Both India and Pakistan have conducted nuclear weapons testing, once in 1974, and again in 1988. Israel is believed to have sufficient power to produce nuclear warheads, and even our closest neighbor, the Democratic People's Republic of Korea, announced on Oct. 9, 2006 that the government was successful in conducting nuclear tests.

Although fewer than 10 countries possess nuclear weapons, the total number of warheads is stunningly high. More than 22,000 nuclear warheads exist around the globe, and 8,000 of these can be activated instantly.

The numbers listed above demonstrate two alarming facts: first, nuclear weapons have the potential to cause mass destruction, despite the global community's efforts to reduce catastrophic events. The Stockpile Steward Program is one such effort. Second, there is still a possibility that countries like North Korea and Iran are producing more nuclear weapons in order to compensate for their political weakness and to defend themselves from outside forces.

Some proponents argue that nuclear weapons serve as deterrents against war between countries. That said, a single question remains: Can nuclear weapons truly guarantee a country's national security? The answer is an emphatic no.

These are stark realities. Yet, the truth is that the importance of atomic power, which is often associated with the production of nuclear weapons, cannot be ignored.

Last year's nuclear meltdown and ensuing tsunami in Fukushima, Japan as a result of a massive earthquake - measuring an astonishing 9.0 on the Richter scale -was another reminder of the consequences of atomic power.

Recent reports in Japan indicate that there were shortfalls in preparatory measures against the possibility of accidents that could have reduced the impact of the natural phenomenon.

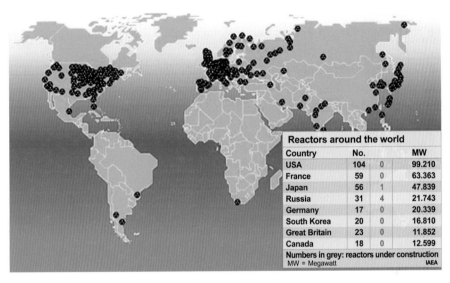

Reactors around the world			
Country	No.		MW
USA	104	0	99.210
France	59	0	63.363
Japan	56	1	47.839
Russia	31	4	21.743
Germany	17	0	20.339
South Korea	20	0	16.810
Great Britain	23	0	11.852
Canada	18	0	12.599
Numbers in grey: reactors under construction			
MW = Megawatt			IAEA

Environment info: nuclear energy

As a result of the Fukushima accident, Germany has declared that it will move to power down all nuclear plants in the country by 2022, even as the United States commissions the construction of a new nuclear facility for the first time in decades.

What are the implications for South Korea? Most experts believe that for a country with virtually no natural resources and increasing demands for energy, there are few viable alternatives.

In a world where climate change and its consequences are the concerns of countries everywhere, it is important to remember that nuclear power is cost-effective, and, more importantly, generates virtually no pollution. No gases that cause global warming or any other pollutants generated by fossil fuels are emitted.

We should also take note of the fact that many countries with nuclear power plants have not resorted to uranium enrichment programs, unlike North Korea. Most have been successful in the preservation of safe energy.

Acknowledging dangers

Korean monk Tan-huh was renowned for his ability to foresee the future. He did so from a Buddhist perspective, also based on his deep knowledge of "The Book of Changes." He once remarked, "The people who will eventually be damaged the most by nuclear warheads are not the ones living in countries without nuclear weapons, but rather, those residing in nations possessing the most nuclear warheads."

According to Tan-huh, it is highly unlikely for humanity to be pushed to the verge of extinction by another world war. Instead, natural disasters such as earthquakes that humans can neither prevent nor avoid might inadvertently cause nuclear warheads to explode.

His warning, once been disregarded by scientists overseeing the security of nuclear warheads, has proven prophetic. The recent earthquakes in Japan and the ensuing nuclear fallout and radioactive contamination illustrate his foresight.

It is of paramount importance to consider that the decision of implementing nuclear warheads in real-life situations is made by imperfect human beings who make mistakes.

Suppose a world leader suffering from a psychological disorder decides to attack other countries with nuclear weapons? There are numerous psychological conditions that result in impaired judgment.

The first nuclear weapon was invented to address this very concern. Einstein worried about the destructive powers of nuclear weapons when German and Soviet leaders first introduced them. He sent a letter to President Franklin D. Roosevelt, urging him to make the United States the first country to possess nuclear warheads. Consequently, the Manhattan Project was initiated, and the United States was able to induce the surrender of Japan by dropping atomic bombs on Nagasaki and Hiroshima for the first time in history. If the Nazi leader, Adolf Hitler, or the Japanese militarist, Hirohito, had used the atomic bomb earlier than the Americans, the outcome would have been much more devastating.

Notorious leaders such as Hitler and Jung-il Kim clearly suffered from personality disorders and posed threats to the entire world. However, they were not genetically programmed to have mental disorders, since humans develop their personalities throughout their lives.

Prevailing implications

This leads to the argument that the availability of nuclear power inadvertently leads to the possibility of weapons build-ups.

Therein lies the importance of efforts like the second nuclear security summit, which will take place in Seoul this year [2012], where political leaders from more than 50 countries will gather to find solutions for possible nuclear warfare and terrorism.

I would like to ask every world leader to take violence off the table. Even if some countries such as North Korea and Iran flout the rules and are headed in the wrong direction, no country should use force to oppress them. Violence will only beget more violence, rather than make the world a safer place.

Another valid point would be to separate the need for nuclear energy from the potential for a weapons build-up. The Seoul Nuclear Security Summit will hopefully go a long way in this direction.

One Korean spiritual leader argued that the new era requires us to become "unified and co-dependent" rather than "confrontational and antagonistic." Every human being and country should foster a stronger sense of community. Therefore, instead of punishing countries like North Korea and Iran, we should always remain empathetic, and encourage them to give up their nuclear weapons voluntarily while preserving the possibility of the peaceful use of nuclear technology.

At the end of the day, there will continue to be long and conflicting discussions on the safety of nuclear power and whether mankind needs to resort to this source when there are alternatives.

Atomic power debate

The atomic power debate is about the controversy that has surrounded the deployment and use of nuclear fission reactors to generate electricity from nuclear fuel for civilian purposes. The debate about nuclear power peaked during the 1970s and 1980s, when it reached an intensity unprecedented in the history of technology controversies, in some countries.

Proponents of nuclear energy argue that it is a sustainable energy source that reduces carbon emissions and can increase energy security if its use supplants dependence on imported fuels.

Proponents advance the notion that nuclear power produces virtually no air pollution, in contrast to the chief alternative of fossil fuel. Proponents also believe that atomic power is the only viable course to achieve energy independence for most Western countries.

They emphasize that the risks of storing the waste are small and can be further reduced by using the latest technology and newer reactors. The operational safety record in the Western world is excellent when compared to the other major kinds of power plants.

Destructive weapons or a peaceful source of virtually unlimited energy? Only time will tell.

Epilogue
Contributors
Index

Epilogue

The Earth is a terrible thing to waste.

The environment is indeed a serious business. It affects every aspect of our lives and anything and everything that roams or exists on our planet.

As a consequence of industrial expansion across the world, global warming has occurred due to the emission of greenhouse gases such as carbon dioxide and numerous other adverse, perhaps irreversible, effects.

As South Korean President Myung-bak Lee commented in his contribution as the concluding article of the 50-part series, we should not pass on an Earth in danger to our posterity. Novel ways of thinking and behavior are needed. "We should choose a path that would ensure a new path sustainable prosperity and safety for future generations."

He also mentioned that the OECD has adopted green growth as a core strategy for achieving sustainable economic development in its 50th Anniversary Vision Statement.

United Nations Secretary-General Ki-moon Ban for his part warned in his contribution that "the world continues on a dangerous path in which economic growth has been achieved at the expense of natural resources and ecosystems."

He went on to say: "Climate change is an existential threat. Biodiversity loss is accelerating, desertification and land degradation are imperiling lives and incomes in all regions, and the marine environment is under assault pollution to over-fishing."

It became obvious through the presentation of the series that the concept of the Earth in danger is not confined to any country, region, or segment of society and industry.

The most important thing we have come to learn is how we embrace the environment affects every aspect of the lives of every single one of the 7 billion people who inhabit our planet.

And it is through this recognition that there is true meaning to the commitment the Korea Institute of Public Administration and The Korea Times made in inviting some of the most prominent figures in the world

of the environment and environmental protection to raise
awareness of the need to make extra efforts to make certain that we
don't leave future generations a world that is less livable and more
difficult to protect.

The Earth, after all, is a terrible thing to waste.

Moo-jong Park
President-Publisher
The Korea Times

Contributors

Global Leader

Myung-bak Lee

Myong-bak Lee was elected the 17th President of the Republic of Korea (2008-2013). He chaired the 2010 G20 Summit in Seoul and the 2011 Nuclear Summit on Jeju Island. Lee served two terms in the Korean National Assembly as a lawmaker before being elected Mayor of Seoul in 2002. Often dubbed a "CEO-turned-head of state," Lee was the first person to go from a rank-and-file company worker to the status of the President of South Korea.

Ki-moon Ban

Secretary-General of the United Nations. Served as Minister of Foreign Affairs and Trade in Korea, including foreign policy adviser to the President, chief national security adviser to the President, Deputy Minister for policy planning and director-general of American Affairs. Served as Chairman of the Preparatory Commission for the Comprehensive Nuclear Test Ban Treaty Organization and Chef de Cabinet during the Republic of Korea's 2001-2002 presidency of the UN General Assembly.

Jeffrey Sachs

American economist and Director of the Earth Institute at Columbia University. One of the youngest economics professors in the history of Harvard University, Sachs became known for his role as an adviser to Eastern European and developing country governments during the transition from communism to a market system or during periods of economic crisis. Subsequently he has been known for his work on the challenges of economic development, environmental sustainability, poverty alleviation, debt cancellation and globalization.

Jeremy Rifkin

President of the Foundation on Economic Trends in Washington, D.C., and teaches at the Wharton School's Executive Education Program at the University of Pennsylvania. He has advised the European Commission, the European Parliament, and several EU heads of state, including Prime Minister Jose Luis Rodriguez Zapatero of Spain and Prime Minister Romano Prodi of Italy.

Scholar

Komal Raj Aryal

Professor of Northumbria University in Great Britain. His current research explores local risks and the impact of disaster vulnerability risks on local environment. This research has been used to develop local risk and resilience tools (LRRT). The aims of LRRT are linked with current and future development needs associated with local and global sustainability.

Bernard Rowan

Professor and coordinator of political science and international studies at Chicago State University, where he has taught for 18 years. A former fellow of the Korea Foundation, Rowan is an advisor to the Korea Institute of Public Administration and a former visiting professor of the Graduate School of Local Autonomy, Hanyang University.

Sang-ok Choi

Associate professor in the Department of Public Administration at Korea University in Korea. He was an assistant professor at Virginia Tech and California State University-Dominguez Hills for seven years before he joined Korea University in August 2011.

Geoff O'Brien

Senior Lecturer in Geography and Environmental Management at Northumbria University in Britain. Prior to joining Northumbria University, Dr. O'Brien was involved in the geophysical industry with a global remit, focusing on environmental responsibility.

Jim Dator

Professor and director of the Hawaii Research Center for Futures Studies, Department of Political Science, and adjunct professor in the Program in Public Administration, the College of Architecture, and the Center for Japanese Studies, of the University of Hawaii at Manoa. Professor Dator is co-chair of Space and Society Division, International Space University, Strasbourg, France, and former president of World Futures Studies Federation.

International Organization

Richard Samans

Executive Director of the Global Green Growth Institute, which is headquartered in Seoul. He was Managing Director of the World Economic Forum until March 2011, overseeing the Forum's policy and public-private partnership initiatives as well as its relations with international organizations, governments, NGOs, unions and other non-business constituencies.

John L. Casti

Senior research scholar at the International Institute for Applied Systems Analysis in Laxenburg bei Wien, Austria. He is also the founder of the X-Center, a Vienna-based society for exploration of extreme events and uncertainty. His most recent book is Mood Matters: From Rising Skirt Lengths to the Collapse of World Powers.

Leena Ilmela

Senior Researcher in the International Institute for Applied Systems Analysis (IIASA) in Vienna, Austria. 20 countries fund IIASA's research, South Korea is one of them. Leena Ilmela's research theme is uncertainty, and her group is developing pragmatic tools for decision-making.

Brindusa Fidenza

Associate Director and deputy head of Climate Change Initiatives at the World Economic Forum, where she engages governments, the private sector and development institutions in collaborative approaches to designing public-private financing mechanisms for unlocking low-carbon markets in developing countries.

Margaret Arnold

Senior Social Development Specialist with the World Bank specializing in the social dimensions of climate change, disaster risk management, and community-based and gender-sensitive approaches to risk management. She leads work on pro-poor adaptation and resilience building for the Social Resilience cluster.

Randell Krantz

Director at the World Economic Forum located in Switzerland. Randell joined the Forum in 2005 to help promote the foundations of a nascent climate change initiative. As head of the Sustainability Initiative at the Forum, Randell works with business leaders to explore the transformational changes required to decouple consumption of energy and resources from environmental degradation.

Climate Institute

In the over 25 years since its founding in 1986 as the first environmental organization on the Earth focused on climate protection, the Climate Institute has been instrumental in moving climate protection onto the international agenda, fostering collaboration between developing countries and richer nations, and launching and implementing pioneering studies and initiatives on such subjects as environmental refugees.

Martin Kruse

Senior researcher at the Copenhagen Institute for Futures Studies (CIFS). Kruse has extensive experience in advising top management on issues of strategic concerns in various industries, including retail, financial services, manufacturing and energy, as well as in the public sector. He primarily works with innovation and strategic issues concerning the water-energy-food-climate nexus.

Government (Executive and Legislature)

Seung-Soo Han

Dr Han served as Prime Minister of Republic of Korea(2008-09). He is currently Member of the UN Secretary-General's Advisory Board on Water and Sanitation and Chair of High-Level Expert Panel on Water and Disaster. He was Special Envoy of the UN Secretary-General on Climate Change(2007-08), Member of the UN Secretary-General's High-Level Panel on Global Sustainability(2010-12), Founding Chair of Global Green Growth Institute(2010-12) and Chair of the 2009 OECD Ministerial Council Meeting, President of the 56th Session of the United Nations General Assembly(2001-02).

Young-sook Yoo

Yoo spent most of her career in scientific research at the Korea Institute of Science and Technology (KIST), was appointed as Environment Minister in May last year. In between her work at KIST, she also undertook research at the Korean Chemical Society and served as director at the Korean Society for Biochemistry and Molecular Biology. For her work in chemical research, Yoo was presented with the 3rd Amore Pacific Award for outstanding women in the sciences in 2008.

Do-youp Kwon

Kwon Do-youp was appointed as the first Minister of Land, Transport and Maritime Affairs in 2011 after a long career at the Ministry of Construction and Transportation. Prior to the appointment, he was president of the Korea Expressway Corporation.

Won-soon Park

Mayor of Seoul. After years of activities in the judiciary and universities, including a position on the Council of the Constitutional Court, he was elected as Mayor in 2011. He also helped found the Beautiful Foundation and acted as its general executive director in 2002-2010.

Soo-gil Young

Young has been Chairman of the Presidential Committee on Green Growth since its founding in 2009. He also serves on the Council for Green Growth Leaders launched by the Monday Morning think tank in Copenhagen in 2010 and co-chairs the Advisory Board for the Green Growth Forum launched by the Danish government in 2011.

Kyoo-yong Lee

Former Environment Minister Lee is a career bureaucrat who began his service in government in 1978 at the Ministry of Government Legislation and joined the Environment Ministry in 1990. At present, Lee is senior advisor for environment-related cases at the law firm Kim & Chang.

Dae-won Park

President of the Korea International Cooperation Agency (KOICA). He began his career in 1974 at the foreign ministry. Previously, Park also served as a member of the Presidential Council on Nation Branding.

Mi-ae Choo

A member of the Supreme Council of the Democratic United Party. She made her entry in politics as a member of the 15th Korean National Assembly in 1996 after serving as a judge for over 10 years. Between 2008 and 2010, she was chairwoman of the House Environment and Labor Committee.

Hee-bong Chae

Chae has been at the Knowledge Economy Ministry since 1990, during which time he was engaged in a number of energy-related bureaus, including director of energy policy. He is now director general of the Presidential Committee on Regional Development.

Do-soo Jang

Director of the Center for International Cooperative Programs of the Korea Ocean Research and Development Institute (KORDI). He is also working as Chairman of the Drafting Committee for the Yeosu Declaration. Before Jang was appointed to be in charge of international affairs at KORDI, he had been a senior advisor to the president of KORDI during the period 2008-2009.

World Governments

Christian Friis Bach

Danish Minister for Development and Cooperation in 2011. Friis is an agronomist and holds a Ph.D. in international economics from the University of Copenhagen. Bach has more than 20 years of experience in development work. He has also worked for the World Bank, UNEP and DansChurchAid.

Torbjørn Holthe

Ambassador Holthe began his public career at the Norwegian Ministry of Justice in 1979. He moved on to the Ministry of Foreign Affairs in 1982 and spent a number of years overseas. Holthe was ambassador for Caribbean Affairs from 2008 before coming to Korea as the envoy in November 2011.

Ilan Kelman

Senior Research Fellow at the Center for International Climate and Environmental Research, Oslo. His main research and application interests are disaster diplomacy and sustainability in island communities. See www.ilankelman.org

JC Gaillard

Senior Lecturer at the School of Environment of the University of Auckland, New Zealand. His research, policy and practical interests span a wide range of topics related to disaster risk reduction.

Thani Al-Zeyoudi

Head of the Directorate of Energy and Climate Change (DECC) within the UAE's Ministry of Foreign Affairs (MOFA), where he leads the country's development of sustainable foreign and domestic policy. He is also the UAE representative for the International Renewable Energy Agency (IRENA) within DECC.

Chin-keun Park

Park completed his doctorate in economics at the University of California, Los Angeles. He has been a professor at Yonsei University in Seoul and advisor to numerous organizations, including the Federation of Korean Industries.

Eung-kyuk Park

President of the Korea Institute of Public Administration (KIPA), a state-run think tank under the Office of the Prime Minister. He worked as a professor of public administration at Hanyang University for 28 years before he was appointed to the research institution. Authored "Good Local Autonomy and Governance" and "Federation Path to Korean Unification: Global and Local Prerequisites."

Chang-seok Park

Resident research fellow at the Korea Institute of Public Administration (KIPA). Park, a former Korea Times managing editor and Kyung Hee University media professor, is the author of "The History of the Korean English Newspaper" and "News English." He is the editor of KIPA's two English books "Korea: From Rags to Riches" and "Discover Korea in Public Administration."

Eun-sung Kim

Associate research fellow at the Korea Institute of Public Administration. He is currently working on disaster and risk management, in particular, decision-making in the face of scientific uncertainty. He has conducted risk studies of mad cow disease, genetically modified organisms, nanotechnology, climate change, and enterprise risk management

Yong-seok Seo

Research fellow at the Research Center of Social Integration at the Korea Institute of Public Administration. Seo earned his Ph.D. in political science at the University of Hawaii at Manoa. His major area of specialization is strategic foresight on social and demographic change.

Journalist

Jake J. Nho

Nho has been a journalist since 1985, has covered the environment beat since around 1990. He has written numerous articles on environmental issues for over 20 years. He also has been working in the area corporate affairs during his career. Nho is currently a part of organizing the "Earth in Danger" series.

Yearn-hong Choi

Choi has written academic articles in Environmental Management, Environmental Conservation, Journal of Environmental Education, Journal of Environmental Sciences, Nuclear Plant Safety, Environmental Engineering, Water Environment and Technology.

Entrepreneur

Joong-kyum Kim

Kim spent a good part of his career with Hyundai Engineering and Construction, playing a critical role in introducing environment-friendly construction techniques. He served as chairman of the Korea Housing Association before assuming his current position as President and CEO of KEPCO.

Keung-hwan Kim

Executive Vice President and head of the Technology Development Center at Samsung C&T. Prior to joining Samsung, Kim had a number of assignments, including the position of Chairman of the Korea Recycled Construction Resource Institute in 2006.

Tae-won Chey

Chairman of SK Group, who maintains core businesses in energy, telecommunications, and trading and services. Through a visionary management philosophy that concentrates on encouraging positive system changes and an entrepreneurial spirit, Chey promotes the group's continued growth and success in areas such as energy exploration and production and advanced mobile communications.

Jean Keijdener

Keijdener assumed the role of Country Manager for Singapore-based Ascott Limited and general manager for the Somerset Palace Seoul in July 2008. Since his appointment, Keijdener has been active in implementing the company's environmental program.

Civil Society

Yul Choi

President of the Korea Green Foundation. In 1988, Choi became the first chairman of the Korean Anti-Pollution Movement (KAPMA). He was put under house arrest for the activities related to nuclear waste disposal problem. In 1992, he worked as director of the Korean NGO Committee for the Earth Summit in Brazil.

Jin-seng Park

As a psychiatrist and psychotherapist, Dr. Park approaches the complexities of humanity with sincerity, passion, and an open mind. In particular, he takes great interest in the elements of life that bring people happiness. From 2000 to 2004, he worked as a visiting professor at Catholic University, lecturing on meditation and counseling.

Index

A

Abu Dhabi 137, 217

Achim Steiner 150

The Act on greenhouse gas emissions trading 14

Adaptation 21, 42-44, 63, 65-68, 99, 163, 232, 235, 285

Africa 16, 21, 29, 84, 97-98, 104, 109, 115, 178, 181, 217

The air safety management 47

Alaska 115

Allocative Efficiency 78-79

Alternative fuels 59

Antarctica 84, 87, 115, 117, 119

Andes 111, 115

Angel Gurria 150

Anti-terrorism 46

The Arctic Council 204-205

The Army Corps of Engineers 49

Arthur C. Clarke 71

The Ascott 286, 288

Asia and the Pacific 39-42, 44, 202

The Asian Development Bank 25

Atomic power 182, 300-301, 303-304

Australia 40, 108, 115, 138

Azerbaijan 169

B

Balhae 240-241

The Baltic Sea 90

Bangladesh 40, 67, 102, 104, 120, 234

The Basic Act on Green Growth 14

BBC news 40

Bernard Rowan 45

Bill Clinton 230

Biochemical oxygen demand (BOD) 188

Biomass 59-60, 110, 130

Bipartisan agreement 200

Bloomberg New Energy Finance 97-98

Bosphorus 84

Brazil 13, 97, 138, 167, 254

Brian Fagan 84

Brindusa Fidenza 95

Building energy management system (BEMS) 279

Building Performance Consulting (BPC) 279

The Bulletin of the Atomic Scientists (BAS) 299

The Bureau International des Expositions (BIE) 192

C

Cambodia 95, 138-139, 169, 201-202, 235

The Carbon Capture and Storage (CCS) 60

Carbon dioxide 28-29, 33-34, 58-61, 87, 125-126, 149, 179-182, 226, 230, 280

Carbon monoxide 106, 224

Central America 102

Chang-seok Park 239

Chernobyl 58, 295

China 29, 40, 97-98, 109, 120, 125, 128, 173-175, 177-178, 180-181, 204, 206, 209-210, 224, 226, 231, 234-235, 240, 242-243, 260, 262, 267, 270, 300

China National Offshore Oil Corporation (CNOOC) 178

Chin-keun Park 223

Christian Friis Bach 199

Clean energy system 30

Climate change adaptation (CCA) 21, 43-44

Climate Institute 115

The Climate Policy Initiative 99

Coastal borders 47

Coastal waterways 47

CO_2 emissions 28, 91,105, 120, 129

Cold waves 39

The Combines Heat and Power (CHP) 60

The Coming Oil Crisis 123

The Comité de Emergencia Garifuna of
Honduras 104

Communication network 35

Community Practitioners' Platform for
Resilience (CPPR) 104

Conventional fuel 34

The Copenhagen climate change conference
179, 226

Corporate social responsibility (CSR) 281

The crisis of the 1970s 124

Cross-sector working 44

Cyclone 40, 64, 102, 235

D

Dae-won Park 167

Danish Building Evaluation Centre 130

Davos 112

The Day After Tomorrow 85

Decarbonization 30

Deforestation 24, 96, 105, 110, 139, 169,
210, 231, 237, 270

The Demilitarized Zone (DMZ) 144

Denmark 30, 125, 129, 137-138, 176, 199-
201

The Department of Homeland Security (DHS)
49, 53, 55

De-prioritization 48

Desertification 14, 17, 24, 27, 231, 266

Disaster diplomacy 209-214

Disaster management 45-49

Disaster-prone areas 40

Disaster risk assessments 43

Disaster risk reduction (DRR) 41-43, 46-47

Divorce rates 45

Do-soo Jang 191

Do-youp Kwon 147

Drought 14, 19, 29, 40, 42, 52, 64-65, 67,
97, 104, 149-150, 152, 169, 188, 210, 231,
235

Durban, South Africa 16, 21

E

Earth in Danger 17-18, 21-22

Earthquake 51, 103, 174, 211-212, 243,
261, 296, 301-302

Earth Summit 23, 254, 296-297

The East Asian Climate Partnership (EACP) 20

e-Coli bacteria 91

Economic damage 52, 97

Economic multiplier effect 35-36

Ecosystem 24, 33, 46, 52, 64-65, 67, 78, 91,
120, 142, 144, 193, 204-205, 229-231, 233,
236-237, 245, 268, 284

Edith Brown Weiss 255

Effectiveness 41, 44, 105

Electricity 36, 58-60, 71, 80, 110-112, 126,
130-131, 137, 149, 152-154, 164-165, 169,
171, 179, 199-200, 216, 218, 262, 274,
276, 286, 289, 303

The End of Suburbia 123

Energy Crisis 20

Energy Efficiency 26, 30, 34, 60, 97, 152-
153, 162-164, 171, 200, 274, 278-279

Energy efficient power generation 15

Energy Security 178, 183, 205, 218, 303

Energy Storage system 15

The Energy Systems Research Unit (ESRU)
279

England 84

Entropy 236-237

The European Environmental Agency (EEA)
176

Environmental emergency management
system (E2MS) 53

The Environmental Information and
Observation Network (EIONET) 176

Environmental laws 175, 270

Environmental Protection Agency (EPA) 52, 120, 245

Environmental Response Laboratory Network (ERLN) 52

Ethical Consumerism 225

Ethiopia 97, 138-139

Eung-kyuk Park 229

Eun-sung Kim 245

The European Union (EU) 34, 36, 90, 124, 129, 176, 205

Exclusive Economic Zones (EEZs) 265

F

The Federal Civil Defense Administration 55

The Federal Disaster Relief Act 54

The Federal Emergency Management Agency (FEMA) 55

Federalism 45, 48-49

The Federal Reserve 49

The Federal Response Plan 55

Federal system 46-47

Felipe Calderon 98-99

Finland 91-92, 296

The First Five-Year Green Growth Plan 136

The first great recession 48

Fiscal dilemmas 48

Floodplains 47, 211

Florida 47

Food security 29

The Four River Water Quality Upgrading Plan 186

Forest fire 39, 235

Fossil fuel 28, 33-34, 58, 60, 62, 96, 98, 122, 135, 138, 179, 200, 230, 262, 301, 304

The Four Major Rivers Restoration Project 19

Framework Act on Low Carbon 18, 136, 163

FTA 175

Fukushima 58, 152-154, 173, 180, 182, 215, 261, 296, 301

G

Geoff O'Brien 57, 63

George Bush 55

Geothermal energy 59, 218

Germany 58, 61, 91, 99, 138, 180, 182, 301

Global economy 13, 14, 24, 31, 35, 40, 90, 121, 136-137

Global Green Growth Institute (GGGI) 15, 20, 79, 97, 137, 201

Global Green Growth Partnership 15, 20

The Global Humanitarian Forum 68

Global warming 14, 17, 19, 34, 54, 60, 85, 90, 149, 152, 163-164, 230-231, 238, 260-262, 287, 295, 300-301

Golden thread 26

Gonggeumji 144

Governance 30, 40-44, 54, 80-81, 104, 173-176, 245, 249, 269

The Government of Indonesia and the Free Aceh Movement (GAM) 102

Grassroots organizations 104

Great Ocean Conveyor 85

Green Climate Fund 16, 21, 68, 98

Green economy 16, 25, 30-31, 77, 80, 167, 170, 192, 215, 219

Green Growth 14-22, 30, 77-81, 95, 97-99, 135-140, 142, 145, 149, 161-163, 168-171, 191, 199-202, 217, 219, 274

Green Growth Forum 201

Green growth plan (GGP) 18, 80, 136, 138-139, 201, 219

Green Growth Knowledge Platform 15, 21

Greenhouse gas emissions (GHG) 14, 18, 57, 65, 96-97, 99, 109, 193-195, 233, 274

Greenhouse Gas Target Management System 163

Green new deal 15, 150

Green Technology 15, 19-20, 136, 139, 286

The Green Technology Center Korea (GTCK) 20

GROOTS International 103

Gross Domestic Product (GDP) 18, 29, 45, 67, 78-79, 95, 98, 125, 129, 270

Group of 20 (G20) 21, 79, 81, 98-99

H

Hard-wiring of energy 29

Hawaii 69-73

Heat blanket 87

Heat waves 39

Hee-bong Chae 177

Himalayas 115

Hiroshi Machida 240

Holland 84

Honda 40

Hongneung 21

Huairou Commission 104

The Hudson Institute 49

Human-made disaster 51

Hunters in the Snow 83

Hurricane 47-49, 51, 55 102, 104, 212, 230-231

Hydroelectric power 59

Hydrogen 35-36, 59-60, 130, 153, 242

Hyogo Framework for Action (HFA) 41, 43-44

I

Ilan Kelman 209

India 40, 97-99, 102-104, 120, 125, 143, 178, 211, 234-235, 296, 300

Indonesia 97, 102, 104, 120, 138-139, 169-171, 211, 235

The Industrial Revolution 58

Infant mortality 45

Information Technology (IT) 80, 181, 245, 282

The Intergovernmental Panel on Climate Change (IPCC) 64-65, 90, 118-120, 179, 235

The Integrated Consortium of Laboratory Networks (ICLN) 53

The International Atomic Energy Agency 218

The International Development Finance Club 99

The International Ecotourism Society (TIES) 143

The International Energy Agency (IEA) 96, 123

The International Forum on Globalization (IFG) 232

International Institute of Applied Systems analysis (IIASA) 92

The International Renewable Energy Agency (IRENA) 217

The International Thermonuclear Experimental Reactor (ITER) 59

The International Union for Conservation of Nature and Natural Resources (IUCN) 150

Italy 241

J

Jake J. Nho 259

Japan 30, 58, 96, 101, 125, 138, 152-154, 173-174, 176, 180, 204, 206, 215, 226, 231, 234-235, 240, 242-243, 261, 279, 296, 300, 302

JC Gaillard 209

Jean Keijdener 285

Jeremy Rifkin 33, 236

Jerry Marden 232

Jim Dator 69

Jimmy Carter 55

The Johannesburg Declaration on Sustainable Development 192

John L. Casti 83

K

Katrina 47-48, 55, 212
Kazakhstan 138-139, 178
Kenya 97, 99
KEPCO 215, 218, 273-276
Keung-hwan Kim 277
Keynesian 73
KFW 99
Ki-moon Ban 17, 23, 194, 216, 304
Knowledge-sharing 44
Komal Raj Aryal 39
Korea Gas Corporation (KOGAS) 183
The Korea Institute of Public Administration 267
The Korea Institute for International Economic Policy (KIEP) 202
The Korea International Cooperation Agency (KOICA) 169
The Korea Legislative Research Institute (KLRI) 202
The Korea National Oil Corporation (KNOC) 181
The Korea Times 17, 135, 267
The Kunsthistorisches Museum 83
Kyoo-yong Lee 155, 185
The Kyoto Protocol 226

L

Lake Superior 84
Laura Bush 268
Leena Ilmela 89
Liquefied natural gas (LNG) 182
Little Ice Age (LIA) 83-84, 87
Low Carbon, Green Growth 18, 168, 171

M

Maharashtra 103
The Maldives 120, 143
Margaret Arnold 101

Martin Freer 261
Martin Kruse 121, 127
Mass electrification of transport system 31
McKinsey 109
Meteor dust 86
The Mexican Business 20 Summit(B20) 98
Mexico 85, 97, 99, 268
Mi-ae Choo 173
The Middle East and Asia 96
Migratory species 267
The Millennium Development Goals (MDGs) 25, 57
Ministry of Construction and Transportation 186
Ministry of Home Affairs 187
Montreal Protocol 24-25
Mt. Baekdu 239-243
Mount Kilimanjaro 115
Mongolia 169, 173-174, 234-235
Mudslides 39-40, 213
Myanmar 40, 235
Myung-bak Lee 13, 17, 79, 137, 161-162, 281

N

The Nairobi Declaration 192
Nakdong River 157, 185-187
Nargis 40
National Adaptation Program 44
National defense 49
National development 46, 99, 216
National disaster areas 49
The National Emergency Management Agency 54
National Green Growth Master Plan (NGGMP) 201
The National Incident Management Strategy 55
the National Institute for Civil Protection (INDECI) 104

The National Petroleum Corporation(CNPC) 178

The National Response Framework 48

The National Response Plan 56

National security 48-49, 51, 55, 164, 300

Natural disaster 46-48, 55,101-102,143,168, 176, 193, 229-230, 241, 243, 302

Natural gas 29-30, 24-35, 59, 98, 178, 182 210, 218, 232, 262, 294

Natural hazard 41

Nepal 40, 104, 234

New Green Deal 150

New People's Army (NPA) 213

New York City 51

Nicaragua 104

Nitrogen 106, 186, 236

Non-Governmental Organization (NGO) 49, 98, 246

North America 84, 204, 206

The North Atlantic 85, 87

The Northern Hemisphere 85, 91, 253

North Korea 145, 181-182, 209-211, 214, 240, 242-243, 300, 302-303

The Norwegian shelf 124

Northwest Pacific Action Plan (NOWPAP) 174, 269

Noxious gases 106

The Nuclear Non-proliferation Treaty (NPT) 300

Nuclear power 31, 58, 126, 151-154, 175, 179-182, 215, 243, 261, 295-269, 301-303

Nuclear war 87, 299-300

Nuclear Winter 87

O

Official development assistance (ODA) 15, 20, 168

The Official Journal of the European Union 129

The Organization for Economic Cooperation and Development (OECD) 77, 164, 174

Ozone (O3) 24-25, 106, 224, 259-260

P

Pakistan 40, 97, 214, 235, 300

Pan-National Water Purification Plan 186

Peak oil 34, 123-124, 232

Peer-to-peer 35

The Pet Evacuation and Transportation Standards Act 55

Phenol incident 186

Philippins 40, 97, 120, 169, 213-214, 235

Pieter Brueghel 83

Pollution-related disasters 52

Posco 164, 263

Post-Katrina Emergency Management Reform Act 55

Power grid development 15

Power to the people 36

Precipitation 52, 64, 115, 117

Presidential Committee on Green Growth 18, 21, 136

Presidential election cycle 46

The ProVention Consortium 103

Purchasing Power Parity (PPP) 28

R

The Ramsar Convention 142

Randell Krantz 107

Rasmussen 137

Reducing Emissions from Deforestation and Forest Degradation (REDD) 105

Renewable technologies 58-59, 62

Research and Development (R&D) 245

The Renewable Energy Network (REN21) 97

Richard Samans 77

Richard Weitz 49

Rio+20 13, 21, 24-25, 27, 81, 97, 138, 167, 170, 281, 283

The Rio Declaration on Environment and

Development 192, 254

Risk management 41, 53, 90-92, 102, 246, 248

Risk reduction 41-44, 46, 47

River Thames 84

The Robert T. Stafford Disaster Relief and Emergency Assistance Act (Stafford Act) 55

Russia 40, 89, 91, 124, 174, 182, 206, 235, 240-243, 300

S

San Giorgio Group 99

Sangju 144

Sang-ok Choi 51

Sarah Waterman 48

Saudi 123, 179-181

Scarcity 64, 110, 237

Second-generation information system 35

Seung-Soo Han 135

Sheikh Zaki Yamani 123, 126

Shell Oil Company 294

Shinawatra 150

Siberia 85, 141, 234

Sir David King 58

Smart Fish Aggregating Device (Smart FAD) 195

Smart intergrids 35

Social entrepreneurship (SE) 282

Social safety net 26

Solar power system 30

Songdo 40

Sony 40

South Africa 16, 21, 97

Southeast Asia 142

South Korea 97, 182, 201-202, 217-218, 239, 243, 263, 301

Space clouds 86

Spain 91, 108, 217

Sri Lanka 40, 102, 169, 171, 211, 234

Stakeholder engagement 288

Steam power technology 35

The Stockholm Declaration 192, 253

Storm surges 39, 119, 235

Sub-Saharan Africa 98, 109

Sulfur dioxide 106

Suncheon Bay 142, 145

Sustainable development 13, 15-16, 24-25, 31, 40-44, 57, 80, 103, 142, 145, 167, 170, 192, 204, 215-216, 245, 253-254, 269, 270

Sustainable world economy 98

Switzerland 293

T

Tae-won Chey 281

Technology cooperation 15

Terrorism 46, 49, 55-56, 303

Texas 47, 51

Thailand 40, 97

Thani Al-Zeyoudi 215

Thomas Birkalnd 48

Tim Conlan 48

Tomakomai 240

Torbjørn Holthe 203

Tornadoes 51-52

Tsunamis 64, 143, 211, 265

Tundra 65, 85

Turkey 84, 103

U

Unemployment 78, 91, 283

The United Arab Emirates (UAE) 139, 215

The U.K. 58, 138

The United Nations Climate Change Conference 21

The UN Conference on Sustainable Development (UNCSD) 167

The United Nations Convention on the Law of the Sea (UNCLOS) 267

The UN Development Programme (UNDP) 67

The United Nations Economic and Social

Commission for Asia and the Pacific
(UNESCAP) 202
The United Nations Environment Program
(UNEP) 14, 77, 150, 192, 269
The United Nations Framework Convention
on Climate Change (UNFCCC) 16, 58
United Nations Global Compact (UNGC) 284
The United Nations International Strategy for
Disaster Reduction (UNISDR) 104
UN Secretary General 17
The United States 29-30, 45-48, 51-55, 74,
85, 96, 106, 124-125, 128, 175, 178-179,
181, 209, 212, 224, 226, 230, 249, 260,
268, 270, 294, 296, 300-302
The United Nations World Conference on
Disaster Risk Reduction 41
Upo Wetland 141-142, 145
Uranium-based energies 36
Uranium enrichment programs 302
Urbanization 24, 127-128

V

Vanuatu 40, 120
Venezuela 178
The Vienna Declaration 254
Vietnam 40, 97, 99, 120-121, 235
Voluntarism 54
Vulnerability 42-43, 52, 54, 65-66, 91, 102,
105, 178, 214, 235, 252

W

Water-food-energy-climate nexus 110
Water management 168-169, 186-188
Weather-related disasters 52
Wind Power 30, 71, 179, 280
Wireless communication technologies 34
Won-soon Park 151
The World Bank 15, 68, 99, 105, 128, 269
The World Conference on Disaster Reduction
46

The World Economic Forum 96, 98-99, 110,
112-113, 188
World economy 29, 34, 95, 98
The World Wide Web 34

Y

Yearn-hong Choi 265
Yellow dust 173-175
The Yellowstone National Park 87
Yeosu Declaration 191-194
Yongin 148, 277
Yongsan 148, 187
Yong-seok Seo 251
Young-sook Yoo 141
Yul Choi 293

Z

Zero Hunger Challenge 26
Zipcar 112

Appendix

Environment Info
Forum(40) and Conference(48)

Environment Info

Climate change

The most general definition of climate change is a change in the statistical properties of the climate system when considered over long periods of time, regardless of cause. Accordingly, fluctuations over periods shorter than a few decades, such as El Nino, do not represent climate change.

The term sometimes is used to refer specifically to climate change caused by human activity, as opposed to changes in climate that may have resulted as part of the Earth's natural processes. In this sense, especially in the context of environmental policy, the term climate change has become synonymous with anthropogenic global warming.

Cars, trucks and other road transport vehicles, while essential for commercial and humanitarian work, exert a considerable adverse impact on the environment. Estimates are that road vehicles consume more than a third of the world's supply of petroleum and contribute nearly one-fifth of global carbon dioxide emissions. These vehicles also are a significant source of air pollution that can adversely affect human health and the environment.

CO_2 emissions in Seoul

South Korea is the 9th largest CO_2 emitter in the world.

It experienced a growth in fossil fuel CO_2 emissions with an average annual growth rate of 11.5 percent from 1946-1997. Coal consumption accounts for 43.5 percent of South Korea's fossil fuel CO_2 emissions.

Since the nation is the world's 5th largest importer of crude oil, oil consumption has been a major reason for CO_2 emissions since late 1960s. Then natural gas became the major source for emission of CO_2, as it increased the imports of liquid natural gas in 1987.

Due to the reduced production of secondary petroleum fuels and reduced imports of crude oil, South Korea's emissions fell 14.7 percent from 1997-1998. Since 1998, fossil fuel emissions have risen 37.7 percent and in 2007 it reached an all time high of 137 million metric tonnes of CO_2. Now South Korea emits about 514 million metric tons of

CO_2 and it is Asia's fourth biggest polluter.

South Korea (1.4 percent per year) is the only OECD country other than Mexico for which average emissions growth exceeds 1 percent per year. The Ministry of Knowledge Economy reported that South Korea's per capita CO_2 output of 10.1 tons ranked it 23rd place word wide, up from 25th place in 2006.

Consumption

Today's consumption is undermining the environmental resource base. It is exacerbating inequalities. And the dynamics of the consumption-poverty-inequality-environment nexus is accelerating. Will the trends continue without change? Not redistributing from high-income to low-income consumers, not shifting from polluting to cleaner goods and production technologies, not promoting goods that empower poor producers, not shifting priority from consumption for conspicuous display to meeting basic needs? Failure to do so will worsen today's problems of consumption and human development.

The real issue is not consumption itself but its patterns and effects. Inequalities in consumption are stark. Globally, the 20 percent of the world's people in the highest-income countries account for 86 percent of total private consumption, the poorest 20 percent, a minuscule 1.3 percent.

More specifically, the richest fifth consumes: 45 percent of all meat and fish, the poorest fifth just five percent; 58 percent of total energy, the poorest fifth less than 4 percent; have 74 percent of all telephone lines, the poorest fifth 1.5 percent; consume 84 percent of all paper, the poorest fifth 1.1 percent; own 87 percent of the world's vehicles, the poorest fifth less than one percent.

Disaster management

Disaster management is a strategy that is implemented to respond to any type of catastrophic event. Sometimes referred to as disaster recovery management, the process may be initiated when anything threatens to disrupt normal operations or puts human lives at risk.

Governments at all levels, as well as many businesses, devise some sort of disaster plan in preparation to overcome a potential catastrophe and return to normal function as quickly as possible.

One of the essential elements of disaster management involves defining the types of catastrophes that could possibly disrupt the day-to-day operation of a city, town, business, or country. Identifying those potential disasters makes it possible to create contingency plans, assemble supplies, and outline procedures that can be initiated when and if a given disaster does come to pass.

A truly comprehensive disaster management plan encompasses a wide range of possibilities that can easily be adapted in the event one disaster sets off a chain reaction of other types of disasters in its wake.

Disaster recovery

Disaster recovery is a concept developed in the mid to late 1970s as computer center managers began to recognize the dependence of their organizations on computer systems. At that time, most systems were batch-oriented mainframes that in many cases could be down for a number of days before significant damage would be done to the organization.

As awareness of disaster recovery grew, an industry developed to provide backup computer centers, with Sun Information Systems (which later became Sungard Availability Systems) becoming the first major U.S. commercial hot site vendor, established in 1978 in Philadelphia.

During the 1980s and 1990s, IT disaster recovery awareness and the disaster recovery industry grew rapidly, driven by the advent of open systems and real-time processing (which increased the dependence of organizations on their IT systems). Another driving force in the growth of the industry was increasing government regulations mandating business continuity and disaster recovery plans for organizations in various sectors of the economy.

Eco-friendly Seoul

As an important case of a city administration's governance, Mayor Park introduced the city's specific goals to save energy and eliminate the need for one nuclear power plant; the city's leadership in opening swap meets in all districts at least once a month to recycle unused household items; its decision to collect unwanted electronic items for free by removing the charge to discard large consumer appliances; and its efforts to promote urban agriculture. This has combined to draw many highly favorable responses from citizens, as well as stressed the importance of collaboration between the public and private sector in pursuing all energy saving efforts.

High-speed electric cars first began to operate in Seoul in 2010 and recharging stations were set up in more than a dozen locations. During the G20 Seoul Summit in

2010, a total of 53 eco-friendly cars, including electric cars and hydrogen- fuel-cell vehicles were mobilized and used successfully. This demonstrated Korea's advanced technology in this area to the whole world. Most notably, electric buses operate regularly now in Seoul: as an early adaptor electric buses were successfully fabricated and launched for use in the city in December 2010, for the first time in the world

Eco-friendly Tourism

Sound environmental management of tourism facilities and especially hotels can increase the benefits to natural areas. But this requires careful planning for controlled development, based on analysis of the environmental resources of the area. Planning helps to make choices between conflicting uses, or to find ways to make them compatible. By planning early for tourism development, damaging and expensive mistakes can be prevented, avoiding the gradual deterioration of environmental assets significant to tourism.

Cleaner production techniques can be important tools for planning and operating tourism facilities in a way that minimizes their environmental impact. For example, green building (using energy-efficient and non-polluting construction materials, sewage systems and energy sources) is an increasingly important way for the tourism industry to decrease its impact on the environment. And because waste treatment and disposal are often major, long-term environmental problems in the tourism industry, pollution prevention and waste minimization techniques are especially important for the tourism industry. A guide to sources of information on cleaner production (free) is available here.

Ecological construction

Eco-friendly or ecological construction is building a structure that is beneficial or non-harmful to the environment and resource efficient. Otherwise known as green building, this type of construction is efficient in its use of local and renewable materials, in the energy required to build it, and the energy generated while within it.

Eco-friendly construction has developed in response to the knowledge that buildings often have a negative impact on our environment and our natural resources. This includes transporting materials hundreds or thousands of miles, requiring even more energy in order to move them, and also in the emission of hazardous chemicals from poorly designed buildings that create and trap them.

Many options are now available to those wishing to design and build an eco-friendly dwelling. This is in response to local environmental concerns and the physical resource opportunities available, coupled with 21st century technological refinements.

Ecosystem

An ecosystem (short for "ecological system") is generally defined as a community of organisms living in a particular environment and the physical elements with which they interact. An ecosystem is an open functional unit that results from the interactions of abiotic (soil, water, light, inorganic nutrients and weather), biotic (plants, animals, and microorganisms usually categorized as either producers or consumers), and cultural (anthropogenic) components.

An ecosystem can be as small as a field or as large as the ocean. It is used to describe the world's major habitat types. Terrestrial ecosystems include arctic and alpine ecosystems, dominated by tundra with scarce vegetation; forest ecosystems, which can be subdivided into a whole range of types including tropical rainforests, Mediterranean evergreen forests, boreal forests, and temperate coniferous, deciduous and mixed forests; grasslands and savannas; and deserts and semi-arid ecosystems. Freshwater ecosystems include lakes, rivers, and marshlands. Marine ecosystems comprise an enormous range, from coral reefs, mangroves, sea-grass beds, and other shallow coastal water ecosystems to open-water forms, including the mysterious, little-known ecosystems of the abyssal plains and trenches of the world's oceans.

Ecosystems sustain human societies and allow them to prosper, due to the nutritional, environmental, cultural, recreational and aesthetic resources they provide. We all depend directly or indirectly on the products and services of ecosystems, including crops, livestock, fish, wood, clean water, oxygen, and wildlife.

Energy Efficiency

In September 2007, the Department of Energy of the United States and the National Development and Reform Commission of China signed a Memorandum of Understanding for Cooperation on Industrial Energy Efficiency. At the fifth Strategic Economic Dialogue in December 2008, the United States and China agreed to include energy efficiency as an area of cooperation through the U.S.-China Framework for the 10-Year Cooperation on Energy and Environment agreement (hereinafter referred to as the "TYF").

In July 2009, the Department of Energy of the United States and the Ministry of Housing and Urban-Rural Development of China signed a Memorandum of

Understanding for Cooperation in Energy Efficient Buildings and Communities. In December 2008, the Export-Import Bank and Trade and Development Agency of the United States and the National Development and Reform Commission and the Export-Import Bank of China signed a Memorandum of Understanding on Cooperation in the Areas of Energy Conservation and Environmental Protection. In July 2009, the Export-Import Banks of both countries agreed on an Implementation Plan for Energy Efficiency and Environmental Exports.

Environmental laws

Environmental laws are a complex, interlocking body of statutes encompassing common law, treaties, conventions, regulations and policies to protect the people's right to a healthy and pleasant environment and to protect the natural environment, all in accordance with Article 35 of the Constitutional Law of the Republic of Korea.

Environmental issues are closely related to land, energy and industrial policies. Therefore, it is appropriate to understand environmental laws as a broad concept when it comes to preservation and improvements made.

Starting with the enactment and promulgation of the Environmental Pollution Prevention Act in 1963, which was designed to deal with environmental pollution generated from state-led industrialization efforts in the 1960s, including the first round of five-year economic development projects, the Korean government has introduced various environmental policies.

Since 2000, the government has established the foundation for precautionary measures to protect the environment, breaking away from the conventional end-of-pipe environmental management approach. Through this effort, the number of environmental laws regulated by the Ministry of Environment has grown to a total of 46, along with the diversification and specialization of management targets.

Environmental restoration

Environmental restoration is a term common in the citizens environmental movement.

Environmental restoration is closely allied with (or perhaps sometimes used interchangeably with) ecological restoration or environmental remediation. In the U.S., remediation is the term used more in the realms of industry, public policy, and the civil services.

Environmental restoration involves many different approaches and technologies depending on the requirements of the situation.

It can involve heavy equipment like cranes, graders, bulldozers or excavators and also handle processes like the planting of trees and other vegetation. It can involve high-tech processes such as those applied in the careful environmental control required in fish-hatchery procedures. Today, computerized regulation is often being utilized in these processes. Computer-based mapping has also become an important dimension of restorative work, as has computer modeling.

In some situations, environmental restorative work is handled entirely by professionals working with skilled operators and technicians. In others, ordinary local community members may do much of the work, acquiring skills as the project proceeds.

Food waste composting

As many as one billion people, mostly women and children, are regularly exposed to levels of indoor air pollution exceeding WHO guidelines by up to 100 times.

This startling statistic was quoted at a WHO strategy meeting on Air Quality and Health held in Geneva this year.

Air pollution is a major environmental health problem affecting both developed and developing countries. This is a truly global concern involving ambient air quality in cities as well as indoor air quality at the workplace, in both rural and urban areas. The highest air pollution exposures occur in the indoor environment, particularly in developing countries. Cooking and heating with solid fuel that is with wood, coal, dung, crop residues and charcoal still predominates for over half the world's population. A deadly combination of solid fuels, inefficient stoves, and poor ventilation trigger a complex mix of health damaging pollutants in homes.

Hydrogen car

The Norwegian environmental organization Zero has driven two hydrogen-powered cars from Oslo to Monaco without requiring extra fuel. Observers had said the feat, undertaken in Hyundai Motor cars, would be impossible to achieve.

Zero's Marius Bornstein and Bjrnar Kruse were sun-bathing by the Mediterranean following the 2,260-kilometer-long drive. After five days of travel, they finally rolled up in Monte Carlo. They drove from Oslo to the Mediterranean without a support vehicle or extra fuel supplies.

A fuel cell driven hydrogen car is basically an electric car in which fuel cells convert hydrogen into electricity. In essence, one could say that the car comes with its own electricity-producing power plant. Yet, the best part is that the only thing coming out of the exhaust is pure water.

In Norway, hydrogen-powered cars are also eligible for the same user-incentives as electric cars. Hence they are exempt from normal car taxes and road tolls, can use public transport lanes, and can park free of charge in public car parks. Few countries can boast of more hydrogen-filling stations than Norway.

Industrial revolution

Most products that people in the industrialized nations use today are turned out swiftly by the mass production, by people (and sometimes, robots) working on assembly lines using power-driven machines.

People of ancient and medieval times had no such products. They had to spend long, tedious hours of hand labor even on simple objects. The energy or power they employed in work came from their own and from animals' muscles. The Industrial Revolution is the name given the movement in which machines changed people's way of life as well as their methods of manufacturing.

The most important of the changes that brought about the Industrial Revolution were (1) the invention of machines to do the work of hand tools; (2) the use of steam, and later, other kinds of power in place of the muscles of human beings and of animals, and (3) the adoption of the factory system.

It is almost impossible to imagine what the world would be like if the effects of the Industrial Revolution were swept away. Electric lights would go out. Automobiles and airplanes would vanish. Telephones, radios, and television would disappear. Most of the abundant stocks on the shelves of department stores would be gone.

Kyoto Protocol

The Kyoto Protocol is an international agreement linked to the United Nations Framework Convention on Climate Change. The major feature of the Kyoto Protocol is that it sets binding targets for 37 industrialized countries and the European community to reduce greenhouse gas (GHG) emissions to an average of five per cent against 1990 levels over the five-year period 2008-2012.

The major distinction between the Protocol and the Convention is that while the Convention encouraged industrialized countries to stabilize GHG emissions, the Protocol commits them to do so.

Recognizing that developed countries are principally responsible for the current high levels of GHG emissions in the atmosphere as a result of more than 150 years of industrial activity, the Protocol places a heavier burden on developed nations under the principle of "common but differentiated responsibilities."

The Kyoto Protocol is generally seen as an important first step toward a truly global emission reduction regimen that will stabilize GHG emissions. It provides the essential architecture for future international agreements on climate change.

By the end of the first commitment period of the Kyoto Protocol in 2012, a new international framework needs to have been negotiated and ratified that can deliver the stringent emission reductions that the Intergovernmental Panel indicated on Climate Change (IPCC) has clearly are needed.

Law of the Sea

The United Nations Convention on the Law of the Sea (UNCLOS), also called the Law of the Sea Convention or the Law of the Sea Treaty, is the international agreement that resulted from the Third United Nations Conference on the Law of the Sea (UNCLOS III), which took place from 1973 through 1982. The Law of the Sea Convention defines the rights and responsibilities of nations in their use of the world's oceans, establishing guidelines for businesses, the environment, and the management of marine natural resources.

The Convention, concluded in 1982, replaced four 1958 treaties. UNCLOS came into force in 1994, a year after Guyana became the 60th state to sign the treaty. To date, 162 countries and the European Community have joined the Convention. However, it is uncertain to what extent the Convention codifies customary international law.

While the Secretary General of the United Nations receives instruments of ratification and accession and the UN provides support for meetings of states party to the Convention, the UN has no direct operational role in the implementation of the Convention. There is, however, a role played by organizations such as the International Maritime Organization, the International Whaling Commission, and the International Seabed Authority (the latter was established by the UN Convention).

Nuclear energy

Industry leaders meet in Korea to discuss the relevance of nuclear energy and security implications prior to the Nuclear Security Summit Monday and Tuesday. Nuclear power is the use of sustained nuclear fission to generate heat and electricity. Nuclear power plants provide about six percent of the world's energy and 13-14 percent of the world's electricity, with the U.S., France, and Japan together accounting for about 50 percent of nuclear generated electricity. In 2007, the IAEA reported there were 439 nuclear power reactors in operation in the world, operating in 31 countries. Also, more than 150 naval vessels using nuclear propulsion have been constructed.

There is an ongoing debate about the use of nuclear energy. Proponents such as the World Nuclear Association and IAEA contend that nuclear power is a sustainable energy source that reduces carbon emissions. Opponents such as Greenpeace International and NIRS believe that nuclear power poses many threats to people and the environment. Nuclear power plant accidents include the Three Mile Island accident (1979), the Chernobyl disaster (1986), and the Fukushima Daiichi nuclear disaster (2011).

Ocean levels

The possible causes and specific contributions to fast sea level rising and the uncertainties are very large, particularly for Antarctica.

However, in general it appears that the observed rise can be explained by thermal expansion of the oceans and by the increased melting of mountain glaciers and the margin of the Greenland ice sheet. From present data, it is impossible to judge whether the Antarctic ice sheet as a whole is currently out of balance and is contributing, either positively or negatively, to changes in sea level.

Future changes in sea level were estimated for each of the Intergovernmental Panel on Climate Change (IPCC) forcing scenarios in future predictions.

For each scenario, three projections - best estimate, high and low - were made corresponding to the estimated range of uncertainty in each of the potential contributing factors.

It was found that for the IPCC Business-as-Usual Scenario, at year 2030, global-mean sea level will be 8-29cm higher than today, with a best-estimate of 18cm. At the year 2070, the rise will be 21-71cm, with a best estimate of 44cm.

Most of the contribution is estimated to derive from thermal expansion of the oceans and the increased melting of mountain glaciers and small ice caps.

Ocean pollution

Pollution in the ocean is a major problem affecting the ocean and the rest of the Earth. Pollution in the ocean directly affects ocean organisms and indirectly affects human health and resources. Oil spills, toxic wastes, and dumping of other harmful materials are all major sources of pollution in the ocean. People should learn more to learn how to stop it.

What are toxic wastes?

Toxic wastes are poisonous materials that are being dumped into the ocean. They harm many plants and animals in the ocean and have a huge impact on our health. Toxic waste is the most harmful form of pollution to sea life and humans. When toxic waste harms an organism, it can quickly be passed along the food chain and may eventually end up being in our seafood. In the food chain, one toxic organism gets eaten by another larger animal, which is eaten by another animal, ending up as our seafood.

Toxic waste gets into seas and oceans by leaking and seepage from landfills, dumps, mines, and farms. Farm chemicals and heavy metals from factories can have a very harmful effect on marine life and humans.

When toxic waste harms an organism, it can quickly be passed along the food chain. In the food chain, one toxic organism is eaten by another larger animal, which is eaten by another animal, and ultimately can end up being our seafood.

Ozone layer

Ozone (O_3) is a gas composed of three oxygen atoms. It is not usually emitted directly into the air but is created at ground level by a chemical reaction between oxides of nitrogen and volatile organic compounds (VOC), in the presence of sunlight. Ozone has the same chemical structure whether it occurs miles above the earth or at ground level and can be "good" or "bad," depending on its location in the atmosphere.

In the earth's lower atmosphere, ground level ozone is considered "bad." Motor vehicle exhaust and industrial emissions, gasoline vapors, chemical solvents, and natural sources emit nitrogen and VOC that help form ozone. Ground level ozone is the primary constituent of smog. Sunlight and hot weather cause ground level ozone to form in the air in harmful concentrations. As a result, it is known as a summertime air pollutant. Many urban areas tend to have high levels of "bad" ozone, but even rural areas are subject to increased ozone levels because wind carries it hundreds of miles away from the original sources.

Pollution solution

In the United States and other developed nations, there are strong laws to protect clean water. Unfortunately, good starts are not always accompanied by strong follow-though. For instance, the implementation of the U.S. Clean Water Act in the 1970s did improve water quality over the subsequent decade or two. But the act called for zero discharge of pollutants into navigable waters by 1985, and fishable and swimmable waters by 1983.

"Yet almost all surface waters in the U.S. still suffer some level of pollution; discharges are still permitted; the EPA still categorizes roughly 40 percent of lakes, rivers, and streams as unsafe for fishing or swimming; and the number of U.S. river miles on which people have been advised to restrict their consumption of fish has risen sharply since the early 1990s."

Our first water pollution solution is simple: enforce existing laws. Politicians pontificating about a great new anti-pollution law they've sponsored means little if they continue to allow existing laws to go unenforced.

Beyond laws, there are some practical water pollution solutions that can be implemented by society and by you as an individual.

Resource depletion

The quality of water in the upper reaches of the Han River has in fact been improving in recent years, as is the case for many other rivers in Korea. Experts say this is the result of residents and visitors taking more care when they are in the vicinity to ensure less water pollution.

The past 210 years have seen some of the most amazing developments in human science and technology, thanks to the Industrial Age and its successor, the Information Age. However, the elements that make our highly sophisticated society possible are rapidly being depleted, prompting growing concern among scientists and environmentalists about human survival.

The reason for this concern is really simple. Today's industrial civilization is based on a trinity of resources: metals, hydrocarbons (fossil fuels) and electricity. Each of these elements is dependent upon the other two. Without electricity and metals, there would be no way to extract the hydrocarbons, or fossil fuels, that create more electricity and process more metals from ore. Without fossil fuels, there would be no efficient way to generate electric power.

Rio+20

The United Nations Conference on Sustainable Development (UNCSD) is being organized in pursuance of the General Assembly Resolution. The Conference will take place in Rio de Janeiro, Brazil on June 20-22, 2012 to mark the 20th anniversary of the

1992 United Nations Conference on Environment and Development (UNCED) and the 10th anniversary of the 2002 World Summit on Sustainable Development (WSSD) in Johannesburg.

It is envisaged as a Conference at the highest possible level, including Heads of State and Governments or other high-ranking representatives. The Conference will result in a focused political document.

The objective of the Conference is to secure renewed political commitment for sustainable development, to assess the progress to date and remaining gaps in the implementation of outcomes for the major summits on sustainable development, and to address new and emerging challenges.

The Conference will focus on two themes: (a) a green economy in the context of sustainable development and poverty eradication and (b) the institutional framework for sustainable development.

Smart grid

Toward the end of the 20th century, electricity demand patterns were established: domestic heating and air-conditioning led to daily peaks that were met by an array of "peak power generators" that are turned on for short periods each day.

The relatively low utilization of these peak generators (commonly gas turbines due to their relatively lower capital cost and faster start-up times) together with the attending redundancy in the electricity grid have resulted in high costs to electricity companies, which were passed on in the form of increased tariffs.

Since the early 21st century, opportunities to take advantage of improvements in electronic communications technology to resolve the limitations and costs of the electrical grid have become apparent.

Technological limitations on metering no longer force peak power prices to be averaged out and passed on to all consumers equally. In tandem, growing concerns over environmental damage from fossil-fired power stations have led to a desire to use large amounts of renewable energy. Dominant forms such as wind and solar power are highly variable, and so the need for more sophisticated control systems became apparent, in order to facilitate the connection of sources to the otherwise highly controllable grid.

Social responsibility

Social sustainability cannot be created simply through the physical design of the community, but then, neither can environmental sustainability be created by physical design alone. Physical design cannot ensure that individuals, families and communities will lead environmentally sustainable lifestyles, although it can help to make such environmentally sustainable choices easier.

Equally, while there is much that can be done on the "design" of the soft community infrastructure to ensure social sustainability, the physical design of the community can make it either easier or more difficult for communities to be socially sustainable. Thus there is a vital need to integrate the physical and social design of communities for sustainability.

In discussing sustainability, both social and environmental, it is important to understand that both require a system of economic activity compatible with and not destructive of either the ecological or the social web of life of which we are a part and upon which we depend for our health, well-being and quality of life.

Waste management

Waste management is an industry that revolves around the collection, storage, and disposal of waste, ranging from ordinary household waste to the waste generated at nuclear power plants. Developing effective waste management strategies is critical for nations all over the world, as many forms of waste can develop into a major problem when they are not handled properly. Numerous firms provide waste management services of a variety of types, and several governments also regulate the waste management industry for safety and efficacy.

Humans generate a great deal of waste as the byproduct of existence, and they always have, as evidenced by dumping pits located in or around archaeological sites. Every task, from preparing a meal to manufacturing a car, is accompanied by the production of waste material, which cannot be used for other things and needs to be disposed of effectively. If not contained and handled appropriately, waste can balloon into a huge problem, as for example when garbage ends up in the open ocean making animals and birds sick.

Water is essential

A considerable amount of water supplied to our households ends up being wasted.

We often inadvertently let water run while brushing our teeth. Even small leaks can waste a large volume of water over time. We thoughtlessly throw away unused water when we get a drink from any potable source. Small changes in our lives can save and conserve significant volumes of water.

If a person saves a cup of water, just a cup of water is conserved, but if 100 persons conserve a cup of water each, then 100 cups of water can be conserved. Each individual's contribution to water conservation may be minuscule, but the cumulative effect of all individuals' saving water can be dramatic.

Water pollution

Water pollution is any chemical, physical or biological change in the quality of water that has a harmful effect on any living thing that drinks, uses or lives (in) it. When humans drink polluted water, it often has serious effects on their health. Water pollution also renders water unsuitable for its desired uses. There are several classes of water pollutants, the main being disease-causing agents. These are bacteria, viruses, protozoa and parasitic worms that enter sewage systems and untreated waste.

Water shortage

Water is scarce. Yet, we take it for granted, we waste it, and we even pay too much to drink it from little plastic bottles. Nonetheless, nearly one billion people in the developing world today don't have access to it.

Clean, safe drinking water is scarce. It is the foundation of life, a basic human need. Yet today, all around the world, far too many people spend their entire day searching for it.

The importance of access to clean water cannot be overstated. Simply put, water scarcity is either the lack of enough water (quantity) or lack of access to safe water (quality).

It's hard for most of us to imagine that clean, safe water is not something that can be taken for granted. But, in the developing world, finding a reliable source of safe water is often time- consuming and expensive. This is known as economic scarcity. Water can be found...it simply requires more resources to do it.

In other areas, the lack of water is a more profound problem. There simply isn't enough. That is known as physical scarcity.

The problem of water scarcity is growing. As more people put ever-increasing demands on limited supplies, the cost and effort to build or even maintain access to water will increase.

Wind power

Like old-fashioned windmills, today's wind machines (also called wind turbines) use blades to collect the wind's kinetic energy. The wind flows over the blades, creating lift like the effect on airplane wings, which causes them to turn. The blades are connected to a drive shaft that turns an electric generator to produce electricity.

With the new wind machines, there is still the problem of what to do when the wind isn't blowing. At those times, other types of power plants must be used to make electricity.

In 2011, wind turbines in the United States accounted for about three percent of total U.S. electricity generation. Although this is a small fraction of the nation's total electricity production, it was equal to the annual electricity use of about 10 million households.

The amount of electricity generated from wind has grown significantly in recent years. Generation in the United States increased from about 6 billion kilowatt-hours in 2000 to about 120 billion kilowatt-hours in 2011.

New technologies have decreased the cost of producing electricity from wind, and growth in wind power has been encouraged by tax breaks for renewable energy and green pricing programs.

Volcanic eruptions

An important measure of eruptive strength is the Volcanic Explosivity Index (VEI), a magnitude scale ranging from 0 to 8 that often correlates to eruptive types.

During a volcanic eruption, lava, tephra (ash, lapilli tuff, volcanic bombs and blocks), and various gases are expelled from a volcanic vent or fissure.

Volcanologists have distinguished several types of volcanic eruptions. These are often named after famous volcanoes where the type of behavior has been observed.

Some volcanoes may exhibit only one characteristic type of eruption during a period of activity, while others may display an entire sequence of types all in one.

Forum and Conference

The following are excerpts from a forum of experts in environmental studies sponsored by the Korea Institute of Public Administration.

Owing to the fact that high-rises tend to use an enormous amount of energy, they must be levied with special taxes when construction permits are approved. Likewise, the energy consumed at COEX, a major convention and exhibition center in southern Seoul, is equivalent to that used in the entire City of Uijongbu, with her population of 600,000.

Just like developed countries, Korea must move in the direction of using small vehicles and increase taxes on large cars by a significant margin so that owners and prospective owners of smaller vehicles are provided with an advantage and incentive.

Another simple measure that can be taken to preserve the environment is to reduce the amount of water used when flushing the toilet, which is an average of 12 liters, by differentiating between lighter and heavier usage. There is the related story that in the name of environmental protection, the late President Chung-hee Park inserted a brick in the toilet basin to reduce the amount of water that is flushed.

Yung-hee Rho, Professor emeritus of the Environment Graduate School of Seoul National University and former chairman of the Korea Environment Institute

Considering fundamental environmental problems, we need to take into account the basic economic situation and how civilization has evolved over time. The past few centuries have been dominated by Western civilization, and there are aspects of this development that we need in terms of environmental implications. In the process, the West affected the rest of global culture and civilization, while Eastern culture made consistent efforts at coexistence between humans and nature.

In terms of trying to find solutions for the depletion of natural resources and identifying viable applications for the development of science and technology, Oriental culture can play a better role.

I actually began to open my eyes to environmental problems when I attended a conference in Japan in 1971 on the dangerous implications of environmental pollution to health. In the following year, the Earth Summit was held in Stockholm, attracting global attention to the direction in which our planet is headed and what needs to be done to prevent further adverse effects.

The market economy may give rise to competition, but sustainability means man and nature should recognize the other's needs to create a win-win strategy.

Sang-chul Choe, Professor emeritus of the Environment Graduate School of Seoul National University and former chairman of the Presidential Commission on Regional Development

Recognition of the importance of environmental change goes back to the 1972 Stockholm meeting and the Roma Club reports. "Man and the Environment" and "Limits to Growth," which declared that the Earth would come to an end in 2020.

As anticipated, the depletion of natural resources has grown worse and worse, as has environmental pollution. Despite the ominous warnings, problems continue to be buried, despite their continuation and worsening. It is high time that we recognize the problems at hand and find appropriate solutions.

Another important issue is the environment in education. It has reached a stage when teachers are avoiding environmental education, probably because students are not excited by it. Steps must be taken to train teachers in environmental education and ensure that they become more aware of environmental concerns and implications.

Changes also have to take place in the very way we live. Korea and the United States are about the only countries in the world where the demand for large vehicles continues to increase. In Japan, the majority of vehicles on the road have engine displacements of less than 1,000cc, while the consumption of water there is a fourth of what it is in Korea.

We are probably the only country in the world in which each household has at least three refrigerators - one that is built into the apartment, the one being used and a kimchi fridge (a unique type of refrigerator used to store Korean pickled cabbage).

There must be an effective change to the way that Koreans live their lives.

An-jae Kim, Professor emeritus of the Environment Graduate School of Seoul National University, chairman of the Korea Local Government Development Institute

There is a distinctive difference between disasters such as the eruption of volcanic mountains and earthquakes and those that are man-made. There is need to review the relationship between nature, the environment and mankind since they are intimately related, along with resulting damage to the environment, including forms of pollution and ecological hazards that are basically man-made.

It is time that we analyze the basics of the relationship between humans and nature, perhaps finding common ground along the way. The truth is that mankind has been seeking too much convenience in life, and this has inevitably led to increasing pollution. In addition, excessive competition for economic and financial growth has also contributed to a far worse environment.

There must be social justice between man and nature, since this is particularly important in addressing the issue of environmental pollution. A combination of wisdom and courage is necessary as we address nature and our very survival. There must be greater cooperation among governments and organizations, and we must live less conveniently and less competitively so as to prolong our survival and put off the end of our planet.

Hyung-kook Kim, Professor emeritus of the Environment Graduate School of Seoul National University, former civilian chairman of the Presidential Commission on Green Growth

The Korean government has recognized the seriousness of environmental problems and has presented low carbon, green growth as a new paradigm in pursuing national development. But there seems to be a lack of understanding regarding prevalent issues. The fact is that the term 'global warming,' even when expressed in Korean, is more positive than negative.

There needs to be a language with which the public can have a better and clearer understanding of the dangers we are facing in terms of the environment. Companies have been reluctant to participate in the introduction of a carbon tax and laws on the emission of greenhouse gases. Despite this reality, the truth is that despite the pursuit of green transportation in large cities, there are not enough places in the world that emit small amounts of carbon dioxide.

Chang-seok Park, Professor at Kyunghee University and visiting fellow at the Korea Institute of Public Administration

In 40 years, Korea will become a sub-tropical country with banana trees lining the streets instead of gingko trees. We used to have a climate of three warm days and four cold days in the winter, but this is now something of the past. We suddenly find ourselves in an environment in which we have summer and winter. This is perhaps because of the extreme conflict between nature and humanity where there is no form of co-prosperity whatsoever.

But not all is lost. Recently, Environment Minister Young-sook Yoo visited Nigeria where the Korean government has been funding a project to purify polluted streams. A lot of environmental solutions are about international cooperation.

And it is perhaps no coincidence that we are holding this forum on the environment at a time when leaders of the world are attending the Earth Summit as part of the Rio+20 Conference. Such conferences are necessary at a time when people are using terms like "hot Earth" resulting from global warming, a term that is much more powerful than warming.

New opportunities for global cooperation

The following are excerpts from presentations that are scheduled to be made during an international conference on conflict management organized under the theme of "From Environmental Challenges to Environmental Conflicted: New Opportunities for Global Cooperation" at the Seoul Press Center in downtown Seoul at 2 p.m. today. - ED.

Eung-kyuk Park, Ph.D. President of the Korea Institute of Public Administration

Today, environmental challenges have become increasingly significant in producing conflicts. As a result of unsustainable developments without taking due account of ecological consequences, we have witnessed a raised sea levels, and significant increase in temperature that has altered global climate cycle.

Nowadays, the threat posed by global climate change often leads to conflicting interests among people and nations surrounding resource scarcity and waste disposals issues. And the Northeast Asian countries are no exception to this trend.

Policymakers are indeed having a hard time in crafting efficient measures to counteract those issues, since these conflicts may be intensified in combination with other factors, such as inefficient governance system, economic instability, and the lack of regional cooperation.

There have been some proposals on how to prevent and manage conflicts and ways of promoting regional cooperation in Northeast Asia.

Jim Dator, University of Hawaii at Manoa

In 2008, the Hawaii Research Center for Futures Studies wrote a report titled, "10 Things Every Korean Leader Must Know About Climate Change in the 21st Century-plus Four Alternative Futures. I was asked to prepare my talk today as an update of that report.

There is no greater challenge for governments, economic systems, and all of humanity everywhere in the coming decades than dealing with the causes and consequences of human-created climate change.

Among the vast amount of research and opinion on climate change and climate policy, there are several fundamental points that must be understood, internalized, and used as a guide for our individual and collective actions, especially in Korea. I will present eleven points that I believe every leader - and citizen - in Korea must know about climate change.

I will then ask one question that I challenge you to consider and answer.

1. Climate change is real, it is here, and more are coming.
2. Global warming leads to climate change leads to global change.

3. Climate change is global, but its impacts are local.
4. It is too late to prevent climate change, but we can stop making it worse.
5. Climate change is a critical issue for national security.
6. The poor are both the most vulnerable to climate change, and yet in many ways the best prepared to adapt to it.
7. Climate change can be good, and should be grasped as a wonderful opportunity.
8. Climate change must be governed.
9. We have the technology to do the job.
10. We may not have the energy needed to do the job.
11. Climate change is a complex, interconnected, systemic phenomenon

Prof. Dong-chun Shin, Dept. of Preventive Medicine, College of Medicine, Yonsei University

Environmental health issues in Korea in the 20th century may be summarized as follows:
1. Environmental diseases issue in Onsan, a non-ferrous metal complex
2. Pneumoconiosis in residents near a coal fuel-brick factory
3. Tap water contamination from phenol leakage into the Nakdong river
4. Dioxins emission by various solid waste incinerator
5. Heavy metal poisoning near decommissioned mines

Prof. Geoff O'Brien, Northumbria University

This is about addressing extremes as well as long term change. But there are huge uncertainties associated with climate change and many different views: It may not be happening, or it might not happen as fast as some think or it may be already too late!

Ideally we would want "no regrets" adaptation solutions - that is solutions that work for a range of climate scenarios and offer co-benefits

Climate change is a wicked problem: There is little opportunity to learn by trial and error or any exit point from the problem.

Human actions are leading to a series of "produced" unknowns: We can generalise about the type of threats we face but we cannot predict the "what" and "when."

Conventional scientific methods cannot provide sufficient data for robust policy making - climate change uncertainties and the interactivity between systems at micro, meso and macro scales militates against gathering enough empirical data for robust decision-making. Climate decision making falls into the Post Normal Science (PNS) domain.

PNS can be used where there are differences of opinion and uncertainties and it is not possible to gather sufficient empirical data to resolve those differences. Climate change mitigation and adaptation are such a problem

An effective climate change policy is an iterative one that considers and incorporates this new learning at regular intervals.

Prof. Huang Chongfu, Beijing Normal University

Thirty years ago, there was a railway station in my home town in China where the railway was only two feet (0.6 meter) wide.

Thirty years ago, our environment was so clean but now there is serious pollution!

Thirty years ago, we were poor but happy!

Now, not so poor, but too busy and face much risks: Today's China is badly different from past China. Now, there are much risks we have to face.

The Chinese government is paying more attention on risk management. Until now, the main role of risk analysis in China is to server for the government and giant companies.

The key projects have soundly promoted the researches of risk analysis in China.

Prof. Isao Sakaguchi, Gakushuin University

Middle power diplomacy has been a dominant model for Japan, involving dependence on stable international order since reputation matters for non-great power

There has been active participation in international institutions because there is a need for civil political diplomacy, more so than the ordinary model for western countries

Also, there had to be active movement in the Japanese civil society since it was too weak to influence the environmental diplomacy of the government of Japan.

As a result, local governments are more environmentally enlightened, and can lead the environmental diplomacy from bottom-up.

Historically, local governments were the primary supporters of Japan's anti-pollution or nature conservation movements, helping to enforce stricter environmental regulations more strictly than the national government.

With the internationalization of local cities, they began to seek local diplomacy in 1980s with know-how in environmental regulations.

Prof. Suh-Yong Chung, Korea University

Looking at global problems for local solutions, we must recognize that there are various level of developments in different regions.

There are impacts of different political, economic, diplomatic, scientific, and cultural environments on the institution building process.

And there are all types of environmental problems:

- Yellow Dust (Korea vs. China)
- Acid rain (Japan vs. China)
- Marine environment (Korea vs. China)

- Fisheries (China vs. Korea)
- Movements of hazardous wastes (China vs. Korea)
- Climate change (China, Korea, and Japan)

As a means to try and resolve some of these problems, certain steps have to be taken:
- 1st step: individual small scale of cooperation mechanisms
- 2nd step: institutionalization of individual mechanisms
- 3rd step: institutional competitions among the mechanisms
- 4th step: formation of a region-wide environment (green) governance

Ji-bum Chung, Ph.D., Korea Institute of Public Administration

Korea is one of the world's 10 major energy consumers.

However, the country has few natural resources and its dependency on overseas energy sources has risen from 87.9 percent in 1990 to 96.7 percent in 2005.

The Korean energy policy has been driven by the considerations of national energy security to support the nation's high economic growth and minimization of foreign oil dependency.

This has resulted in a policy that continues to have nuclear power as a major element of electricity production.

Since the startup of the first nuclear power plant Gori Unit 1 in 1977, the Korean nuclear industry has achieved continuous high growth.

Now, a total of 21 units are in operation, which ranked sixth globally (accounting for about 40 percent of the total domestic power generation).

Further, under the country's fifth long-term power development plan finalized in January 2000, eight more nuclear power plants will be constructed by 2015.